Book of Catholic Prayer

BOOK OF Catholic Prayer

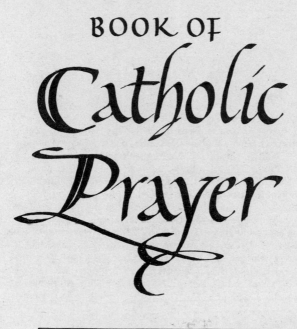

Edmond Bliven

OREGON CATHOLIC PRESS
✝

Nihil Obstat:
The Reverend Richard Huneger, STL

Imprimatur:
† William J. Levada, STD
Archbishop of Portland
August 1, 1992

In memory of
H.A. Reinhold,
dedicated priest,
pioneer liturgist,
herald of social justice,
faithful friend and mentor,
who first opened to me
the spiritual treasures
of the Bible and the liturgy.

TABLE OF CONTENTS

FOREWORD

In the Gospel we read that the disciples of Jesus, on an occasion when He had just finished praying, asked Him: "Lord, teach us to pray." The result was the classic prayer that each Christian and all Christians have prayed in public and private since the time of the Apostles, the Lord's Prayer.

But Jesus did not intend the Our Father to exhaust the repertory of our prayer. The Catholic Church has imitated the Lord Himself in praying the Psalms daily in its official prayer of the Liturgy of the Hours. And the prayers, short and long, which have enriched the spiritual life of generations of disciples of Jesus have been inspired by the words of the Bible and the sacraments of the Church.

No wonder, then, that a priest like Father Edmond Bliven, Pastor of St. Michael's Church in Portland, Oregon, would want to respond with the priestly heart of Jesus, the Good Shepherd, when he hears the request of many of the Lord's disciples today to teach them to pray. This book of prayers is the fruit of his desire to give a shepherd's care to his people.

For many the presentation of the Psalms for daily use will be a first introduction to this treasury of prayer of the Church. Linking our daily prayer with the privileged moments of encounter with Jesus in the sacraments will surely enrich and strengthen the spiritual growth of Catholics who avail themselves of this book.

Father Bliven deserves our thanks for responding to a present and perennial need to learn how to pray by organizing a book of prayers which is both comprehensive in its scope and practical in its presentation. May all who use it rely on the Lord's own words, "If you know how to give *your* children good things, how much *more* will the heavenly Father give the Holy Spirit to those who ask Him (Luke 11:13).

The Most Reverend William J. Levada
Archbishop of Portland in Oregon

August 1, 1992

TO THE READER

This *Book of Catholic Prayer* is a parish priest's attempt to make the Emmaus experience more accessible to today's Christian.

One of my favorite stories is told in the Gospel of Luke:

Now on that same day [Easter Sunday] two of the disciples of Jesus were going to a village called Emmaus, about seven miles from Jerusalem, and talking with each other about all these things that had happened.

While they were walking and discussing, Jesus himself came near and went with them. But their eyes were kept from recognizing him. And he said to them, "What are you discussing with each other as you walk along?"

They stood still, looking sad. Then one of them, whose name was Cleopas, answered him, "Are you the only stranger in Jerusalem who does not know the things that have taken place there in these days?"

He asked them, "What things?"

They replied, "The things about Jesus of Nazareth, who was a prophet mighty in deed and word before God and all the people, and how our chief priests and leaders handed him over to be condemned to death and crucified him. But we had hoped that he was the one to redeem Israel. Yes, and besides all this, it is now the third day since these things took place. Moreover, some women of our group astounded us. They were at the tomb early this morning, and when they did not find his body there, they came back and told us that they had indeed seen a vision of angels who said that he was alive. Some of those who were with us went to the tomb and found it just as the women had said; but they did not see him."

Then he said to them, "Oh, how foolish you are, and how slow of heart to believe all that the prophets have declared! Was it not necessary that the Messiah should suffer these things and then enter into his glory?"

Then beginning with Moses and all the prophets, he interpreted to them the things about himself in all the scriptures.

As they came near the village to which they were going, he walked ahead as if he were going on. But they urged him strongly, saying, "Stay with us, because it is almost evening and the day is now nearly over."

So he went in to stay with them. When he was at the table with them, he took bread, blessed and broke it, and gave it to them. Then their eyes were opened, and they recognized him; and he vanished from their sight. They said to each other, "Were not our hearts burning within us while he was talking to us on the road, while he was opening the scriptures to us?"

Now let's examine what the story tells us. The disciples were joined by Jesus, who walked with them. He listened to them. Then they listened to him. When he broke bread for them (an early Christian expression for celebrating the Eucharist), their eyes were opened and they recognized him.

Just as the disciples came to a knowledge of Jesus gradually, most of us grow in intimacy with him step by step. We begin by walking with him, generally by growing up in a Christian home, although many of us probably follow a meandering path.

Eventually we realize a deeper need for God. If we are fortunate, we find God in a community of believers. We search for guidance in the Scriptures as understood by the Church and in the prayer of the Church, which reaches its apex in the Sacraments, especially the Eucharist, which is also the climax of the Emmaus story.

It is my hope that this book will assist the reader's own Emmaus journey.

The prayer book is divided into four sections:

- WALKING WITH THE LORD (GUIDE-LINES FOR CHRISTIAN LIVING)
- TALKING WITH THE LORD (PRAYING WITH THE CHURCH)
- LISTENING TO THE LORD (MEDITA-TIVE OR CONTEMPLATIVE PRAYER)
- KNOWING THE LORD (THE SACRA-MENTS AND CHRISTIAN LIFE)

This prayer book is for Roman Catholics, but I invite other Christians to make use of it. Over the past several decades, Christians of all denominations have become increasingly open not only to the Scriptures but also to the almost 2,000-year prayer tradition of the Church. For Western Christians, Protestant as well as Catholic, that tradition has been centered in Rome since Apostolic times.

Another benefit of the new openness between churches and ecclesial communities is the desire of Christians of the West to know more about the prayer life of their Eastern Christian brothers and sisters. The reader will find prayers from Eastern liturgies in this prayer book. The section on meditative prayer also draws on the wisdom of the Eastern Churches.

One of the principal goals of the liturgical reforms of the Second Vatican Council was to bring the private prayer life of the Catholic laity into closer contact with the Scriptures and the liturgy.

Beginning in the Middle Ages, popular devotion in the Western Church developed parallel to the Scriptures and the liturgy. Sometimes the relationship was close, sometimes not so close. There were many historical reasons for this, but surely one of them was the fact that the liturgy continued to be celebrated in Latin long after it ceased to be a language that most people understood. (Eastern-rite Catholics and Orthodox Christians retained the use of the vernacular, or at least an understandable classical form of the spoken language, in the liturgy. For them the separation between popular devotion and liturgy was not the problem that it became in Western Christianity.)

The liturgical changes of Vatican Council II have made the riches of the Bible and the liturgy more accessible to the Catholic laity, by reintroducing the use of the language of the people in the liturgy, and by introducing a three-year cycle of Scripture readings at Sunday celebrations of the Eucharist and a two-year cycle on weekdays.

But the goal of nourishing the laity's private prayer life with the Bible and the liturgy would be further aided, I believe, by the publication of a good personal prayer book drawn from biblical and liturgical sources.

In the period immediately preceding the Second Vatican Council, many Catholics owned a missal that contained a translation of the Mass and also a selection of popular prayers.

Nowadays most parishes furnish parishioners with a variety of participation aids for Mass, including the publications of Oregon Catholic Press: *Today's Missal* and *Breaking Bread*. But few Catholics today have a prayer book of their own.

The very abundance of the Church's liturgical publications makes the compiling of a modern layperson's prayer book a daunting task.

Besides the reform of the Mass, the Second Vatican Council (or Vatican II) also expressed the hope that the riches of the Church's liturgy of the hours would be opened to the laity. The complete American edition is published in four volumes by Catholic Book Publishing Co. There are several publications which contain excerpts from the liturgy of the hours. They are listed in the SUG-GESTED BOOKS FOR FURTHER READING section of this prayer book.

This *Book of Catholic Prayer* is offered as an introduction to these official liturgical publications, as well as an aid to women and men living in today's world who wish to nourish their private prayer from the Bible and the liturgy. It also presents a selection of beloved traditional prayers, many of them in a new version by the International Committee for English in the Liturgy (ICEL). I share the hope of the ICEL translators that "a modified translation of these texts, with words and expressions congenial to our times, will encourage their use among new generations of Catholics."

The French, who seem to provide an aphorism for every occasion, have a saying, "The best is the enemy of the good." Perhaps others more capable than I have shied away from publishing a biblical-liturgical prayer book for fear that theirs would not be the best. I have no illusions that this prayer book will be the best. It is my prayer that it will be helpful.

If the *Book of Catholic Prayer* helps more people to "taste and see that the Lord is good" (Psalm 34:8), it will have been worth all the effort. Together with a good edition of the Bible, it will offer an introduction to the Church's rich tradition of prayer.

We live in times when people are becoming more sensitive to sexism in language. In their "Criteria for the Evaluation of Inclusive Language

Translations of Scriptural Texts Proposed for Liturgical Use," November 15, 1990, the U.S. bishops ruled that "the language of biblical texts for liturgical use should facilitate the full, conscious and active participation of all members of the Church, women and men, in worship." The first fruits of this directive are the revised Psalms of the New American Bible (NAB), approved by the American bishops at their November 1991 meeting. The Psalms in this prayer book, except where specifically noted, are taken from this revised NAB psalter. The remainder of Scripture is taken from the New Revised Standard Version, which also uses inclusive language. A few passages, which are noted in the text, are taken from other versions.

The Reverend Edmond Bliven
Church of St. Michael the Archangel
Portland, Oregon

SUGGESTIONS FOR USING THIS BOOK

This book is intended to be a daily companion on the reader's daily journey with God.

I suggest that you set aside some quiet time to acquaint yourself with the contents of the book. Read the table of contents and leaf through the different sections. You will find some pages suitable for daily use; others will be useful weekly or monthly. Other sections are appropriate for times of reflection, such as a retreat. Some parts are intended for milestones in life, such as preparation for baptism or entrance into the Church, marriage or reception of the diaconate or priesthood.

Each person faces times of special difficulty, such as sickness and death, when the Church offers the consolation of our loving God.

I hope you will familiarize yourself with the book and become aware of the treasury of Bible and liturgy that the Church offers, like the householder mentioned in the Gospel, who "brings forth both old things and new" (Matthew 13:52).

If you have been wondering just what is morally right and wrong nowadays, I hope the section WALKING WITH THE LORD will help you form your conscience. It should also be helpful in preparing to receive the Sacrament of Penance.

If the Psalms have not yet become a part of your daily prayer, I encourage you to read the sec-

tion on the Psalms in TALKING WITH THE
LORD.

If you are searching for ways to deepen your
relationship with God through prayer, you will
find suggestions in LISTENING TO THE LORD.

KNOWING THE LORD offers you guidance
in your journey with the Church.

Many people have found it helpful to have a
plan for daily Bible reading. For this reason,
READING THE BIBLE provides a suggested plan
for reading the Bible with the Church.

No matter where you are in your pilgrim
journey with the Lord, you will find reading for
daily living in SUGGESTED BOOKS FOR FUR-
THER READING.

Happy reading. I pray you will experience
some of the joy in using this book that I found in
putting it together.

E.B.

THANKS

In the first place, I wish to express my gratitude to my Ordinary, the Most Reverend William Levada, STD, Archbishop of Portland, Oregon, for his encouragement and helpful suggestions.

Then to the many people without whom this book would not have come to be: To Mary Jo Tully, chancellor of the Archdiocese of Portland, for her valuable counsel and advice; to my publisher, Owen Alstott, for his patience and abiding support; to Jan Bear, for her indefatigable labor and helpful advice; to Geri Ethen, for countless hours at the computer keyboard; to Leanna Nudo for obtaining permissions and negotiating contracts to use copyrighted material; to Robert Pfohman, genial leader of the editorial team; and to all the others at Oregon Catholic Press who worked to make this prayer book a reality.

To Robert Palladino for the calligraphy, a witness to his dedication to the good, the true and the beautiful.

To Celeste Granato, pastoral minister of the Church of Saint Michael the Archangel, whose generous cooperation helped make time available for my writing and editing. To the monks of Mount Angel Abbey for their living witness to the perennial power of a spiritual life based on the Bible and the liturgy. To Sister Antoinette Traeger, OSB, for her good-humored and inspiring counsel. To the numerous friends and parishioners who were pressed into service for their reactions, suggestions and corrections. To Valerie Evans for reading the proofs, correcting typographical errors and making suggestions for stylistic improvements. A special mention must be made of the 1991-92 class of candidates and catechumens who were received or baptized into the Church at the Easter Vigil, 18 April 1992, at St. Michael's. The class willingly acted as a living laboratory for trying out this new venture in Catholic publishing. It is my hope that they will be the first of a large company of readers who will benefit from using this *Book of Catholic Prayer.*

— E.B.

1
Walking with the Lord

הוֹרֵנִי יהוה דַּרְכֶּךָ אֲהַלֵּךְ בַּאֲמִתֶּךָ

Teach me your way
O LORD
that I may walk
in your truth

PSALM 86 · 11

WALKING WITH THE LORD

GUIDELINES FOR CHRISTIAN LIVING

In the Bible, walking is often a metaphor for the way one lives. Thus, one of the Hebrew words for "sin" means to stray from the path. The *Didache*, "Teaching of the Twelve Apostles," perhaps the first Christian document written after the New Testament, speaks of the Two Ways, the way of following God and the way of evil. The first Psalm invites readers to follow the law of the Lord. The word "follow" in our translation is literally "walk" in Hebrew. The Hebrew word translated "law" is "Torah," which also means teaching or guidance. As Lawrence Boadt emphasizes in the Reading Guide of the *Catholic Study Bible*, it is important for Christians to realize that "in Judaism, 'Torah' does not have the narrow and constricting meaning of 'Law' so common among modern people." Torah is always associated with joy. Therefore the first Psalm begins with the word "happy" referring to those who walk in the way of the LORD.*

---

* "The LORD" or "GOD" takes the place of "YHWH," the name God called himself when he spoke to Moses from the burning bush; see Exodus 3:14-15. Israel considered the name too holy to speak, and most Christian Bibles use small capitals to indicate the name. "The Lord" and "God" translate different Hebrew words.

Psalm 1

True Happiness in God's Law

Happy those* who do not follow
the counsel of the wicked,
Nor go the way of sinners,
nor sit in company with scoffers.
Rather the law of the LORD is their joy;
God's law they study day and night.
They are like a tree
planted near streams of water,
that yields its fruit in season;
Its leaves never wither;
whatever they do prospers.

But not the wicked!†
They are like chaff driven by the wind.
Therefore the wicked will not survive judgment,
nor will sinners in the assembly of the just.
The LORD watches over the way of the just,
but the way of the wicked leads to ruin.

The Ten Commandments

Deuteronomy, Chapter 5

I vss. 6-8 — I am the LORD your God, who brought
you out of the land of Egypt, out of the house

---

* "Those": literally, "the man." The word is used here and
in many of the Psalms as typical, and therefore is translated
"those" or "they."
† "The wicked": Those who by their actions distance
themselves from God's life-giving presence.

of slavery; you shall have no other gods before me. You shall not make for yourself an idol, whether in the form of anything that is in heaven above, or that is on the earth beneath, or that is in the water under the earth. You shall not bow down to them or worship them.

II vs. 11 — You shall not make wrongful use of the name of the LORD your God, for the LORD will not acquit anyone who misuses his name.

III vss. 12-13,15 — Observe the sabbath day and keep it holy, as the LORD your God commanded you. Six days you shall labor and do all your work. But the seventh day is a sabbath to the LORD your God. Remember that you were a slave in the land of Egypt, and the LORD your God brought you out from there with a mighty hand and an outstretched arm; therefore the LORD your God commanded you to keep the sabbath day.

IV vs. 16 — Honor your father and your mother, as the LORD your God commanded you, so that your days may be long and that it may go well with you in the land that the LORD your God is giving you.

V vs. 17 — You shall not murder.

VI vs.18 — Neither shall you commit adultery.

VII vs. 19 — Neither shall you steal.

VIII vs. 20 — Neither shall you bear false witness against your neighbor.

IX vs. 21 — Neither shall you covet your
    neighbor's wife.

X — Neither shall you desire your neighbor's
    house, or field, or male or female slave, or ox,
    or donkey, or anything that belongs to your
    neighbor.

<hr />

Sh'ma Israel

Deuteronomy 6:4-9

Hear, O Israel; The LORD is our God, the
LORD alone. You shall love the LORD your God
with all your heart, and with all your soul, and
with all your might.

<hr />

This passage, which is prayed every day by
devout Jews was quoted by Jesus in answer to the
question, Which commandment is first of all?
Then, citing Leviticus 19:18, he said, the second is
this:

You shall love your neighbor as yourself.

*These two commandments summarize the Ten Com-
mandments. (See Mark 12:28-31.)*

<hr />

Personal Obligations
Based on the Ten Commandments

I — To realize that God is the center of all being. To
    nourish my faith by reading the Scriptures
    with the Church and by prayer. To see the
    world and my fellow creatures through the

eyes of God. To worship God and not the idols of this world: wealth and power.

II — To have a sense of awe and reverence for God who created me and sustains me in existence and for his Name which represents him. (The Bible calls this awe and reverence "fear of the Lord.")

III — To develop a sense of sacred time: by setting aside time to worship God regularly with my fellow Christians. To sanctify daily living by growing in knowledge and love of the Church's liturgical year.

IV — To have respect for those who are close to me, particularly those who reared me and first taught me about God. To respect and celebrate their individual gifts, to understand and help them to overcome their weaknesses, if possible. To give a Christian upbringing to my children, teaching them by example as well as word.

V — To develop a consistent pro-life ethic. To have respect for all human life, especially for those who cannot defend themselves: the unborn, the newborn and children, the handicapped and the elderly. To work for peaceful solutions to conflicts: local, national and international. To avoid all that is harmful to others, physically or psychologically. To respect my own body by living moderately, including the use of food and drink. To avoid drug abuse.

VI — For all: To keep my body chaste as a temple of the Holy Spirit, and as a sign of God's faithful love for men and women, a sign that is seen most perfectly in the sacrament of matrimony. To avoid dishonoring my own body or the bodies of others by impure actions or words. Not to encourage others to sin sexually by my behavior.

If I am married: to rejoice in the sexual love which I share with my spouse; to allow nothing or no one to come between us; to refuse to exploit anyone sexually, including my spouse; to give, accept and appreciate loving affection between my spouse and myself.

If I am a religious: to avoid any exclusive friendship which is dangerous to chastity and which offends against the love which should exist among all the members of my community.

VII — To respect the property of others, as well as public property and, especially important today, the environment, which is the heritage of future generations. To make restitution for property I may have stolen or damaged. To be truly honest and not just stay within the law. To live within my means and not to endanger the security of those dependent on me by an irresponsible use of money.

VIII — To respect the reputation of others and refuse to take part in harmful gossip. To respect the confidences of others. To tell the truth.

IX — To respect my own sexuality and that of others. To avoid making sex objects of others. To avoid reading, conversation and entertainment that offend against Christian and human decency.

X — To observe justice in dealings with others. To avoid envy of others' good fortune. To give an honest day's work for my salary. To pay a fair wage to my employees. To be faithful to promises and contracts. To be mindful of social justice in business dealings and when I vote.

~∞∞∞~

The Precepts of the Church

Among the specific obligations of Catholic Christians, the principal ones are these:

1 — To keep holy the day of Christ's resurrection (Sunday). To worship God by participating in Mass every Sunday and every holy day of obligation. To avoid activities that hinder recreation of soul and body, for example, unnecessary work and business activities.

2 — To participate in the sacramental life of the Church, to receive holy Communion frequently and the Sacrament of Penance regularly. The minimum requirement is to receive the Sacrament of Penance once a year (if one is in a state of serious sin). The minimum re-

quirement is to receive holy Communion
once a year between the first Sunday of Lent
and Trinity Sunday, unless, for a just cause, it
is fulfilled at some other time of the year.

3 — To observe the marriage laws of the Church.

4 — To give religious instruction to one's children,
by word and example. To take advantage of
the religious education services of one's local
church.

5 — To strengthen and support the Church finan-
cially and by giving of one's talent in service
to others.

6 — To do penance, including fasting and abstaining on the days appointed.

The Beatitudes

Matthew 5:3-10 (REB)

Blessed are the poor in spirit;
　　the kingdom of heaven is theirs.

Blessed are the sorrowful;
　　they shall find consolation.

Blessed are the gentle;
　　they shall have the earth for their possession.

Blessed are those who hunger and thirst to see
　　　　right prevail;
　　they shall be satisfied.

Blessed are those who show mercy;
　　mercy shall be shown to them.

Blessed are those whose hearts are pure;
  they shall see God.

Blessed are the peacemakers;
  they shall be called God's children.

Blessed are those who are persecuted in the cause
    of right;
  the kingdom of God is theirs.

―∽◦◦◦∾―

The Last Judgment
Matthew 25:31-46

When the Son of Man comes in his glory, and
all the angels with him, then he will sit on the
throne of his glory. All the nations will be gathered
before him, and he will separate people one from
another as a shepherd separates the sheep from
the goats, and he will put the sheep at his right
hand and the goats at the left.

Then the king will say to those at his right
hand, "Come, you that are blessed by my Father,
inherit the kingdom prepared for you from the
foundation of the world; for I was hungry and you
gave me food, I was thirsty and you gave me
something to drink, I was a stranger and you welcomed me, I was naked and you gave me clothing,
I was sick and you took care of me, I was in prison
and you visited me."

Then the righteous will answer him, "Lord,
when was it that we saw you hungry and gave
you food, or thirsty and gave you something to
drink? And when was it that we saw you a
stranger and welcomed you, or naked and gave

you clothing? And when was it that we saw you sick or in prison and visited you?

And the king will answer them, "Truly I tell you, just as you did it to one of the least of these who are members of my family, you did it to me."

Then he will say to those at his left hand, "You that are accursed, depart from me into the eternal fire prepared for the devil and his angels; for I was hungry and you gave me no food, I was thirsty and you gave me nothing to drink, I was a stranger and you did not welcome me, naked and you did not give me clothing, sick and in prison and you did not visit me."

Then they also will answer, "Lord, when was it that we saw you hungry or thirsty or a stranger or naked or sick or in prison, and did not take care of you?"

Then he will answer them, "Truly I tell you, just as you did not do it to one of the least of these, you did not do it to me."

And these will go away into eternal punishment, but the righteous into eternal life.

A Life Guided by the Spirit

Galatians 5:13-25 (REB)

You, my friends, were called to be free; only beware of turning your freedom into license for your unspiritual nature. Instead, serve one another in love; for the whole law is summed up in a single commandment: "Love your neighbor as yourself." But if you go on fighting one another, tooth and nail, all you can expect is mutual destruction.

What I mean is this: Be guided by the Spirit and you will not gratify the desires of your unspiritual nature. That nature sets its desires against the Spirit, while the Spirit fights against it. They are in conflict with one another, so that you cannot do what you want. But if you are led by the Spirit, you are not subject to law.

Anyone can see the behavior that belongs to the unspiritual nature: fornication, indecency, and debauchery; idolatry and sorcery; quarrels, a contentious temper, envy, fits of rage, selfish ambitions, dissensions, party intrigues, and jealousies; drinking bouts, orgies and the like. I warn you, as I warned you before, that no one who behaves like that will ever inherit the kingdom of God.

But the harvest of the Spirit is love, joy, peace, patience, kindness, goodness, fidelity, gentleness and self control. Against such things there is no law. Those who belong to Christ Jesus have crucified the old nature with its passions and desires. If the Spirit is the source of our life, let the Spirit also direct its course.

THE PENITENTIAL TRIAD

Prayer, Fasting and Almsgiving

On February 17, 1966, after the conclusion of the Second Vatican Council, Pope Paul VI issued an *Apostolic Constitution on Penance.* The pope reminded modern Catholics of the continuing necessity to do penance. He said, "The Church has gained a clearer awareness that, while it is by divine vocation holy and without blemish, it is defective in its members and in continuous need of conversion and renewal, a renewal which must be implemented not only internally and individually but also externally and socially."

Pope Paul cited the history of prayer, fasting and almsgiving in the Jewish tradition and the example of Christ himself in honoring this tradition, which was continued after his resurrection and ascension by the Apostles and the early Church.

Although penitential practices have varied throughout the centuries, the necessity of continuing them remains.

At the same time the pope warned against formalism and hypocrisy: "penitential acts done for show and not accompanied by inner conversion, prayer and acts of charity."

After asserting general principles for fasting and abstinence, Pope Paul left it to national bishops' conferences to make specific applications.

Although modifications in the Church's penitential discipline have been made, the general obligation to do acts of penance remains. As Pope Paul stated, "In the New Testament and in the history of the Church — although the duty of doing penance is motivated above all by participating in the sufferings of Christ — the necessity of an asceticism which disciplines the body and brings it into subjection is affirmed with special insistence by the example of Christ himself."

Most Catholics are aware that the American bishops abrogated, for the United States, the strict obligation of abstaining from meat on Fridays outside of Lent. Many Catholics are not aware, however, of an important invitation issued to them by their bishops.

In their letter, "The Challenge of Peace: God's Promise and Our Response," the bishops wrote, "As a tangible sign of our need and desire to do penance we, for the cause of peace, commit ourselves to fast and abstinence on each Friday of the year. We call upon our people voluntarily to do penance on Friday by eating less food and by abstaining from meat. This return to a traditional practice of penance, once well observed in the U.S. Church, should be accompanied by works of charity and service toward our neighbors. Every Friday should be a day significantly devoted to prayer, penance, and almsgiving for peace."

Prayer for Fridays

All praise be yours, God our Creator,
as we wait in joyful hope
for the coming of justice

and the fullness of peace.

All praise for this day, this Friday.
By our weekly fasting and prayer
cast out the spirit of war, of fear and mistrust,
and make us grow hungry for human kindness,
thirsty for solidarity
with all the people of your dear earth.

May all our prayer, our fasting and our deeds
be done in the name of Jesus.

Amen.

II.
Talking with the Lord

Moses did not know
that the skin of his face
SHONE
because he had been
talking with GOD

משה לא־ידע
כי קרן עור
פניו בדברו אתו

EXODUS
34 · 29

TALKING WITH THE LORD

PRAYING WITH THE CHURCH

When Jesus walked with the disciples on the road to Emmaus, he listened to them as they explained all their sorrow, confusion and hope concerning events in Jerusalem over the preceding few days. One might ask why he would hear the disciples retelling events that the risen Christ surely would know. Obviously, he listened for their sake, because it was important for them to talk about this crisis they faced, and not for his own information.

The people of God continue to talk to the Lord in all their sorrow, confusion and hope. And the Lord continues to listen.

The prayers in this chapter range from the informal to the formal; they come to us from across the centuries and from widely different cultures. Some will be immediately accessible for a reader; others will take more study and contemplation.

The sections in this chapter are these:

- Hebrew and Greek Acclamations
    (page 231)

You will find more information about these prayers in the beginning of each section.

BASIC PRAYERS

Basic prayers are fundamental to the prayer life of a Catholic Christian. They are essential elements in all the prayers of the Church. They should be memorized.

~∞∞~

In the name of the Father, and of the Son, and of the Holy Spirit. Amen.

Lord's Prayer*

Traditional Version

Our Father, who art in heaven,
   hallowed be thy name;
thy kingdom come;
   thy will be done
   on earth as it is in heaven.
Give us this day our daily bread;
   and forgive us our tresspasses
as we forgive those
   who trespass against us;
and lead us not into temptation,
      but deliver us from evil. Amen.

Hail Mary

Traditional Version

Hail Mary, full of grace, the Lord is with thee; blessed art thou among women, and blessed is the fruit of thy womb, Jesus. Holy Mary, Mother of God, pray for us sinners, now and at the hour of our death. Amen.

---

* The Amen is omitted in the Mass because the priest develops the final phrase: "deliver us . . . ."

Gloria Patri

Traditional Version

Glory be to the Father, and to the Son, and to the Holy Spirit, as it was in the beginning, is now, and ever shall be, world without end. Amen.

Apostles' Creed

Traditional Version

I believe in God, the Father Almighty, Creator of heaven and earth, and in Jesus Christ, his only Son, our Lord, who was conceived by the Holy Spirit, born of the Virgin Mary, suffered under Pontius Pilate, was crucified, died, and was buried. He descended into hell; the third day he rose again from the dead; he ascended into heaven, sits at the right hand of God, the Father almighty; from thence he shall come to judge the living and the dead. I believe in the Holy Spirit, the Holy Catholic Church, the communion of saints, the forgiveness of sins, the resurrection of the body, and life everlasting. Amen.

Lord's Prayer

Contemporary Version

Our Father in heaven,
   hallowed be your name,
   your kingdom come,
   your will be done,
      on earth as in heaven.
Give us today our daily bread.
Forgive us our sins
   as we forgive those who sin against us.
Save us from the time of trial

and deliver us from evil.
Amen.

Hail Mary

Contemporary Version

Hail Mary, full of grace,
    the Lord is with you.
Blessed are you among women,
    and blessed is the fruit
    of your womb, Jesus.
Holy Mary, Mother of God,
    pray for us sinners,
    now and at the hour
    of our death.
Amen.

Gloria Patri

Contemporary Version

Glory to the Father,
and to the Son,
and to the Holy Spirit:
As it was in the beginning,
is now,
and will be for ever. Amen.

Apostles' Creed

Contemporary Version

I believe in God, the Father almighty,
    creator of heaven and earth.
I believe in Jesus Christ, his only Son, our Lord,
    who was conceived by the Holy Spirit,
    born of the Virgin Mary,
    suffered under Pontius Pilate,
    was crucified, died and was buried;

he descended to the dead.
On the third day he rose again;
he ascended into heaven,
he is seated at the right hand of the Father,
and he will come to judge the living and the
    dead.
I believe in the Holy Spirit,
the holy catholic Church,
the communion of saints,
the forgiveness of sins,
the resurrection of the body,
and the life everlasting. Amen.

<hr>

Prayers of Contrition

When we see the high vocation to which we are all called, we are struck with our continuing need of conversion. One of the principal means of this conversion is the Sacrament of Penance (see KNOWING THE LORD, page 272). At other times, one of the following prayers of contrition will be helpful.

<hr>

Lord Jesus Christ, Son of God,
have mercy on me, a sinner.

or

Our Savior Jesus Christ
    suffered and died for us.
In his name, my God, have mercy.
Amen.

or Luke 15:18, 18:13

Father, I have sinned against heaven
   and against you. I am not worthy
   to be called your child.
Be merciful to me, a sinner.

or

Lord Jesus,
   you opened the eyes of the blind,
   healed the sick,
   forgave the sinful woman,
   and after Peter's denial
   confirmed him in your love.
Listen to my prayer:
   Forgive all my sins,
   renew your love in my heart,
   help me to live in perfect
   unity with my fellow Christians
   that I may proclaim your saving
   power to all the world.

or

Lord Jesus,
   you chose to be called the friend of sinners.
By your saving death and resurrection
   free me from my sins.
May your peace take root in my heart
   and bring forth a harvest
   of love, holiness and truth.

or

I confess to almighty God
and to you, my brothers and sisters
that I have sinned through my own fault
in my thoughts and in my words,
in what I have done,

and in what I have failed to do,
and I ask blessed Mary, ever virgin,
all the angels and saints
and you, my brothers and sisters,
to pray for me to the Lord our God.

DAILY PRAYERS

Daily prayers help us to bring our relationship with God into all the ordinary times of our life. You may want to memorize some of these prayers.

Prayers on Awaking

In the name of the Father, and of the Son, and of the Holy Spirit. Amen.

Psalm 51:17

Lord, open my lips,
  and my mouth will proclaim your praise.
Holy, holy, holy Lord, God of power and might,
  heaven and earth are full of your glory.
Hosanna in the highest.

Prayers from Our Jewish Heritage

Blessed are you, Lord, God of all creation:
  You raise the dead to life.
Blessed are you, Lord, God of all creation:
  You open the eyes of the blind.

Deuteronomy 6:4-5

Hear O Israel!
The LORD is our God, the LORD alone!
You shall love the LORD your God, with all your heart,
  and with all your soul, and with all your strength.

Washing and Dressing

Blessed are you, Lord, God of all creation:
    You take the sleep from our eyes
    and the slumber from our eyelids.
Blessed are you, Lord, God of all creation:
    You clothe the naked.

Doxology

Glory to the Father,
and to the Son,
and to the Holy Spirit:
As it was in the beginning,
is now,
and will be for ever. Amen.

Table Prayers

Before Meals

    In the name of the Father, and of the Son, and of the Holy Spirit. Amen.

Psalm 104:14

You bring bread from the earth
    and wine to gladden our hearts.

or

Psalm 104:27-28

All [creatures] look to you
    to give them food in due time.
When you give to them, they gather it;
    when you open your hand,
    they are well filled with good things.

Our Father . . .*

Bless us, O Lord, and these your gifts which we are
     about to receive from your goodness.
Through Christ our Lord.
Amen.

or

A Hymn before Meals†

Be present at our table, Lord.
Be here and everywhere adored.
Thy creatures bless and grant that we
May feast in Paradise with thee.

After Meals

We give you thanks for all your gifts, almighty
    God,
   living and reigning now and for ever.
Amen.

For the sake of your name, O Lord,
   reward those who have been good to us
   and give them eternal life.
Amen.

or

Lord, give all people the food they need,
   so that they may join us in giving you thanks.
Amen.

---

   * See page 21 for the traditional version of the Lord's
Prayer; page 22 for a contemporary version.
   † This hymn may be sung to the tune of "Praise God from
Whom All Blessings Flow"

For other table prayers, see *Catholic House-hold Blessings and Prayers* in SUGGESTED BOOKS FOR FURTHER READING, page 384.

Morning and Evening Prayer

The Liturgy of the Hours grew out of the Jewish daily prayers, which sanctify the hours of the day by the praying of Psalms.

The Book of Acts tells us that, after the death and resurrection of Jesus, Peter and John continued to go to the Temple at the hour of prayer (Acts 3:1). But gradually the early Christians became estranged from the Jewish community because of their different attitudes toward Jesus.

But Christians continued to gather for the hours of prayer in their own homes. From this practice the Christian Liturgy of the Hours developed. It remains based on the Psalms. The principal hours, Morning and Evening Prayer, were especially popular with lay people.

In the Western (Roman) Church, the liturgy was still celebrated in Latin long after the laity no longer understood it. So the Liturgy of the Hours became the prayer of the clergy and vowed Religious. An abbreviated version (breviary) for private recitation became the clergy's prayer book.

The Second Vatican Council expressed the hope that the Liturgy of the Hours, reformed and in the vernacular, would become again the prayer of the entire Church, laity as well as clergy. Unfortunately this change has not yet happened.

One of the purposes of this prayer book is to help people use the Psalms as their personal prayers. Tradition has selected certain Psalms as most appropriate for morning and evening. Many people have found that by following the Church's example in using these Psalms, they have come to love them. The following plan is based on the Church's official Morning and Evening Prayer (Liturgy of the Hours).

To make it easier for the reader to use the Psalms in daily prayer, here is a proposal for Morning and Evening Prayer based on the Liturgy of the Hours:

Outline of Morning and Evening Prayer
Based on the Liturgy of the Hours

Morning	Evening
Lord, open my lips	God, come to my
Invitatory, Psalm 95	assistance
with its antiphon	
Glory to the Father	Glory to the Father
Hymn or poem	Hymn or poem
Psalm(s)	Psalm(s)
Canticle	Canticle
Glory to the Father	Glory to the Father
Scripture reading(s)	Scripture reading(s)
Canticle of Zechariah	Canticle of Mary
Glory to the Father	Glory to the Father
The Lord's Prayer	The Lord's Prayer
Concluding Prayer	Concluding Prayer

Morning Prayer

We begin by asking the Holy Spirit to open our lips and our hearts to pray:

Lord, open my lips;
    my mouth will proclaim your praise.
Glory to the Father,
and to the Son,

and to the Holy Spirit:

As it was in the beginning,

is now,

and will be for ever. Amen.

Invitatory Psalm — Invitation to Prayer

The following seasonal antiphons may be said at the beginning and the end of the Invitatory Psalm:

I Sunday of Advent to December 16

Come let us worship the Lord, the King who is to come.

December 17-23

The Lord is close at hand; come, let us worship him.

December 24

Today you will know the Lord is coming, and in the morning you will see his glory.

Christmas to the Epiphany

Christ is born for us; come, let us adore him.

Epiphany until the Baptism of the Lord

Christ has appeared to us; come, let us adore him.

Ash Wednesday to Palm Sunday

Oh, that today you would hear God's voice: Do not harden your hearts.

Come, let us worship Christ the Lord,
who for our sake endured temptation and
suffering.

The Lord is risen, alleluia.

Come, let us adore Christ the Lord,
who promised to send the Holy Spirit on his
people, alleluia.

The Spirit of the Lord has filled the whole world,
come, let us worship, alleluia.

Come, let us sing joyfully to the Lord;
cry out to the rock of our salvation.

or

Let us bow down in worship,
let us kneel before the Lord who made us.

or

Come, let us worship the Lord, whose people we
are,
God's well-tended flock.

Psalm 95

A Call to Praise and Obedience

Invitatory

Come, let us sing joyfully to the LORD;
cry out to the rock of our salvation.
Let us greet him with a song of praise,
joyfully sing out our psalms.

For the LORD is the great God,
   the great king over all gods.
Whose hand holds the depths of the earth;
   who owns the tops of the mountains.
The sea and the dry land belong to God,
   who made them, formed them by hand.

Enter, let us bow down in worship;
   let us kneel before the LORD who made us,
For this is our God,
   whose people we are,
God's well-tended flock.

Oh, that today you would hear his voice:
   Do not harden your hearts as at Meribah,
   as on the day of Massah in the desert.
There your ancestors tested me;
   they tried me though they had seen my works.
Forty years I loathed that generation;
   I said: "This people's heart goes astray,
   they do not know my ways."
Therefore I swore in my anger:
   "They shall never enter my rest."

Glory to the Father,
and to the Son,
and to the Holy Spirit:
As it was in the beginning,
is now,
and will be for ever. Amen.

Psalms

One or two Psalms are now prayed. Psalms for Morning Prayer are so designated in the Psalter or Psalm section following this outline. Also, there is a plan for one to pray all the Psalms over four weeks; it is located at the beginning of THE PSALTER, page 53.

"Glory to the Father . . ." is prayed at the end of each Psalm.

An Old Testament canticle may be substituted for one of the Psalms on Sunday. See OLD TESTAMENT CANTICLES, page 173.

Readings

One or two Scripture readings may be read. See the list of readings in READING THE BIBLE, page 355.

Canticle of Zechariah

Benedictus

Luke 1:68-79

Blessed are you, Lord, the God of Israel,
    you have come to your people and set them
        free.
You have raised up for us a mighty Savior,
    born of the house of your servant David.
Through your holy prophets, you promised of old
    to save us from our enemies,
    from the hands of all who hate us,
    to show mercy to our forebears,
    and to remember your holy covenant.

This was the oath you swore to our father
  Abraham:
    to set us free from the hands of our enemies,
    free to worship you without fear,
    holy and righteous before you,
    all the days of our life.

And you, child, shall be called the prophet of the
  Most High,
    for you will go before the Lord to prepare the
    way,
    to give God's people knowledge of salvation
    by the forgiveness of their sins.
    In the tender compassion of our God
    the dawn from on high shall break upon us,
    to shine on those who dwell in darkness and
    the shadow of death,
    and to guide our feet into the way of peace.

Glory to the Father,
and to the Son,
and to the Holy Spirit:
As it was in the beginning,
is now,
and will be for ever. Amen.

The Lord's Prayer*

Contemporary Version

Our Father in heaven,
  hallowed be your name,
  your kingdom come,

---

* When English was first introduced in the Mass, the
American bishops decided to retain the traditional form of the
Lord's Prayer. You may wish to use the contemporary version
in private prayer. (See page 21 for the traditional version.)

your will be done,
        on earth as in heaven.
Give us today our daily bread.
Forgive us our sins
        as we forgive those who sin against us.
Save us from the time of trial
        and deliver us from evil.
Amen.

Prayer of the Day

Sunday

O God,
        you make us glad
        by the weekly remembrance
        of the glorious resurrection
        of your Son our Lord.
Give us today your blessing
        so that the week to come
        may be lived in your grace.
We ask this through Christ our Lord.
Amen.

or Sunday's Opening Prayer from the missal

Monday

Lord,
        may everything we do
        begin with your inspiration
        and continue with your saving help.
Let our work always find its origin in you
        and through you reach completion.
Grant this through Christ our Lord.
Amen.

or

God our Creator,
 you gave us the earth to cultivate
 nd the sun to serve our needs.
Help us to spend this day
 for your glory and our neighbor's good.
We ask this in the name of Jesus the Lord.
Amen.

Tuesday

Lord our God,
 hear our morning prayer
 and let the radiance of your love
 scatter the gloom of our hearts.
The light of heaven's love has restored us to life;
 free us from the desires that belong to darkness.
We ask this in the name of Jesus the Lord.
Amen.

or

Lord Jesus Christ,
 true light of the world,
 you guide us to salvation.
Give us the courage, strength and grace
 to build a world of justice and peace,
 ready for the coming of that kingdom
 where you live with the Father and the Holy
  Spirit,
 one God, for ever and ever.
Amen.

Wednesday

God our Savior,
 hear our morning prayer:
Help us to follow the light
 and live the truth.
In you we have been born again

as sons and daughters of light;
may we be your witnesses before all the world.
Grant this through Christ our Lord.
Amen.

or

Lord,
as daylight fills the sky,
fill us with your holy light.
May our lives mirror our love for you
whose wisdom has brought us into being,
and whose care guides us on our way.
We ask this in the name of Jesus the Lord.
Amen.

Thursday

Lord,
let the knowledge of salvation
enlighten our hearts,
so that freed from fear and from the power of
our enemies,
we may serve you faithfully all the days of our
life.
Grant this through Christ our Lord.
Amen.

or

All-powerful and ever-living God,
shine with the light of your radiance
on a people who live in the shadow of death.
Let the dawn from on high break upon us:
your Son our Lord Jesus Christ,
who lives and reigns with you and the Holy
Spirit,

One God, for ever and ever.
Amen.

Lord our God,
    you conquer the darkness of ignorance
    by the light of your Word.
Strengthen within our hearts
    the faith you have given us;
    let not temptation ever quench the fire
    that your love has kindled in us.
We ask this through Christ our Lord.

or

Lord,
    fill our hearts with your love
    as morning fills the sky.
By living your law may we have
    your peace in this life
    and endless joy in the life to come.
Grant this through Christ our Lord.
Amen.

Lord,
    free us from the dark night of death.
Let the light of resurrection
    dawn within our hearts
    to bring the radiance of eternal life.
We ask this in the name of Jesus the Lord.
Amen.

or

Lord,
    we praise you
    with our lips,

and with our lives and hearts.
Our very existence is a gift from you;
    to you we offer all we have and are.
Grant this through Christ our Lord.
Amen.

Let us bless the Lord.
— Thanks be to God.

Evening Prayer

    We begin by asking God's Spirit to help us
pray.

God, come to my assistance.
    Lord make haste to help me.

Glory to the Father,
and to the Son,
and to the Holy Spirit:
As it was in the beginning,
is now,
and will be for ever. Amen.

    A hymn or poem may be prayed. See
POEMS AND HYMNS, page 194.
    The most ancient Christian evening hymn,
Phos Hilaron, dating from the early second century,
is still used by the Eastern Orthodox and Byzantine-rite Catholics:

Joyous Light

Phos Hilaron

O joyous Light,

pure brightness of the ever-living Father in
heaven,

O Jesus Christ, holy and blessed.

Now as we come to the setting of the sun,

and our eyes behold the vesper light,

we sing your praises, God: Father, Son, and
Holy Spirit.

It is fitting at all times to raise a song of praise

in measured melody to you, O Son of God,
giver of life.

Behold, the universe sings your glory.

Psalms

One or two Psalms are prayed. Psalms for
Evening Prayer are so designated in the Psalter
(the Psalter begins on page 53). Also, at the beginning of the Psalter is a plan to pray the Psalms
over four weeks.

After each Psalm, "Glory to the Father . . ." is
prayed.

Readings

One or two readings from Scripture as found
in READING THE BIBLE.

Canticle of Mary

Magnificat

Luke 1:46-55

My soul proclaims the greatness of the Lord,
my spirit rejoices in God my Savior,
for you, Lord, have looked with favor on your
     lowly servant.
From this day all generations will call me blessed:
You, the almighty, have done great things for me
and holy is your name.
You have mercy on those who fear you,
from generation to generation.
You have shown strength with your arm
and scattered the proud in their conceit,
casting down the mighty from their thrones
and lifting up the lowly.
You have filled the hungry with good things
and sent the rich away empty.
You have come to the aid of your servant Israel,
to remember the promise of mercy,
the promise made to our forebears,
to Abraham and his children for ever.

Glory to the Father,
and to the Son,
and to the Holy Spirit:
As it was in the beginning,
is now,
and will be for ever. Amen.

Lord's Prayer*

Contemporary Version

Our Father in heaven,
   hallowed be your name,
   your kingdom come,
   your will be done,
      on earth as in heaven.
Give us today our daily bread.
Forgive us our sins
   as we forgive those who sin against us.
Save us from the time of trial
   and deliver us from evil.
Amen.

Prayer of the Day

Sunday

Lord God,
   your Son our Savior Jesus Christ
   triumphed over the powers of death
   and prepared for us
   a place in the new Jerusalem.
Grant that we,
   who have this day given thanks
   for his resurrection,
   may praise you in that city
   of which he is the light,
   and where he lives and reigns
   for ever and ever.
Amen.

   or Sunday's Opening Prayer from the missal.

---

* See page 21 for the traditional version of the Lord's Prayer.

O Lord,
    may this evening pledge of our service to you
    bring you glory and praise.
For our salvation you looked with favor
    on the lowliness of the Virgin Mary;
    lead us to the fullness of the salvation
    you have prepared for us.
We ask this in the name of Jesus the Lord.
Amen.

or

Stay with us, Lord Jesus,
    for evening draws near,
    and be our companion on our way
    to set our hearts on fire with new hope.
Help us to recognize your presence among us
    in the Scriptures we read,
    and in the breaking of the bread.
You live and reign with the Father and the Holy
        Spirit,
    one God, for ever and ever.
Amen.

Almighty God,
    we give you thanks
    for bringing us safely
    to this evening hour.
May this lifting up of our hands in prayer
    be a sacrifice pleasing in your sight.
Grant this through Christ our Lord.
Amen.

or

Lord,
    may our evening prayer rise up to you,
    and your blessing come down upon us.
May your help and salvation be ours
    now and through all eternity.
We ask this in the name of Jesus the Lord.
Amen.

Wednesday

Lord,
    watch over us by day and by night.
In the midst of life's countless changes
    strengthen us with your never-changing love.
We ask this in the name of Jesus the Lord.
Amen.

or

God our Father,
    you have filled the hungry
    with the good things of heaven.
Keep in mind your infinite compassion.
Look upon our poverty;
    and let us share the riches of your life and love.
Grant this through Christ our Lord.
Amen.

Thursday

Lord God,
    you illumine the night
    and bring the dawn to scatter darkness.
Let us pass this night in safety,
    free from Satan's power,
    and rise when morning comes
    to give you thanks and praise.

We ask this through Jesus Christ our Lord.
Amen.

or

Lord,
hear the evening prayers we bring before you:
Help us to follow in the footsteps of your Son
so that we may produce an abundant harvest of
goodness
in patience and in faith.
Grant this through Christ our Lord.
Amen.

Friday

God our Father,
help us to follow the example
of your Son's patience in suffering.
By sharing the burden he carries,
may we come to share his glory
in the kingdom where he lives with you and the
Holy Spirit,
one God, for ever and ever.
Amen.

or

O God,
the contradiction of the cross
proclaims your infinite wisdom.
Help us to see that the glory of your Son
is revealed in the suffering he freely accepted.
Give us faith to claim as our only glory
the cross of our Lord Jesus Christ,
who lives with you and the Holy Spirit,
one God for ever and ever.
Amen.

Lord God,
    the source of eternal light,
    shine your day on us
    who watch for you,
    that our lips may praise you,
    our lives may serve you,
    and our worship tomorrow
    give you glory.
Grant this through Christ our Lord.
Amen.

    or Sunday's Opening Prayer from the missal.

NIGHT PRAYER

The office of night prayer is based on the Liturgy of the Hours.

~~~~∽∞∽∞∽~~~~

God, come to my assistance.
　Lord, make haste to help me.
　　Examination of conscience

Prayer of Contrition*

Lord Jesus,
you opened the eyes of the blind,
healed the sick,
forgave the sinful woman,
and after Peter's denial
confirmed him in your love.
Listen to my prayer:
forgive all my sins,
renew your love in my heart,
help me to live in perfect
unity with my fellow Christians
that I may proclaim your saving
power to all the world.

Psalm 91

Security under God's Protection

You who dwell in the shelter of the Most High,
　who abide in the shadow of the Almighty,
Say to the LORD, "My refuge and fortress,
　my God in whom I trust."
God will rescue you from the fowler's snare,

---

* See page 210 for other prayers of contrition.

from the destroying plague,
Will shelter you with pinions,
spread wings that you may take refuge;
God's faithfulness is a protecting shield.
You shall not fear the terror of the night
nor the arrow that flies by day,
Nor the pestilence that roams in darkness,
nor the plague that ravages at noon.
Though a thousand fall at your side,
ten thousand at your right hand,
near you it shall not come.
You need simply watch;
the punishment of the wicked you will see.
You have the LORD for your refuge;
you have made the Most High your stronghold.
No evil shall befall you,
no affliction come near your tent.
For God commands the angels
to guard you in all your ways.
With their hands they shall support you,
lest you strike your foot against a stone.
You shall tread upon the asp and the viper,
trample the lion and the dragon.

Whoever clings to me I will deliver;
whoever knows my name I will set on high.
All who call upon me I will answer;
I will be with them in distress;
I will deliver them and give them honor.
With length of days I will satisfy them
and show them my saving power.

Glory to the Father . . .

Canticle of Simeon

Nunc Dimittis

Luke 2:29-32

Now, Lord, you let your servant go in peace:
Your word has been fulfilled.
My own eyes have seen the salvation
which you have prepared in the sight of every
      people:
a light to reveal you to the nations
and the glory of your people Israel.

Glory to the Father . . .
Lord,
   give our bodies restful sleep
   and let the work we have done today
bear fruit in eternal life.
We ask this through Christ our Lord.
Amen.

Hail Mary . . .*

or

A hymn to Mary†.

For additional night prayers, see Catholic
Household Blessings and Prayers *in SUGGESTED
BOOKS FOR FURTHER READING, page 384.*

---

* See page 21.
† See POEMS AND HYMNS, page 222 and following.

The Psalter

The Psalter, or Book of Psalms, is the oldest prayer book of both Jews and Christians. It is still our best prayer book.

Jesus, as a devout Jew, prayed the Psalms faithfully. Matthew and Mark cite the opening words of Psalm 22, "My God, my God, why have you abandoned me?" as the last words of Jesus on the cross.

In the earliest period of the Church, the Psalter was the Church's only hymnal. The Psalms have remained the foundation of the Church's daily liturgical prayer. One of the goals of the Second Vatican Council was that the Psalms should again be at the center of lay people's prayer life as they were in the early Church.

At first the Psalms may seem strange. Most of us do not spend much time reading poetry, and the Psalms are poetry. The poet makes us look beneath the surface of life, which many modern people try to avoid. But that is precisely what we must do if our relationships with God and with our fellow humans are to become real and not just superficial.

Eugene H. Peterson, in his book *Answering God: The Psalms as Tools for Prayer* (see SUGGESTED BOOKS FOR FURTHER READING, page 375), says that human beings use three languages:

Language I is the first language we use as infants, even before we can speak words. It is the language of feelings, at first expressed by wordless sounds.

As we grow up, we learn Language II, by which information is communicated. This is the language of school and casual conversation.

Finally, we learn Language III, the language of motivation: the medium of business, politics and advertising.

Languages II and III are the dominant languages of our culture. Language I is largely neglected except by lovers and saints. It is a language we need to recover. At death, it will be the only language we will have.

Language I is the language of the Psalms. Praying them is a good way to rediscover your feelings. God gave you feelings, and you should not be afraid to acknowledge them. At first, the vehemence of some of the Psalms may make you uneasy, but as you continue to pray them, you will feel at home with them.

This prayer book follows the example of the Church's Liturgy of the Hours in omitting a few Psalm verses that a modern Christian may not find appropriate for prayer. But the strong expressions of feelings remain in this collection of Psalms. You will find that by expressing these feelings to God, you can let them go, knowing that God will take care of them.

But suppose you are praying the Psalms in a systematic way, following their order in Morning and Evening Prayer, and you find a Psalm that does not at all express your feelings? St. Augustine reminds us that the Psalms are the prayer of the whole Church, or as he loved to say, the Whole Christ: the Head and the members. When Christ prayed Psalm 22 on the cross, he expressed not only his own feeling of abandonment, but that of every person who ever had or ever will feel forsaken by God. He taught us that we should identify with and pray for all our sisters and brothers.

If the Psalms do not appeal to you at first, persevere. Whenever Jesus talked about prayer, he stressed the importance of faithfulness. If you are faithful in praying the Psalms, the time will soon come when you will wonder how you ever lived without them.

On the following page is a chart that shows a plan for praying the Psalter over a four-week period. The numbers in the chart refer to Psalm numbers; the two Canticles are included in OLD TESTAMENT CANTICLES, page 173.

Four-Week Psalm Readings

	Week			
	1	2	3	4
Sunday				
Evening I*	141 142	16	113 116	122 130
Morning	63 149	118 150	93 148	118 150
Evening II	110 114	110 115	110 111	110 112
Monday				
Morning	5 29	42 19	84 96	91 135
Evening	11 15	45	123 124	136
Tuesday				
Morning	24 33	43 65	67 85	101 144
Evening	20 21	49	125 131	137 138
Wednesday				
Morning	36 47	77 97	86 98	108 146
Evening	27	62 67	126 127	139
Thursday				
Morning	48 57	80 81	87 99	143 147
Evening	30 32	72	132	144
Friday				
Morning	51 100	51 147	51 100	51 147
Evening	41 46	116 121	135	145
Saturday				
Morning	Moses† 117	8 92	Wisdom† 117	8 92

*"Sunday evening I" is Saturday evening.
†"Moses": Canticle of Moses; "Wisdom": Canticle of Lady Wisdom. (See Old Testament Canticles.)

Psalm 1

True Happiness in God's Law

Happy those* who do not follow
   the counsel of the wicked,
Nor go the way of sinners,
   nor sit in company with scoffers.
Rather the law of the LORD is their joy;
   God's law they study day and night.
They are like a tree
   planted near streams of water,
   that yields its fruit in season;
Its leaves never wither;
   whatever they do prospers.

But not the wicked!†
   They are like chaff driven by the wind.
Therefore the wicked will not survive judgment,
   nor will sinners in the assembly of the just.
The LORD watches over the way of the just,
   but the way of the wicked leads to ruin.

Psalm 2‡

A Psalm for a Royal Coronation

Why do the nations protest
   and the peoples grumble in vain?
Kings on earth rise up

---

   * "Those": literally, "the man." The word is used here and
in many of the Psalms as typical, and therefore is translated
"those" or "they."
   † "The wicked": Those who by their actions distance
themselves from God's life-giving presence
   ‡ This Psalm has a messianic meaning for the Church; the
New Testament understands it of Christ. (Acts 4:25-27; 13:33;
Hebrews 1:5).

and princes plot together
  against the LORD and his anointed:*
"Let us break their shackles
  and cast off their chains!"
The one enthroned in heaven laughs;
  the Lord derides them,
Then speaks to them in anger,
  terrifies them in wrath:
"I myself have installed my king
  on Zion, my holy mountain."
I will proclaim the decree of the LORD
  who said to me, "You are my son;
  today I am your father.
Only ask it of me,
  and I will make your inheritance the nations,
  your possession the ends of the earth.
With an iron rod you shall shepherd them,
  like a clay pot you will shatter them."
And now, kings, give heed;
  take warning, rulers on earth.
Serve the LORD with fear;
  with trembling bow down in homage,
Lest God be angry and you perish from the way
  in a sudden blaze of anger.
Happy are all who take refuge in God!

Psalm 4

Trust in God

Night Prayer

Answer me when I call, my saving God.
  In my troubles, you cleared a way;

---

  * "Anointed": Hebrew "mashiah"; Greek "christos,"
whence English Messiah and Christ.

show me favor; hear my prayer.

How long will you people mock my honor,
  love what is worthless, chase after lies?
Know that the LORD works wonders for the
      faithful;
  the LORD hears when I call out.
Tremble* and do not sin;
  upon your beds ponder in silence
Offer fitting sacrifice
  and trust in the LORD.

Many say, "May we see better times!
  LORD, show us the light of your face!"
But you have given my heart more joy
  than they have when grain and wine abound.
In peace I shall both lie down and sleep,
  for you alone, LORD, make me secure.

Psalm 5:2-10, 12-13

Prayer for Divine Help

Morning Prayer

Hear my words, O LORD;
  listen to my sighing.
Hear my cry for help,
  my king, my God!
To you I pray, O LORD;
  at dawn you will hear my cry;
  at dawn I will plead before you and wait.

You are not a god who delights in evil;
  no wicked person finds refuge with you;
  the arrogant cannot stand before you.

---

* "Tremble": Be moved deeply with religious awe.

You hate all who do evil;
    you destroy all who speak falsely.
Murderers and deceivers
    the LORD abhors.

But I can enter your house
    because of your great love.
I can worship in your holy temple
    because of my reverence for you, LORD.
Guide me in your justice because of my foes;
    make straight your way before me.

Then all who take refuge in you will be glad
    and forever shout for joy.
Protect them that you may be the joy
    of those who love your name.
For you, LORD, bless the just;
    you surround them with favor like a shield.

Psalm 6

Prayer in Distress

Do not reprove me in your anger, LORD,
    nor punish me in your wrath.
Have pity on me, LORD, for I am weak;
    heal me, LORD, for my bones are trembling.
In utter terror is my soul —
    and you, LORD, how long . . . ?*
Turn, LORD, save my life;
    in your mercy rescue me.

---

* "How long . . . ?": elliptical for "How long will it be
before you answer my prayer?"

For who among the dead remembers you?*
Who praises you in Sheol?

I am wearied with sighing;
all night long tears drench my bed;
my couch is soaked with weeping.
My eyes are dimmed with sorrow,
worn out because of all my foes.

Away from me, all who do evil!
The LORD has heard my weeping.
The LORD has heard my prayer;
the LORD takes up my plea.
My foes will be terrified and disgraced;
all will fall back in sudden shame.

Psalm 7

God the Vindicator

LORD my God, in you I take refuge;
rescue me; save me from all who pursue me,
Lest they maul me like lions,
tear me to pieces with none to save.

LORD my God, if I am at fault in this,†
if there is guilt on my hands,
If I have repaid my friend with evil —
I spared even those who hated me without

---

* "For who among the dead . . . ?": a motive for God to
preserve the psalmist from death: In the shadowy world of the
dead no one offers you praise. Sheol is the biblical term for the
underworld where the insubstantial souls of the dead dwelt. It
was similar to the Hades of Greek and Latin literature. Only in
the second century B.C. do biblical books begin to speak posi-
tively of life with God after death. See Daniel 12:1-3; Wisdom 3.

† "At fault in this": in the accusation enemies have made
against the psalmist.

        cause —
Then let my enemy pursue and overtake me,
    trample my life to the ground,
    and leave me dishonored in the dust.

Rise up, LORD, in your anger;
    rise against the fury of my foes.
    Wake to judge as you have decreed.
Have the assembly of the peoples gather about
        you;
    sit on your throne high above them,
    O LORD, judge of the nations.
Grant me justice, LORD, for I am blameless,
    free of any guilt.
Bring the malice of the wicked to an end;
    uphold the innocent,
O God of justice,
    who tries hearts and minds.

A shield before me is God
    who saves the honest heart.
God is a just judge,
    who rebukes in anger every day.
If sinners do not repent,
    God sharpens his sword,
    strings and readies the bow,
Prepares his deadly shafts,
    makes arrows blazing thunderbolts.

Sinners conceive iniquity;
    pregnant with mischief,
    they give birth to failure.
They open a hole and dig it deep,
    but fall into the pit they dug.
Their mischief comes back upon themselves;

their violence falls on their own heads.

I praise the justice of the LORD;
  I celebrate the name of the LORD Most High.

Psalm 8

O LORD, our Lord,
  how awesome is your name through all the
    earth!
  You have set your majesty above the heavens!
Out of the mouths of babes and infants
  you have drawn a defense against your foes,
  to silence enemy and avenger.
When I see your heavens, the work of your
    fingers,
  the moon and stars that you set in place —
What are humans that you are mindful of them,
  mere mortals that you care for them?
Yet you have made them little less than a god,*
  crowned them with glory and honor.
You have given them rule over the works of your
    hands,
  put all things at their feet:
All sheep and oxen,
  even the beasts of the field,
The birds of the air, the fish of the sea,
  and whatever swims the paths of the seas.
LORD, our Lord,

---

* "Little less than a god": Hebrew "elohim," the ordinary
word for "God" or "the gods" or members of the heavenly
court. The Greek version translated "elohim" by "angels." Several ancient and modern versions follow the Greek. The meaning seems to be that God created human beings almost at the
level of the beings in the heavenly world. Hebrews 2:9 finds the
eminent fulfillment of this verse in Jesus Christ.

how awesome is your name through all the
earth!

Psalm 8 (NAB 1970)

Divine Majesty and Human Dignity

Morning Prayer

O LORD, our Lord,
how glorious is your name over all the earth!
You have exalted your majesty above the
heavens.
Out of the mouths of babes and sucklings
you have fashioned praise because of your foes,
to silence the hostile and the vengeful.

When I behold your heavens, the work of your
fingers,
the moon and the stars which you set in
place —
What is man that you should be mindful of him,
or the son of man that you should care for him?

You have made him little less than the angels,
and crowned him with glory and honor.
You have given him rule over the works of your
hands,
putting all things under his feet:

All sheep and oxen,
yes, and beasts of the field.
The birds of the air, the fishes of the sea,
and whatever swims the paths of the seas.
O LORD, our Lord,
how glorious is your name over all the earth.

Psalm 11

Confidence in the Presence of God

In the LORD I take refuge;
　　how can you say to me,
　　"Flee like a bird to the mountains!"
See how the wicked string their bows,
　　fit their arrows to the string
　　to shoot from the shadows at the upright.
When foundations* are being destroyed,
　　what can the upright do?

The LORD is in his holy temple;
　　the LORD's throne is in heaven.
God's eyes keep careful watch;
　　they test all peoples.
The LORD tests the good and the bad,
　　hates those who love violence,
And rains upon the wicked
　　fiery coals and brimstone,
　　a scorching wind their allotted cup.†
The LORD is just and loves just deeds;
　　the upright shall see his face.

Psalm 15

The Righteous Israelite

Evening Prayer

LORD, who may abide in your tent?
　　Who may dwell on your holy mountain?

---

* "Foundations": usually understood of public order.
† "Their allotted cup": The cup that God gives people to drink is a common figure for their destiny. See Matthew 20:22, Revelation 14:10.

Whoever walks without blame,
     doing what is right,
     speaking truth from the heart;
Who does not slander a neighbor,
     does no harm to another,
     never defames a friend;
Who disdains the wicked,
     but honors those who fear the LORD;
Who keeps an oath despite the cost,
     lends no money at interest,*
     accepts no bribe against the innocent.

Whoever acts like this
     shall never be shaken.

Psalm 16

God the Supreme Good

Evening Prayer

Keep me safe, O God;
     in you I take refuge.
I say to the LORD,
     you are my Lord,
     you are my only good.
Worthless are all the false gods of the land.
     Accursed are all who delight in them.
They multiply their sorrows
     who court other gods.
Blood libations to them I will not pour out,
     nor will I take their names upon my lips.

---

* "Lends no money at interest": Lending money in the
Old Testament was often seen as assistance to the poor in their
distress, not as an investment. Making money off the poor by
charging interest was thus forbidden. See Exodus 22:24; Deuteronomy 23:20.

LORD, my allotted portion and my cup,
   you have made my destiny secure.
Pleasant places were measured out for me;
   fair to me indeed is my inheritance.

I bless the LORD who counsels me;
   even at night my heart exhorts me.
I keep the LORD always before me;
   with the Lord at my right, I shall never be
      shaken.
Therefore my heart is glad, my soul rejoices;
   my body also dwells secure,
For you will not abandon me to Sheol,
   nor let your faithful servant see the pit.
You will show me the path to life,
   abounding joy in your presence,
   the delights at your right hand forever.

Psalm 19

God's Glory in the Heavens and in the Law

Morning Prayer

The heavens declare the glory of God;
   the sky proclaims its builder's craft.
One day to the next conveys that message;
   one night to the next imparts that knowledge.
There is no word or sound;*
   no voice is heard;
Yet their report goes forth through all the earth,
   their message to the ends of the world.

---

* "No word or sound": Without words, the regular func-
tioning of the heavens and the alternation of day and night
inform human beings of the creator's power and wisdom.

God has pitched there a tent for the sun;*
   it comes forth like a bridegroom from his
      chamber,
   and like an athlete joyfully runs its course.
From one end of the heavens it comes forth;
   its course runs through to the other;
   nothing escapes its heat.

The law of the LORD is perfect,
   refreshing the soul.
The decree of the LORD is trustworthy,
   giving wisdom to the simple.
The precepts of the LORD are right,
   rejoicing the heart.
The command of the LORD is clear,
   enlightening the eye.
The fear of the LORD is pure,
   enduring forever.
The statutes of the LORD are true,
   all of them just;
More desirable than gold,
   than a hoard of purest gold,
Sweeter also than honey
   or drippings from the comb.
By them your servant is instructed;
   obeying them brings much reward.

Who can detect heedless failings?
   Cleanse me from my unknown faults.
But from willful sins keep your servant;

---

* "The sun": In other (non-biblical) religious literature,
the sun is a judge and lawgiver since it sees all in its daily
course. The verses about the sun form a transition to praise of
the law.

let them never control me.
Then shall I be blameless,
    innocent of grave sin.
Let the words of my mouth meet with your favor,
    keep the thoughts of my heart before you,
    LORD, my rock and my redeemer.

Psalm 20

Prayer for the King in Time of War

Evening Prayer

The LORD answer you in time of distress;
    the name of the God of Jacob defend you!
May God send you help from the temple,
    from Zion be your support.
May God remember your every offering,
    graciously accept your holocaust,
Grant what is in your heart,
    fulfill your every plan.
May we shout for joy at your victory,
    raise the banners in the name of our God.
    The LORD grant your every prayer!

Now I know victory is given
    to the anointed of the LORD.
God will answer him from the holy heavens
    with a strong arm that brings victory.
Some rely on chariots, others on horses;
    but we rely on the name of the LORD our God.
They collapse and fall,
    but we stand strong and firm.
LORD, grant victory to the king;
    answer when we call upon you.

Psalm 21:2-8, 14

Thanksgiving and Assurances for the King

Evening Prayer

LORD, the king finds joy in your power;
 in your victory how greatly he rejoices!
You have granted him his heart's desire;
 you did not refuse the prayer of his lips.
For you welcomed him with goodly blessings;
 you placed on his head a crown of pure gold.
He asked life of you;
 you gave it to him,
 length of days forever.
Great is his glory in your victory;
 majesty and splendor you confer upon him.
You make him the pattern of blessings forever,
 you gladden him with the joy of your presence.
For the king trusts in the LORD,
 stands firm through the love of the Most High.

Arise, LORD, in your power!
 We will sing and chant the praise of your
 might.

Psalm 22

My God, my God, why have you abandoned me?*
 Why so far from my call for help,
 from my cries of anguish?
My God, I call by day, but you do not answer;
 by night, but I have no relief.

---

* This Psalm is important in the New Testament. Its opening words occur on the lips of the crucified Jesus. (Matthew 27:46; Mark 15:34.) Several other verses are quoted or alluded to in the account of his passion (Matthew 27:35, 43; John 19:24).

Yet you are enthroned as the Holy One;
   you are the glory of Israel.
In you our ancestors trusted;
   they trusted and you rescued them.
To you they cried out and they escaped;
   in you they trusted and were not disappointed.
But I am a worm, hardly human,
   scorned by everyone, despised by the people.
All who see me mock me;
   they curl their lips and jeer;
   they shake their heads at me;
"You relied on the LORD — let him deliver you;
   if he loves you, let him rescue you."
Yet you drew me forth from the womb,
   made me safe at my mother's breast.
Upon you I was thrust from the womb;
   since birth you are my God.
Do not stay far from me,
   for trouble is near,
   and there is no one to help.

Many bulls surround me;
   fierce bulls of Bashan* encircle me.
They open their mouths against me,
   lions that rend and roar.
Like water my life drains away;
   all my bones grow soft.
My heart has become like wax,
   it melts away within me.
As dry as a potsherd is my throat;

---

* "Bulls of Bashan": The enemies of the psalmist are also portrayed in less-than-human form, as wild animals. Bashan was a famous grazing land east of the Jordan (Deuteronomy 32:14; Ezekiel 39:18; Amos 4:1).

my tongue sticks to my palate;
    you lay me in the dust of death.
Many dogs surround me;
    a pack of evildoers closes in on me.
So wasted are my hands and my feet
    that I can count all my bones.
They stare at me and gloat;
    they divide my garments among them;
    for my clothing they cast lots.
But you LORD, do not stay far off;
    my strength, come quickly to help me.
Deliver me from the sword,
    my forlorn life from the teeth of the dog.
Save me from the lion's mouth,
    my poor life from the horns of wild bulls.

Then I will proclaim your name to the assembly;
    in the community I will praise you:
"You who fear the LORD, give praise!
    All descendants of Jacob give honor;
    show reverence, all descendants of Israel!
For God has not spurned or disdained
    the misery of this poor wretch,
Did not turn away from me,
    but heard me when I cried out.
I will offer praise in the great assembly;
    my vows I will fulfill before those who fear
      him.
The poor* will eat their fill;
    those who seek the LORD will offer praise.
    May your hearts enjoy life forever!"

---

    * "The poor": Hebrew "anawim," originally the poor, who were dependent on God. The term "anawim" came to include the religious sense of "humble, pious, devout."

All the ends of the earth
   will worship and turn to the LORD;
All the families of nations
   will bow low before you.
For kingship belongs to the LORD,
   the ruler over the nations.
All who sleep in the earth
   will bow low before God;
All who have gone down into the dust
   will kneel in homage.
And I will live for the LORD;
   my descendants will serve you.
The generation to come will be told of the Lord,
   that they may proclaim to a people yet unborn
   the deliverance you have brought.

Psalm 23

The Lord, Shepherd and Host

The LORD is my shepherd;
   there is nothing I lack.
In green pastures you let me graze;
   to safe waters you lead me;
   you restore my strength.
You guide me along the right path
   for the sake of your name.
Even when I walk through a dark valley,
   I fear no harm for you are at my side;
   your rod and staff give me courage.

You set a table before me
   as my enemies watch;
You anoint my head with oil;
   my cup overflows.
Only goodness and love will pursue me

all the days of my life;
I will dwell in the house of the LORD
    for years to come.

Psalm 23 (EB)

The LORD is my shepherd,
    I shall not want.
In green pastures you give me repose;
    to still waters you lead me; you restore my soul.
You lead me in right paths
    for your name's sake.

Even though I walk through the
    valley of the shadow of death,
I fear no evil, for you are with me;
    your rod and your staff, they comfort me.
You spread a table before me
    in the sight of my foes;
you anoint my head with oil,
    my cup overflows.

Surely goodness and kindness will
    follow me all the days of my life,
and I shall dwell in the house of the LORD forever.

Psalm 24

The Glory of God in Procession to Zion

Morning Prayer

The earth is the LORD's and all it holds,
    the world and those who live there.
For God founded it on the seas,
    established it over the rivers.

Who may go up the mountain of the LORD?
    Who can stand in his holy place?

"The clean of hand and pure of heart,
   who are not devoted to idols,
   who have not sworn falsely."
They will receive blessings from the LORD,
   and justice from their saving God.
Such are the people that love the LORD,
   that seek the face of the God of Jacob.

Lift up your heads, O gates;
   rise up, you ancient portals,
   that the king of glory may enter.
Who is this king of glory?
   The LORD, a mighty warrior,
   the LORD, mighty in battle.
Lift up your heads, O gates;
   rise up, you ancient portals,
   that the king of glory may enter.
Who is this king of glory?
   The LORD of hosts is the king of glory.

Psalm 25:1, 4-22

Confident Prayer for Forgiveness and Guidance

I wait for you, O LORD;
   I lift up my soul to my God.
Make known to me your ways, LORD;
   teach me your paths.
Guide me in your truth and teach me,
   for you are God my savior.
For you I wait all the long day,
   because of your goodness, LORD.
Remember your compassion and love, O LORD;
   for they are ages old.
Remember no more the sins of my youth;
   remember me only in light of your love.

Good and upright is the LORD,
    who shows sinners the way,
Guides the humble rightly,
    and teaches the humble the way.
All the paths of the LORD are faithful love
      toward those who honor the covenant
        demands.
For the sake of your name, LORD,
    pardon my guilt, though it is great.
Who are those who fear the LORD?
    God shows them the way to choose.
They live well and prosper,
    and their descendants inherit the land.
The counsel of the LORD belongs to the faithful;
    the covenant instructs them.
My eyes are ever upon the LORD,
    who frees my feet from the snare.

Look upon me and have pity on me,
    for I am alone and afflicted.
Relieve the troubles of my heart;
    bring me out of my distress.
Put an end to my affliction and suffering;
    take away all my sins.
See how many are my enemies,
    see how fiercely they hate me.
Preserve my life and rescue me;
    do not let me be disgraced, for I trust in you.
Let honesty and virtue preserve me;
    I wait for you, O LORD.
Redeem Israel, God,
    from all its distress!

Psalm 27

Trust in God

Evening Prayer

The LORD is my light and my salvation;
    whom do I fear?
The LORD is my life's refuge;
    of whom am I afraid?
When evildoers come at me
    to devour my flesh,
These my enemies and foes
    themselves stumble and fall.
Though an army encamp against me,
    my heart does not fear;
Though war be waged against me,
    even then do I trust.

One thing I ask of the LORD;
    this I seek:
To dwell in the LORD's house
    all the days of my life,
To gaze on the LORD's beauty,
    to visit his temple.
For God will hide me in his shelter
    in time of trouble,
Will conceal me in the cover of his tent;
    and set me high upon a rock.
Even now my head is held high
    above my enemies on every side!
I will offer in his tent
    sacrifices with shouts of joy;
    I will sing and chant praise to the LORD.

Hear my voice, LORD, when I call;
    have mercy on me and answer me.

"Come," says my heart, "seek God's face";
　　your face, LORD, do I seek!
Do not hide your face from me;
　　do not repel your servant in anger.
You are my help; do not cast me off;
　　do not forsake me, God my savior!
Even if my father and mother forsake me,
　　the LORD will take me in.

LORD, show me your way;
　　lead me on a level path
　　because of my enemies.
Do not abandon me to the will of my foes;
　　malicious and lying witnesses have risen
　　　　against me.
But I believe I shall enjoy the LORD's goodness
　　in the land of the living.
Wait for the LORD, take courage;
　　be stouthearted, wait for the LORD!

Psalm 29

The Lord of Majesty
Acclaimed as King of the World

Morning Prayer

Give to the LORD, you heavenly beings,
　　give to the LORD glory and might;
Give to the LORD the glory due God's name.
　　Bow down before the LORD's holy splendor!

The voice of the LORD* is over the waters;
　　the God of glory thunders,
　　the LORD, over the mighty waters.

---

　　* "The voice of the LORD": The sevenfold repetition of the phrase imitates the sound of crashing thunder.

The voice of the LORD is power;
  the voice of the LORD is splendor.
The voice of the LORD cracks the cedars;
  the LORD splinters the cedars of Lebanon,
Makes Lebanon leap like a calf,
  and Sirion* like a young bull.
The voice of the LORD strikes with fiery flame;
  the voice of the LORD rocks the desert;
  the LORD rocks the desert of Kadesh.†
The voice of the LORD twists the oaks
  and strips the forests bare.
  All in his palace say, "Glory!"

The LORD sits enthroned above the flood!
  The LORD reigns as king forever!
May the LORD give might to his people;
  may the LORD bless his people with peace!

Psalm 30

Thanksgiving for Deliverance

Evening Prayer

I praise you, LORD, for you raised me up
  and did not let my enemies rejoice over me.
O LORD, my God,
  I cried out to you and you healed me.
LORD, you brought me up from Sheol;
  you kept me from going down to the pit.

Sing praise to the LORD, you faithful;
  give thanks to God's holy name.
For divine anger lasts but a moment;

---

  * "Sirion": the Phoenician name of Mount Hermon.
  † "The desert of Kadesh": probably north of Palestine in the neighborhood of Lebanon and Hermon.

divine favor lasts a lifetime.
At dusk weeping comes for the night;
    but at dawn there is rejoicing.
Complacent,* I once said,
    "I shall never be shaken."
LORD, when you showed me favor
    I stood like the mighty mountains.
But when you hid your face
    I was struck with terror.
To you, LORD, I cried out;
    with the Lord I pleaded for mercy:
"What gain is there from my lifeblood,
    from my going down to the grave?
Does dust give you thanks
    or declare your faithfulness?
Hear, O LORD, have mercy on me;
    LORD, be my helper."

You changed my mourning into dancing;
    you took off my sackcloth
    and clothed me with gladness.
With my whole being I sing
    endless praise to you.
O LORD, my God,
    forever will I give you thanks.

Psalm 32

Remission of Sin

Evening Prayer

Happy the sinner whose fault is removed,
    whose sin is forgiven.

---

* "Complacent": Untroubled existence is often seen as a source of temptation to forget God. See Deuteronomy 8:10-18; Hosea 13:6.

Happy those to whom the LORD imputes no guilt,
     in whose spirit is no deceit.

As long as I kept silent,* my bones wasted away;
     I groaned all the day.
For day and night your hand was heavy upon me;
     my strength withered as in dry summer heat.
Then I declared my sin to you;
     my guilt I did not hide.
I said, "I confess my faults to the LORD,"
     and you took away the guilt of my sin.
Thus should all your faithful pray
     in time of distress.
Though flood waters threaten,
     they will never reach them.
You are my shelter; from distress you keep me;
     with safety you ring me round.

I will instruct you and show you the way you
          should walk;
     give you counsel and watch over you.
Do not be senseless like horses or mules;
     with bit and bridle their temper is curbed,
     else they will not come to you.

Many are the sorrows of the wicked,
     but love surrounds those who trust in the LORD.
Be glad in the LORD and rejoice, you just;
     exult, all you upright of heart.

---

* "I kept silent": did not confess the sin before God.

Psalm 33

Praise of the Lord's Power and Providence

Rejoice, you just, in the LORD;
  praise from the upright is fitting.
Give thanks to the LORD on the harp;
  on the ten-stringed lyre offer praise.
Sing to God a new song;
  skillfully play with joyful chant.
For the LORD's word is true;
  all his works are trustworthy.
The LORD loves justice and right
  and fills the earth with goodness.

By the LORD's word the heavens were made;
  by the breath of his mouth all their host.
The waters of the sea were gathered as in a bowl;
  in cellars the deep was confined.

Let all the earth fear the LORD;
  let all who dwell in the world show reverence.
For he spoke, and it came to be,
  commanded, and it stood in place.
The LORD foils the plan of nations;
  frustrates the designs of peoples.
But the plan of the LORD stands forever,
  wise designs through all generations.
Happy the nation whose God is the LORD,
  the people chosen as his very own.

From heaven the LORD looks down,
  and observes the whole human race.
Surveying from the royal throne
  all who dwell on earth.

The one who fashioned the hearts of them all,
    knows all their works.

A king is not saved by a mighty army,
    nor a warrior delivered by great strength.
Useless is the horse for safety;
    its great strength, no sure escape.
But the LORD's eyes are upon the reverent,
    upon those who hope for his gracious help,
Delivering them from death,
    keeping them alive in times of famine.

Our soul waits for the LORD,
    who is our help and shield.
For in God our hearts rejoice;
    in your holy name we trust.
May your kindness, LORD, be upon us;
we have put our hope in you.

Psalm 34

Thanksgiving to God Who Delivers the Just

I will bless the LORD at all times;
    praise shall be always in my mouth.
My soul will glory in the LORD
    that the poor may hear and be glad.
Magnify the LORD with me;
    let us exalt his name together.

I sought the LORD, who answered me,
    delivered me from all my fears.
Look to God that you may be radiant with joy
    and your faces may not blush for shame.
In my misfortune I called,
    the LORD heard and saved me from all distress.
The angel of the LORD, who encamps with them,

delivers all who fear God.
Learn to savor how good the LORD is;
    happy are those who take refuge in him.
Fear the LORD, you holy ones;
    nothing is lacking to those who fear him.
The powerful grow poor and hungry,
    but those who seek the LORD lack no good
       thing.

Come, children,* listen to me;
    I will teach you the fear of the LORD.
Who among you loves life,
    takes delight in prosperous days?
Keep your tongue from evil,
    your lips from speaking lies.
Turn from evil and do good;
    seek peace and pursue it.
The LORD has eyes for the just
    and ears for their cry.
The LORD's face is against evildoers
    to wipe out their memory from the earth.
When the just cry out, the LORD hears
    and rescues them from all distress.
The LORD is close to the brokenhearted,
    saves those whose spirit is crushed.
Many are the troubles of the just,
    but the LORD delivers from them all.
God watches over all their bones;
    not a one shall be broken.
Evil will slay the wicked;
    those who hate the just are condemned.

---

    * "Children": the customary term for students in the Wisdom literature of the Bible.

The LORD redeems loyal servants;
  no one is condemned whose refuge is God.

Psalm 36

Human Wickedness and Divine Providence

Sin directs the heart of the wicked;
  their eyes are closed to the fear of God.
For they live with the delusion:
  their guilt will not be known and hated.*
Empty and false are the words of their mouth;
  they have ceased to be wise and do good.
In their beds they hatch plots;
  they set out on a wicked way;
  they do not reject evil.

LORD, your love reaches to heaven;
  your fidelity, to the clouds.
Your justice is like the highest mountains;
  your judgments, like the mighty deep;
  all living creatures you sustain, LORD.
How precious is your love, O God!
  We take refuge in the shadow of your wings.†
We feast on the rich food of your house;
  from your delightful stream you give us drink.
For with you is the fountain of life,
  and in your light we see light.
Continue your kindness toward your friends,
  your just defense of the honest heart.
Do not let the foot of the proud overtake me,
  nor the hand of the wicked disturb me.

---

* "Hated": punished by God.

† "The shadow of your wings": metaphor for divine protection. It probably refers to the winged cherubim in the holy of holies in the temple (1 Kings 6:23-28; 2 Chronicles 3:10-13).

There make the evildoers fall;
   thrust them down, never to rise.

Psalm 40: 2-14, 17-18

Gratitude and Prayer for Help

I waited, waited for the LORD;
   who bent down and heard my cry,
Drew me out of the pit of destruction,
   out of the mud of the swamp,
Set my feet upon rock,
   steadied my steps,
And put a new song* in my mouth,
   a hymn to our God.
Many shall look on in awe
   and they shall trust in the LORD.

Happy those whose trust is in the LORD,
   who turn not to idolatry
   or to those who stray after falsehood.
How numerous, O LORD, my God,
   you have made your wondrous deeds!
And in your plans for us
   there is none to equal you.
Should I wish to declare or tell them,
   too many are they to recount.

Sacrifice and offering you do not want†
   but ears open to obedience you gave me.
Holocausts and sin-offerings you do not require;

---

   * "A new song": Giving thanks is not merely a human
response but is itself a divine gift.
   † Obedience is better than sacrifice. Hebrews 10:5-9
quotes the somewhat different Greek version and applies it to
Christ's self-oblation.

so I said, "Here I am;
    your commands for me are written in the scroll.
To do your will is my delight;
    my God, your law is in my heart!"
I announced your deed to a great assembly;
    I did not restrain my lips;
    you, LORD, are my witness.
Your deed I did not hide within my heart;
    your royal deliverance I have proclaimed.
I made no secret of your enduring kindness
    to a great assembly.

LORD, do not withhold your compassion from me;
    may your enduring kindness ever preserve me.
For all about me are evils beyond count;
    my sins so overcome me that I cannot see.
They are more than the hairs of my head;
    my courage fails me.

LORD, graciously rescue me!
    Come quickly to help me, LORD!
May all who seek you
    rejoice and be glad in you.
May those who long for your help
    always say, "The LORD be glorified."
Though I am afflicted and poor,
    the Lord keeps me in mind.
You are my help and deliverer;
    my God, do not delay!

Psalm 41

Thanksgiving after Sickness

Happy those concerned for the lowly and poor;*
  when misfortune strikes, the LORD delivers
    them.
The LORD keeps and preserves them,
  makes them happy in the land,
  and does not betray them to their enemies.
The LORD sustains them on their sickbed,
  allays the malady when they are ill.

Once I prayed, "LORD, have mercy on me;
  heal me, I have sinned against you.
My enemies say the worst of me:
  'When will that one die and be forgotten?'
When people come to visit me,
  they speak without sincerity.
Their hearts store up malice;
  they leave and spread their vicious lies.
My foes all whisper against me;
  they imagine the worst about me:
I have a deadly disease, they say;
  I will never rise from my sickbed.
Even the friend who had my trust,†
  who shared my table, has scorned me.
But you, LORD, have mercy and raise me up

---

  * "Happy those": Other psalms use the same formula for
those whom God favors. See Psalm 1:1; 34:9; 40:5; 65:5.
  † "Even the friend": John 13:18 cites this verse to charac-
terize Judas as a false friend.

that I may repay them as they deserve."*

By this I know you are pleased with me,
  that my enemy no longer jeers at me.
For my integrity you have supported me
  and let me stand in your presence forever.

Psalms 42-43

Longing for God's Presence in the Temple

Morning Prayer

As the deer longs for streams of water,
  so my soul longs for you, O God.
My being thirsts for God, the living God.
  When can I go and see the face of God?
My tears have been my food day and night,
  as they ask daily, "Where is your God?"
Those times I recall
  as I pour out my soul,
When I went in procession with the crowd,
  I went with them to the house of God,
Amid loud cries of thanksgiving,
  with the multitude keeping festival.
Why are you downcast, my soul;
  why do you groan within me?
Wait for God, whom I shall praise again,
  my savior and my God.

My soul is downcast within me;
  therefore I will remember you

---

  * "That I may repay them": The healing itself is an act of
judgment through which God decides for the psalmist and
against the false friends. The prayer is not necessarily for
strength to punish enemies.

From the land of the Jordan* and Hermon,
    from the land of Mount Mizar.
Here deep calls to deep† in the roar of your
        torrents.
    All your waves and breakers sweep over me.
At dawn may the LORD bestow faithful love
    that I may sing praise through the night,
    praise to the God of my life.
I say to God, "My rock,
    why do you forget me?
Why must I go about mourning
    with the enemy oppressing me?"
It shatters my bones, when my adversaries
        reproach me.
    They say to me daily: "Where is your God?"
Why are you downcast, my soul,
    why do you groan within me?
Wait for God, whom I shall praise again,
    my savior and my God.

Grant me justice, God;
    defend me from a faithless people;
    from the deceitful and unjust rescue me.
You, God, are my strength.
    Why then do you spurn me?
Why must I go about mourning,
    with the enemy oppressing me?
Send your light and fidelity,

---

    * "Jordan": The sources of the Jordan River are in the foot-
hills of Mount Hermon in present-day southern Lebanon.
Mount Mizar is presumed to be a mountain in the same range.
    † "Deep calls to deep": To the psalmist, the waters arising
in the north are overwhelming and far from God's presence,
like the waters of chaos. Jonah 2:3-6.

that they may be my guide,
And bring me to your holy mountain,
  to the place of your dwelling,
That I may come to the altar of God,
  to God, my joy, my delight.
Then I will praise you with the harp,
  O God, my God.
Why are you downcast, my soul;
  why do you groan within me?
Wait for God, whom I shall praise again,
  my savior and my God.

Psalm 45

Song for a Royal Wedding

Evening Prayer

My heart is stirred by a noble theme,
  as I sing my ode to the king.
  My tongue is the pen of a nimble scribe.

You are the most handsome of men;
  fair speech has graced your lips,
  for God has blessed you forever.
Gird your sword upon your hip, mighty warrior!
  In splendor and majesty ride on triumphant!
In the cause of truth and justice
  may your right hand show you wondrous
    deeds.
Your arrows are sharp;
  peoples will cower at your feet;
  the king's enemies will lose heart.
Your throne, O god,* stands forever;

---

* "O god": The king, in courtly language, is called "god,"
that is, more than human, representing God. Hebrews 1:8-9
applies this and the following verse to Christ.

your royal scepter is a scepter for justice.
You love justice and hate wrongdoing;
    therefore God, your God, has anointed you
    with the oil of gladness above your fellow
        kings.
With myrrh, aloes, and cassia
    your robes are fragrant.
From ivory-paneled palaces
    stringed instruments bring you joy.
Daughters of kings are your lovely wives;
    a princess arrayed in Ophir's gold*
    comes to stand at your right hand.

Listen, my daughter, and understand;
    pay me careful heed.
Forget your people and your father's house,
    that the king might desire your beauty.
He is your lord;
    honor him, daughter of Tyre.
Then the richest of the people
    will seek your favor with gifts.
All glorious is the king's daughter as she enters,
    her raiment threaded with gold;
In embroidered apparel she is led to the king.
    The maids of her train are presented to the king.
They are led in with glad and joyous acclaim;
    they enter the palace of the king.

The throne of your fathers your sons will have;
    you shall make them princes through all the
        land.

---

    * "Ophir's gold": Ophir is mentioned in the Bible as a source of gold. Its location is uncertain.

I will make your name renowned through all
   generations;
   thus nations shall praise you forever.

Psalm 46

God, the Protector of Zion

God is our refuge and our strength,
   an ever-present help in distress.
Thus we do not fear, though earth be shaken*
   and mountains quake to the depths of the sea,
Though its waters rage and foam
   and mountains totter at its surging.
The LORD of hosts is with us;
   our stronghold is the God of Jacob.

Streams of the river gladden the city of God,†
   the holy dwelling of the Most High.
God is in its midst; it shall not be shaken;
   God will help it at break of day.
Though nations rage and kingdoms totter,
   God's voice thunders and the earth trembles.
The LORD of hosts is with us;
   our stronghold is the God of Jacob.

Come and see the works of the LORD,
   who has done fearsome deeds on earth;
Who stops wars to the ends of the earth,
   breaks the bow, splinters the spear;

---

* "Shaken": This verse and the one following use figurative ancient Near Eastern language to describe social and political upheavals.
   † "The city of God": Jerusalem is not situated on a river. This description symbolizes the divine presence as the source of all life. Ezekiel 47:1-12.

and burns the shields with fire.
Who says:
"Be still and confess that I am God!
   I am exalted among the nations,
   exalted on the earth."
The LORD of hosts is with us;
   our stronghold is the God of Jacob.

Psalm 47

The Ruler of All the Nations

Morning Prayer

All you peoples, clap your hands;
   shout to God with joyful cries.
For the LORD, the Most High, inspires awe,
   the great king over all the earth,
Who made people subject to us,
   brought nations under our feet,
Who chose a land for our heritage,
   the glory of Jacob, the beloved.

God mounts the throne amid shouts of joy;*
   the LORD, amid trumpet blasts.
Sing praise to God, sing praise;
   sing praise to our king, sing praise.

God is king over all the earth;
   sing hymns of praise.
God rules over the nations;
   God sits upon his holy throne.
The princes of the peoples assemble
   with the people of the God of Abraham.

---

* "God mounts": The Christian liturgical tradition applies this verse to the ascension of Christ.

For the rulers of the earth belong to God,
    who is enthroned on high.

Psalm 48

The Splendor of the Invincible City

Great is the LORD and highly praised
    in the city of our God:
The holy mountain, fairest of heights,
    the joy of all the earth,
Mount Zion, the heights of Zaphon,*
    the city of the great king.

God is its citadel,
    renowned as a stronghold.
See! The kings assembled,
    together they invaded.
When they looked they were astounded,
    terrified, put to flight!
Trembling seized them there,
    anguish, like a woman's labor,
As when the east wind wrecks
    the ships of Tarshish!†

What we had heard we now see
    in the city of the LORD of hosts,
In the city of our God,

---

* "Zaphon": the mountain abode of the Canaanite storm-god, Baal, in comparable texts. To speak of Zion as it were Zaphon was to claim for Israel's God what Canaanites claimed for Baal. Though topographically speaking, Zion is only a hill, viewed religiously it towers over other mountains as the home of the supreme God.

† "The ships of Tarshish": large ships named after the distant port of Tarshish, probably ancient Tartessus in southern Spain.

founded to last forever.
O God, within your temple
we ponder your steadfast love.
Like your name, O God,
your praise reaches the ends of the earth.
Your right hand is fully victorious.
Mount Zion is glad!
The cities of Judah rejoice
because of your saving deeds!

Go about Zion, walk all around it,
note the number of its towers.
Consider the ramparts, examine its citadels,
that you may tell future generations:
"Yes, so mighty is God,
our God who leads us always!"

Psalm 49

Confidence in God Rather than in Riches

Evening Prayer

Hear this, all you peoples!
Give ear, all who inhabit the world,
You of lowly birth or high estate,
rich and poor alike.
My mouth shall speak wisdom,
my heart shall offer insight.
I will turn my attention to a problem,*
expound my question to the music of a lyre.

Why should I fear in evil days,
when my wicked pursuers ring me round,
Those who trust in their wealth

---

* "Problem": the psalmist's personal solution to the perennial biblical problem of the prosperity of the wicked.

and boast of their abundant riches?
One cannot redeem oneself,
    pay to God a ransom.
Too high the price to redeem a life;
    one would never have enough
To stay alive forever
    and never see the pit.
Anyone can see that the wisest die,
    the fool and the senseless pass away too,
    and must leave their wealth to others.
Tombs are their homes forever,
    their dwellings through all generations,
    though they gave their names to their lands.
For all their riches
    mortals do not abide;
    they perish like the beasts.

This is the destiny of those who trust in folly,
    the end of those so pleased with their wealth.
Like sheep they are herded into Sheol,
    where death will be their shepherd.
Straight to the grave they descend,
    where their form will waste away,
    Sheol will be their palace.
But God will redeem my life,
    will take me* from the power of Sheol.
Do not fear when others become rich,
    when the wealth of their houses grows great.
When they die they will take nothing with them,
    their wealth will not follow them down.

---

* "Will take me": The same Hebrew verb is used of God
"taking up" a favored servant: Enoch in Genesis 5:24; Elijah in
2 Kings 2:11-12.

When living, they congratulate themselves and
    say:
  "All praise you, you do so well."
But they will join the company of their forebears,
    never again to see the light.
For all their riches,
    if mortals do not have wisdom,
    they perish like the beasts.

Psalm 51

The Miserere: Prayer of Repentance

Morning Prayer

Have mercy on me, God, in your goodness;
    in your abundant compassion blot out my
      offense.
Wash away all my guilt;
    from my sin cleanse me.
For I know my offense;
    my sin is always before me.
Against you alone have I sinned;
    I have done such evil in your sight
That you are just in your sentence,
    blameless when you condemn.
True, I was born guilty;
    a sinner, even as my mother conceived me.*
Still, you insist on sincerity of heart;
    in my inmost being teach me wisdom.

---

    * "A sinner, even as my mother conceived me": literally,
"In iniquity was I conceived," an instance of hyperbole: at no
time was the psalmist ever without sin. See Psalm 88:16, "I am
mortally afflicted since youth," i.e., I have always been
afflicted. The verse does not imply that the sexual act of conception is sinful.

Cleanse me with hyssop,* that I may be pure;
   wash me, make me whiter than snow.
Let me hear sounds of joy and gladness;
   let the bones you have crushed rejoice.

Turn away your face from my sins;
   blot out all my guilt.
A clean heart create for me, God;
   renew in me a steadfast spirit.
Do not drive me from your presence,
   nor take from me your holy spirit.
Restore my joy in your salvation;
   sustain in me a willing spirit.
I will teach the wicked your ways,
   that sinners may return to you.
Rescue me from death, God, my saving God,
   that my tongue may praise your healing power.
Lord, open my lips;
   my mouth will proclaim your praise.
For you do not desire sacrifice;†
   a burnt offering you would not accept.
My sacrifice, God, is a broken spirit;
   God, do not spurn a broken, humbled heart.

[Make Zion prosper in your good pleasure;‡

---

   * "Hyssop": a small bush whose many woody twigs make
a natural sprinkler. It was prescribed in the Mosaic law as an
instrument for sprinkling sacrificial blood or lustral water for
cleansing. See Exodus 12:22, Leviticus 14:4, Numbers 19:18.
   † "For you do not desire sacrifice": The mere offering of
the ritual sacrifice apart from good dispositions is not accept-
able to God.
   ‡ Most scholars think that these verses were added to the
psalm some time after the destruction of the temple in 587 B.C.
The verses assume that the rebuilt temple will be an ideal site
for national reconciliation.

rebuild the walls of Jerusalem.
Then you will be pleased with proper sacrifice,
    burnt offerings and holocausts;
    then bullocks will be offered on your altar.]

Psalm 55

A Lament over Betrayal

Listen, God, to my prayer;
    do not hide from my pleading;
    hear me and give answer.
I rock with grief; I groan
    at the uproar of the enemy,
    the clamor of the wicked.
They heap trouble upon me,
    savagely accuse me.
My heart pounds within me;
    death's terrors fall upon me.
Fear and trembling overwhelm me;
    shuddering sweeps over me.
I say, "If only I had wings like a dove
    that I might fly away and find rest.
Far away I would flee;
    I would stay in the desert.
I would soon find a shelter
    from the raging wind and storm."

Lord, check and confuse their scheming.
    I see violence and strife in the city
    making rounds on its walls day and night.
Within are mischief and evil;
    treachery is there as well;
    oppression and fraud never leave its streets.
If an enemy had reviled me,
    that I could bear.

If my foes had viewed me with contempt,
    from that I could hide.
But it was you, my other self,
    my comrade and friend,
You, whose company I enjoyed,
    at whose side I walked
    in procession in the house of God.

Let death take them by surprise;
    let them go down alive to Sheol,
    for evil is in their homes and hearts.
But I will call upon God,
    and the LORD will save me.
At dusk, dawn, and noon
    I will grieve and complain,
    and my prayer will be heard.
God will give me freedom and peace
    from those who war against me,
    though there are many who oppose me.
God, who sits enthroned forever,
    will hear me and humble them.
For they will not mend their ways;
    they have no fear of God.
They strike out at friends
    and go back on their promises.
Softer than butter is their speech,
    but war is in their hearts.
Smoother than oil are their words,
    but they are unsheathed swords.
Cast your care upon the LORD,
    who will give you support.
God will never allow
    the righteous one to stumble.
But you, God, will bring them down

to the pit of destruction.
These bloodthirsty liars
   will not live half their days,
   but I put my trust in you.

Psalm 57

Confident Prayer for Deliverance

Have mercy on me, God,
   have mercy on me.
   In you I seek shelter.
In the shadow of your wings I seek shelter
   till harm pass by.
I call to God Most High,
   to God who provides for me.
May God send help from heaven to save me,
   shame those who trample upon me.
   May God send fidelity and love.
I must lie down in the midst of lions
   hungry for human prey.
Their teeth are spears and arrows;
   their tongue, a sharpened sword.
Show yourself over the heavens, God;
   may your glory appear above all the earth.

They have set a trap for my feet;
   my soul is bowed down;
They have dug a pit before me.
   May they fall into it themselves!
My heart is steadfast, God,
   my heart is steadfast.
   I will sing and chant praise.
Awake, my soul;
   awake, lyre and harp!

I will wake the dawn.*
I will praise you among the peoples, Lord;
    I will chant your praise among the nations.
For your love towers to the heavens;
    your faithfulness, to the skies.
Show yourself over the heavens, God;
    may your glory appear above all the earth.

Psalm 62

Trust in God Alone

Evening Prayer

My soul rests in God alone,
    from whom comes my salvation.
God alone is my rock and salvation,
    my secure height; I shall never fall.
How long will you set upon people,
    all of you beating them down,
As though they were a sagging fence
    or a battered wall?
Even from my place on high
    they plot to dislodge me.
They delight in lies;
    they bless with their mouths,
    but inwardly they curse.

My soul, be at rest in God alone,
    from whom comes my hope.
God alone is my rock and my salvation,
    my secure height; I shall not fall.
My safety and glory are with God,
    my strong rock and refuge.

---

    * "I will wake the dawn": By a bold figure the psalmist imagines that the sound of music and singing will waken a new day.

Trust God at all times, my people!
Pour out your hearts to God our refuge!

Mortals are a mere breath,
the powerful but an illusion;
On a balance they rise;*
together they are lighter than air.
Do not trust in extortion;
in plunder put no empty hope.
Though wealth increase,
do not set your heart upon it.
One thing God has said;
two things I have heard:
Power belongs to God;
so too, Lord, does kindness,
And you render to each of us
according to our deeds.

Psalm 63:2-9

Ardent Longing for God

Morning Prayer

O God, you are my God —
for you I long!
For you my body yearns;
for you my soul thirsts,
Like a land parched, lifeless,
and without water.
So I look to you in the sanctuary
to see your power and glory.

---

* "On a balance they rise": Precious objects were weighed by balancing two pans suspended from a beam. The lighter pan rises.

For your love is better than life;*
    my lips offer you worship!

I will bless you as long as I live;
    I will lift up my hands, calling on your name.
My soul shall savor the rich banquet of praise,
    with joyous lips my mouth shall honor you!
When I think of you upon my bed,
    through the night watches I will recall
That you indeed are my help,
    and in the shadow of your wings I shout for joy.
My soul clings fast to you;
    your right hand upholds me.

Psalm 65

Thanksgiving for God's Blessings

Morning Prayer

To you we owe our hymn of praise,
    O God on Zion;
To you our vows must be fulfilled,
    you who hear our prayers.
To you all flesh must come
    with its burden of wicked deeds.
We are overcome by our sins;
    only you can pardon them.
Happy the chosen ones you bring
    to dwell in your courts.
May we be filled with the good things of your
        house,
    the blessings of your holy temple!

You answer us with awesome deeds of justice,

---

* "For your love is better than life": Only here in the Old
Testament is anything prized above life — God's love.

O God our savior,
The hope of all the ends of the earth
and of far distant islands.
You are robed in power,
you set up the mountains by your might.
You still the roaring of the seas,
the roaring of their waves,
the tumult of the peoples.
Distant peoples stand in awe of your marvels;
east and west you make resound with joy.
You visit the earth and water it,
make it abundantly fertile.
God's stream* is filled with water;
with it you supply the world with grain;
Thus do you prepare the earth:
you drench plowed furrows,
and level their ridges.
With showers you keep the ground soft,
blessing its young sprouts.
You adorn the year with your bounty;
your paths† drip with fruitful rain.
The untilled meadows also drip;
the hills are robed with joy.
The pastures are clothed with flocks,
the valleys blanketed with grain;
they cheer and sing for joy.

---

* "God's stream": The fertile waters of the earth derive from God's fertile waters in the heavenly world.
† "Your paths": probably the tracks of God's storm chariot dropping rain upon earth.

Psalm 67

Harvest Thanks and Petition

May God be gracious to us and bless us;
  may God's face shine upon us.
So shall your rule be known upon the earth,
  your saving power among all the nations.
May the peoples praise you, God;
  may all the peoples praise you!

May the nations be glad and shout for joy;
  for you govern the peoples justly,
  you guide the nations upon the earth.
May the peoples praise you, God;
  may all the peoples praise you!

The earth has yielded its harvest;
  God, our God, blesses us.
May God bless us still;
  that the ends of the earth may revere our God.

Psalm 72

A Prayer for the King

O God, give your judgment to the king;
  your justice to the son of kings;
That he may govern your people with justice,
  your oppressed with right judgment,
That the mountains may yield their bounty for the
      people,
  and the hills great abundance,
That he may defend the oppressed among the
      people,
  save the poor and crush the oppressor.

May he live as long as the sun endures,
    like the moon, through all generations.
May he be like rain coming down upon the fields,
    like showers watering the earth,
That abundance may flourish in his days,
    great bounty, till the moon be no more.

May he rule from sea to sea,
    from the river to the ends of the earth.*
May his foes kneel before him,
    his enemies lick the dust.
May the kings of Tarshish and the islands† bring
       tribute,
    the kings of Arabia and Seba offer gifts.
May all kings bow before him,
    all nations serve him.
For he rescues the poor when they cry out,
    the oppressed who have no one to help.
He shows pity to the needy and the poor
    and saves the lives of the poor.
From extortion and violence he frees them,
    for precious is their blood in his sight.

Long may he live, receiving gold from Arabia,
    prayed for without cease, blessed day by day.
May wheat abound in the land,
    flourish even on the mountain heights.
May his fruit increase like Lebanon's,

---

   * "From sea to sea . . . the ends of the earth": the boundaries of the civilized world known to the psalmist: from the Mediterranean Sea (the western sea) to the Persian Gulf (the eastern sea), and from the Euphrates (the river) to the islands and lands of southwestern Europe, "the ends of the earth."
   † "Tarshish and the islands": the far west; "Arabia and Seba": the far south.

his wheat like the grasses of the land.
May his name be blessed forever;
as long as the sun, may his name endure.
May the tribes of the earth give blessings with his
name;
may all the nations regard him as favored.

* * *

Blessed be the LORD, the God of Israel,
who alone does wonderful deeds.
Blessed be his glorious name forever;
may all the earth be filled with the LORD's glory.
Amen and amen.

Psalm 73

The Trial of the Just

How good God is to the upright,
the Lord, to those who are clean of heart!

But, as for me, I lost my balance;
my feet all but slipped
Because I was envious of the arrogant
when I saw the prosperity of the wicked.
For they suffer no pain;
their bodies are healthy and sleek.
They are free of the burdens of life;
they are not afflicted like others.
Thus pride adorns them as a necklace;
violence clothes them as a robe.
Out of their stupidity comes sin;
evil thoughts flood their hearts.
They scoff and spout their malice;
from on high they utter threats.

They set their mouths against the heavens,*
    their tongues roam the earth.
So my people turn to them
    and drink deeply of their words.
They say, "Does God really know?"
    "Does the Most High have any knowledge?"
Such, then, are the wicked,
    always carefree, increasing their wealth.

Is it in vain that I have kept my heart clean,
    washed my hands in innocence?
For I am afflicted day after day,
    chastised every morning.
Had I thought, "I will speak as they do,"
    I would have betrayed your people.
Though I tried to understand all this,
    it was too difficult for me,
Till I entered the sanctuary of God
    and came to understand their end.

You set them, indeed, on a slippery road;
    you hurl them down to ruin.
How suddenly they are devastated;
    undone by disasters forever!
They are like a dream after waking, Lord,
    dismissed like shadows as you arise.

Since my heart was embittered
    and my soul deeply wounded,
I was stupid and could not understand;
    I was like a brute beast in your presence.

---

   * "They set their mouths against the heavens": In an image probably derived from mythic stories of half-divine giants, the monstrous speech of the wicked is likened to enormous jaws gaping wide, devouring everything in sight.

Yet I am always with you;
  you take hold of my right hand.
With your counsel you guide me,
  and at the end receive me with honor.
Whom else have I in the heavens?
  None beside you delights me on earth.
Though my flesh and my heart fail,
  God is the rock of my heart, my portion forever.
But those who are far from you perish;
  you destroy those unfaithful to you.
As for me, to be near God is my good,
  to make the Lord GOD my refuge.
I shall declare all your works
  in the gates of daughter Zion.

Psalm 77

Confidence in God During National Distress

Morning Prayer

I cry aloud to God,
  cry to God to hear me.
On the day of my distress I seek the Lord;
  by night my hands are raised unceasingly;
  I refuse to be consoled.
When I think of God, I groan;
  as I ponder, my spirit faints.
My eyes cannot close in sleep;
  I am troubled and cannot speak.
I consider the days of old;
  the years long past I remember.
In the night I meditate in my heart;
  I ponder and my spirit broods:
"Will the Lord reject us forever,
  never again show favor?

Has God's love ceased forever?
    Has the promise failed for all ages?
Has God forgotten mercy,
    in anger withheld compassion?"
I conclude: "My sorrow is this,
    the right hand of the Most High has left us."

I will remember* the deeds of the LORD;
    yes, your wonders of old I will remember.
I will recite all your works;
    your exploits I will tell.
Your way, O God, is holy;
    what god is as great as our God?
You alone are the God who did wonders;
    among the peoples you revealed your might.
With your arm you redeemed your people,
    the descendants of Jacob and Joseph.
The waters saw you, God;
    the waters saw you and lashed about,
    trembled even to their depths.
The clouds poured down their rains;
    the thunderheads rumbled;
    your arrows flashed back and forth.
The thunder of your chariot wheels resounded;
    your lightning lit up the world;
    the earth trembled and quaked.
Through the sea was your path;
    your way, through the mighty waters,
    though your footsteps were unseen.
You led your people like a flock
    under the care of Moses and Aaron.

---

    * "Remember": The verb sometimes means to make
present the great deeds of Israel's past by reciting them.

Psalm 80

Prayer to Restore God's Vineyard

Shepherd of Israel, listen,
    guide of the flock of Joseph!
From your throne upon the cherubim reveal
        yourself
    to Ephraim, Benjamin, and Manasseh.
Stir up your power, come to save us.
    O LORD of hosts, restore us.
Let your face shine upon us,
    that we may be saved.

LORD of hosts,
    how long will you burn with anger
    while your people pray?
You have fed them the bread of tears,
    made them drink tears in abundance.
You have left us to be fought over by our
        neighbors;
    our enemies deride us.
O LORD of hosts, restore us;
    let your face shine upon us,
    that we may be saved.

You brought a vine* out of Egypt;
    you drove away the nations and planted it.
You cleared the ground;
    it took root and filled the land.
The mountains were covered by its shadow,
    the cedars of God by its branches.

---

* "A vine": a frequent metaphor for Israel. See Isaiah 5:1-7;
Matthew 21:32.

It sent out boughs as far as the sea,
    shoots as far as the river.
Why have you broken down the walls,
    so that all who pass by pluck its fruit?
The boar from the forest strips the vine;
    the beast of the field feeds upon it.
Turn again, LORD of hosts;
    look from heaven and see;
Attend to this vine,
    the shoot your right hand has planted.
Those who would burn or cut it down —
    may they perish at your rebuke.
May your help be with the man at your right hand,
    with the one whom you made strong.
Then we will not withdraw from you;
    revive us, and we will call on your name.
LORD of hosts, restore us;
    let your face shine upon us,
    that we may be saved.

Psalm 81

An Admonition to Fidelity

Morning Prayer

Sing joyfully to God our strength;
    shout in triumph to the God of Jacob!
Take up a melody, sound the timbrel,
    the sweet-sounding harp and lyre.
Blow the trumpet at the new moon,
    at the full moon, on our solemn feast.*
For this is a law in Israel,

---

* "Our solemn feast": Today this is Rosh Hashanah, Jewish New Year, the first of the High Holy Days. The 10th day is Yom Kippur, the Day of Atonement.

an edict of the God of Jacob,
Who made it a decree for Joseph
    when he came out of the land of Egypt.

I hear a new oracle:
    "I relieved their shoulders of the burden;*
    their hands put down the basket.
In distress you called and I rescued you;
    unseen, I spoke to you in thunder;
At the waters of Meribah I tested you and said:
    'Listen, my people, I give you warning!
    If only you will obey me, Israel!
There must be no foreign god among you;
    you must not worship an alien god.
I, the LORD, am your God,
    who brought you up from the land of Egypt.
    Open wide your mouth that I may fill it.'
But my people did not listen to my words;
    Israel did not obey me.
So I gave them over to hardness of heart;
    they followed their own designs.
But even now if my people would listen,
    if Israel would walk in my paths,
In a moment I would subdue their foes,
    against their enemies unleash my hand.
Those who hate the LORD would tremble,
    their doom sealed forever.
But Israel I would feed with the finest wheat,
    satisfy them with honey from the rock."

_____

* "I relieved their shoulders of the burden": a reference to
the liberation of Israel from slavery in Egypt. "The basket": for
carrying clay to make bricks.

Psalm 84

Prayer of a Pilgrim to Jerusalem

How lovely your dwelling,
  O LORD of hosts!
My soul yearns and pines
  for the courts of the LORD.
My heart and flesh cry out
  for the living God.
As the sparrow finds a home
  and the swallow a nest to settle her young,
My home is by your altars,
  LORD of hosts, my king and my God!
Happy are those who dwell in your house!
  They never cease to praise you.

Happy are those who find refuge in you,
  whose hearts are set on pilgrim roads.
As they pass through the Baca valley,
  they find spring water to drink.
Also from pools the Lord provides water
  for those who lose their way.
They pass through outer and inner wall
  and see the God of gods on Zion.

LORD of hosts, hear my prayer;
  listen, God of Jacob.
O God, look kindly on our shield;
  look upon the face of your anointed.

Better one day in your courts
  than a thousand elsewhere.
Better the threshold of the house of my God
  than a home in the tents of the wicked.

For a sun and shield is the LORD God,
　　bestowing all grace and glory.
The LORD withholds no good thing
　　from those who walk without reproach.
O LORD of hosts,
　　happy are those who trust in you!

Psalm 85

Prayer for Divine Favor

Morning Prayer

You once favored, LORD, your land,
　　restored the good fortune of Jacob.
You forgave the guilt of your people,
　　pardoned all their sins.
You withdrew all your wrath,
　　turned back your burning anger.

Restore us once more, God our savior;
　　abandon your wrath against us.
Will you be angry with us forever,
　　drag out your anger for all generations?
Please give us life again,
　　that your people may rejoice in you.
Show us, LORD, your love;
　　grant us your salvation.

I will listen for the word of God;
　　surely the LORD will proclaim peace
To his people, to the faithful,
　　to those who trust in him.
Near indeed is salvation for the loyal;
　　prosperity will fill our land.
Love and truth will meet;
　　justice and peace will kiss.

Truth will spring from the earth;
    justice will look down from heaven.
The LORD will surely grant abundance;
    our land will yield its increase.
Prosperity will march before the Lord,
    and good fortune will follow behind.

Psalm 86

Prayer in Time of Distress

Morning Prayer

Hear me, LORD, and answer me,
    for I am poor and oppressed.
Preserve my life, for I am loyal;
    save your servant who trusts in you.
You are my God; pity me, Lord;
    to you I call all the day.
Gladden the soul of your servant;
    to you, Lord, I lift up my soul.
Lord, you are kind and forgiving,
    most loving to all who call on you.
LORD, hear my prayer;
    listen to my cry for help.
In this time of trouble I call,
    for you will answer me.

None among the gods can equal you, O Lord;
    nor can their deeds compare to yours.
All the nations you have made shall come
    to bow before you, Lord,
    and give honor to your name.
For you are great and do wondrous deeds;
    and you alone are God.

Teach me, LORD, your way

that I may walk in your truth,
single-hearted and revering your name.
I will praise you with all my heart,
glorify your name forever, Lord my God.
Your love for me is great;
you have rescued me from the depths of Sheol.
O God, the arrogant have risen against me;
a ruthless band has sought my life;
to you they pay no heed.
But you, Lord, are a merciful and gracious God,
slow to anger, most loving and true.
Turn to me, have pity on me;
give your strength to your servant;
save this child of your handmaid.
Give me a sign of your favor;
make my enemies see, to their confusion,
that you, LORD, help and comfort me.

Psalm 87

Zion the Home of God's People

Morning Prayer

The LORD loves the city
founded on holy mountains,
Loves the gates of Zion
more than any dwelling in Jacob.
Glorious things are said of you,
O city of God!

From Babylon and Egypt I count
those who acknowledge the LORD.
Philistia, Ethiopia, Tyre,
of them it can be said:
"This one was born there."

But of Zion it must be said:*
  "They all were born here."
The Most High confirms this;
  the Lord notes in the register of the peoples:
  "This one was born here."
So all sing in their festive dance:
  "Within you is my true home."

Psalm 90

God's Eternity and Human Frailty

Morning Prayer

Lord, you have been our refuge
  through all generations.
Before the mountains were born,
  the earth and the world brought forth,
  from eternity to eternity you are God.
A thousand years in your eyes
  are merely a yesterday,
But humans you return to dust,
  saying, "Return, you mortals!"
Before a watch passes in the night,
  you have brought them to their end;
They disappear like sleep at dawn,
  they are like grass that dies.
It sprouts green in the morning;
  by evening it is dry and withered.

Truly we are consumed by your anger,
  filled with terror by your wrath.
You have kept our faults before you,
  our hidden sins exposed to your sight.

---

* "But of Zion . . .": The bond between the exile and the holy city was so strong as to override the exile's citizenship of lesser cities.

Our life ebbs away under your wrath;
  our years end like a sigh.
Seventy is the sum of our years,
  or eighty, if we are strong;
Most of them sorrow and toil;
  they passed quickly, we are all but gone.
Who comprehends your terrible anger?
  Your wrath matches the fear it inspires.
Teach us to count our days aright,
  that we may gain wisdom of heart.
Relent, O LORD! How long?
  Have pity on your servants!
Fill us at daybreak with your love,
  that all our days we may sing for joy.
Make us glad as many days as you humbled us,
  for as many years as we have seen trouble.
Show your deeds to your servants,
  your glory to their children.
May the favor of the Lord our God be ours.
  Prosper the work of our hands!
  Prosper the work of our hands!

Psalm 91

Security under God's Protection

Night Prayer

You who dwell in the shelter of the Most High,
  who abide in the shadow of the Almighty,
Say to the LORD, "My refuge and fortress,
  my God in whom I trust."
God will rescue you from the fowler's snare,
  from the destroying plague,
Will shelter you with pinions,
  spread wings that you may take refuge;

God's faithfulness is a protecting shield.
You shall not fear the terror of the night
   nor the arrow that flies by day,
Nor the pestilence that roams in darkness,
   nor the plague that ravages at noon.
Though a thousand fall at your side,
   ten thousand at your right hand,
   near you it shall not come.
You need simply watch;
   the punishment of the wicked you will see.

You have the LORD for your refuge;
   you have made the Most High your stronghold.
No evil shall befall you,
   no affliction come near your tent.
For God commands the angels
   to guard you in all your ways.
With their hands they shall support you,
   lest you strike your foot against a stone.
You shall tread upon the asp and the viper,
   trample the lion and the dragon.

Whoever clings to me I will deliver;
   whoever knows my name I will set on high.
All who call upon me I will answer;
   I will be with them in distress;
   I will deliver them and give them honor.
With length of days I will satisfy them
   and show them my saving power.

Psalm 92

A Hymn of Thanksgiving for God's Fidelity

It is good to give thanks to the LORD,
  to sing praise to your name, Most High,
To proclaim your love in the morning,
  your faithfulness in the night,
With the ten-stringed harp,
  with melody upon the lyre.
For you make me jubilant, LORD, by your deeds;
  at the works of your hands I shout for joy.

How great are your works, LORD!
  How profound your purpose!
A senseless person cannot know this;
  a fool cannot comprehend.
Though the wicked flourish like grass
  and all sinners thrive,
They are destined for eternal destruction;
  for you, LORD, are forever on high.
Indeed your enemies, LORD,
  indeed your enemies shall perish;
all sinners shall be scattered.

You have given me the strength of a wild bull;
  you have poured rich oil upon me.
My eyes look with glee on my wicked enemies;
  my ears delight in the fall of my foes.
The just shall flourish like the palm tree,
  shall grow like a cedar of Lebanon.
Planted in the house of the LORD,
  they shall flourish in the courts of our God.
They shall bear fruit even in old age,
  always vigorous and sturdy,

As they proclaim: "The LORD is just;
 our rock, in whom there is no wrong."

Psalm 93

God is a Mighty King

Morning Prayer

The LORD is king, robed with majesty;
 the LORD is robed, girded with might.
The world will surely stand in place,
 never to be moved.
Your throne stands firm from of old;
 you are from everlasting, LORD.
The flood* has raised up, LORD;
 the flood has raised up its roar;
 the flood has raised its pounding waves.
More powerful than the roar of many waters,
 more powerful than the breakers of the sea,
 powerful in the heavens is the LORD.
Your decrees are firmly established;
 holiness belongs to your house, LORD,
 for all the length of days.

Psalm 95

A Call to Praise and Obedience

Invitatory

Come, let us sing joyfully to the Lord;
 cry out to the rock of our salvation.
Let us greet him with a song of praise,
 joyfully sing out our psalms.
For the LORD is the great God,
 the great king over all gods.

---

 * "The flood . . .": The primordial sea was tamed by God
in the act of creation. It is a figure of chaos and rebellion.

Whose hand holds the depths of the earth;
　　who owns the tops of the mountains.
The sea and the dry land belong to God,
　　who made them, formed them by hand.

Enter, let us bow down in worship;
　　let us kneel before the LORD who made us,
For this is our God,
　　whose people we are,
　　God's well-tended flock.

Oh, that today you would hear his voice:
　　Do not harden your hearts as at Meribah,
　　as on the day of Massah in the desert.
There your ancestors tested me;
　　they tried me though they had seen my works.
Forty years I loathed that generation;
　　I said: "This people's heart goes astray,
　　they do not know my ways."
Therefore I swore in my anger:
　　"They shall never enter my rest."

Psalm 96

God of the Universe

Morning Prayer

Sing to the LORD a new song;
　　sing to the LORD, all the earth.
Sing to the LORD, bless his name;
　　announce salvation day after day.
Tell God's glory among the nations;
　　among all peoples, God's marvelous deeds.

For great is the LORD and highly to be praised,
　　to be feared above all gods.
For the gods of the nations all do nothing,

but the LORD made the heavens.
Splendor and power go before him;
    power and grandeur are in his holy place.

Give to the LORD, you families of nations,
    give to the LORD glory and might;
    give to the LORD the glory due his name!
Bring gifts and enter his courts;
    bow down to the LORD, splendid in holiness.
Tremble before God, all the earth;
    say among the nations: The LORD is king.
The world will surely stand fast, never to be
    moved.
    God rules the peoples with fairness.

Let the heavens be glad and the earth rejoice;
    let the sea and what fills it resound;
    let the plains be joyful and all that is in them.
Then let all the trees of the forest rejoice
    before the LORD who comes,
    who comes to govern the earth,
To govern the world with justice
    and the peoples with faithfulness.

Psalm 97

The Divine Ruler of All

Morning Prayer

The LORD is king; let the earth rejoice;
    let the many islands be glad.
Cloud and darkness surround the Lord;
    justice and right are the foundation of his
        throne.
Fire goes before him;
    everywhere it consumes the foes.

Lightning illumines the world;
  the earth sees and trembles.
The mountains melt like wax before the LORD,
  before the Lord of all the earth.
The heavens proclaim God's justice;
  all peoples see his glory.

All who serve idols are put to shame,
  who glory in worthless things;
  all gods* bow down before you.
Zion hears and is glad,
  and the cities of Judah rejoice
  because of your judgments, O LORD.
You, LORD, are the Most High over all the earth,
  exalted far above all gods.
The LORD loves those who hate evil,
  protects the lives of the faithful,
  rescues them from the hand of the wicked.
Light dawns for the just;
  gladness, for the honest of heart.
Rejoice in the LORD, you just,
  and praise his holy name.

Psalm 98

The Coming of God

Morning Prayer

Sing a new song to the LORD,
  who has done marvelous deeds.
Whose right hand and holy arm
  have won the victory.
The LORD has made his victory known;

---

* "All gods": divine beings thoroughly subordinate to Israel's God. The Greek translates "angels," an interpretation adopted by Hebrews 1:6.

has revealed his triumph for the nations to see,
Has remembered faithful love
    toward the house of Israel.
All the ends of the earth have seen
    the victory of our God.

Shout with joy to the LORD, all the earth;
    break into song; sing praise.
Sing praise to the LORD with the harp,
    with the harp and melodious song.
With trumpets and the sound of the horn
    shout with joy to the King, the LORD.

Let the sea and what fills it resound,
    the world and those who dwell there.
Let the rivers clap their hands,
    the mountains shout with them for joy
Before the LORD who comes,
    who comes to govern the earth,
To govern the world with justice
    and the peoples with fairness.

Psalm 99

The Holy King

Morning Prayer

The LORD is king, the peoples tremble;
    God is enthroned on the cherubim,* the earth
        quakes.
The LORD is great on Zion,
    exalted above all the peoples.

---

* "Enthroned on the cherubim": Two cherubim were placed over the ark of the covenant in the holy of holies. Upon them God was believed to dwell invisibly. See Exodus 25:20-22; 1 Samuel 4:4.

Let them praise your great and awesome name:
    Holy is God!

O mighty king, lover of justice,
    you alone have established fairness;
    you have created just rule in Jacob.
Exalt the LORD, our God;
    bow down before his footstool;*
    holy is God!

Moses and Aaron were among his priests,
    Samuel among those who called on God's
        name;
    they called on the LORD, who answered them.
From the pillar of cloud God spoke to them;
    they kept the decrees, the law they received.
O LORD, our God, you answered them;
    you were a forgiving God,
    though you punished their offenses.
Exalt the LORD, our God;
    bow down before his holy mountain;
    holy is the LORD, our God.

Psalm 100

Communal Thanks in the Temple

Morning Prayer

Shout joyfully to the LORD, all you lands;
    worship the LORD with glad shouts;
    come before him with joyful song.
Know that the LORD is God,
    our maker to whom we belong,
    whose people we are, God's well-tended flock.
Enter the temple gates with praise,

---

* "His footstool": the ark of the covenant.

its courts with thanksgiving.
Give thanks to God, bless his name;
   good indeed is the LORD,
Whose love is forever,
   whose faithfulness lasts through every age.

Psalm 101

Norm of Life for Rulers

I sing of love and justice;
   to you, LORD, I sing praise.
I follow in the way of integrity;
   when will you come to me?
I act with integrity of heart
   within my royal court.
I do not allow into my presence
   anyone who speaks perversely.
Whoever acts shamefully I hate;
   no such person can be my friend.
I shun the devious of heart;
   the wicked I do not tolerate.
Whoever slanders another in secret
   I reduce to silence.
Haughty eyes and arrogant hearts
   I cannot endure.

I look to the faithful of the land;
   they alone can be my companions.
Those who follow the way of integrity,
   they alone can enter my service.
No one who practices deceit
   can hold a post in my court.
No one who speaks falsely
   can be among my advisors.

Each morning* I clear the wicked from the land,
and rid the LORD's city of all evildoers.

Psalm 103

Praise of Divine Goodness

Bless the LORD, my soul;
all my being, bless his holy name!
Bless the LORD, my soul;
do not forget all the gifts of God,
Who pardons all your sins,
heals all your ills,
Delivers your life from the pit,
surrounds you with love and compassion,
Fills your days with good things;
your youth is renewed like the eagle's.†

The LORD does righteous deeds,
brings justice to all the oppressed.
His ways were revealed to Moses,
mighty deeds to the people of Israel.
Merciful and gracious is the LORD,
slow to anger, abounding in kindness.
God does not always rebuke,
nurses no lasting anger,
Has not dealt with us as our sins merit,
nor requited us as our deeds deserve.

As the heavens tower over the earth,
so God's love towers over the faithful.
As far as the east is from the west,

---

* "Each morning": the normal time for the administration of justice. See 2 Samuel 15:2.

† "Your youth. . .": The eagle, because of its long life, was a symbol of perennial youth and vigor.

so far have our sins been removed from us.
As a father has compassion on his children,
    so the LORD has compassion on the faithful.
For he knows how we are formed,
    remembers that we are dust.
Our days are like the grass;
    like flowers of the field we blossom.
The wind sweeps over us and we are gone;
    our place knows us no more.
But the LORD's kindness is forever
    toward the faithful from age to age.
He favors the children's children
    of those who keep his covenant,
    who take care to fulfill its precepts.

The LORD's throne is established in heaven;
    God's royal power rules over all.
Bless the LORD, all you angels,
    mighty in strength and attentive,
    obedient to every command.
Bless the LORD, all you hosts,
    ministers who do God's will.
Bless the LORD, all creatures,
    everywhere in God's domain.
    Bless the LORD, my soul!

Psalm 104

Praise of God the Creator

Bless the LORD, my soul!
    LORD, my God, you are great indeed!
You are clothed with majesty and glory,
    robed in light as with a cloak.
You spread out the heavens like a tent;

you raised your palace upon the waters.*
You make the clouds your chariot;
    you travel on the wings of the wind.
You make the winds your messengers;
    flaming fire, your ministers.

You fixed the earth on its foundation,
    never to be moved.
The ocean covered it like a garment;
    above the mountains stood the waters.
At your roar they took flight;
    at the sound of your thunder they fled.
They rushed up the mountains, down the valleys
    to the place you had fixed for them.
You set a limit they cannot pass;
    never again will they cover the earth.

You made springs flow into channels
    that wind among the mountains.
They give drink to every beast of the field;
    here wild asses quench their thirst.
Beside them the birds of heaven nest;
    among the branches they sing.
You water the mountains from your palace;
    by your labor the earth abounds.
You raise grass for the cattle
    and plants for our beasts of burden.
You bring bread from the earth,
    and wine to gladden our hearts,
Oil to make our faces gleam,
    food to build our strength.
The trees of the LORD drink their fill,

---

* "Your palace upon the waters": God's heavenly dwelling above the upper waters of the sky. See Genesis 1:6-7.

the cedars of Lebanon, which you planted.
There the birds build their nests;
  junipers are the home of the stork.
The high mountains are for wild goats;
  the rocky cliffs, a refuge for badgers.

You made the moon to mark the seasons,
  the sun that knows the hour of its setting.
You bring darkness and night falls,
  then all the beasts of the forest roam abroad.
Young lions roar for prey;
  they seek their food from God.
When the sun rises, they steal away
  and rest in their dens.
People go forth to their work,
  to their labor till evening falls.

How varied are your works, LORD!
  In wisdom you have wrought them all;
  the earth is full of your creatures.
Look at the sea, great and wide!
  It teems with countless beings,
  living things both large and small.
Here ships ply their course;
  here Leviathan,* your creature, plays.

All of these look to you
  to give them food in due time.
When you give to them, they gather;
  when you open your hand, they are well filled.
When you hide your face, they are lost.
  When you take away their breath, they perish

---

* "Leviathan": a sea monster symbolizing primeval chaos.
God's omnipotence is demonstrated by turning the monster
into a plaything. See Job 41:1-5.

and return to the dust from which they came.
When you send forth your breath, they are
    created,
  and you renew the face of the earth.

May the glory of the LORD endure forever;
  may the LORD be glad in these works!
If God glares at the earth, it trembles,
  if God touches the mountains, they smoke!
I will sing to the LORD all my life;
  I will sing praise to my God while I live.
May my theme be pleasing to God;
  I will rejoice in the LORD.
May sinners vanish from the earth,
  and the wicked be no more.
Bless the LORD, my soul! Hallelujah!

Psalm 107

God the Savior of Those in Distress

"Give thanks to the LORD who is good,
  whose love endures forever!"
Let that be the prayer of the LORD's redeemed,
  those redeemed from the hand of the foe,
Those gathered from foreign lands,
  from east and west, from north and south.

Some had lost their way in a barren desert;
  found no path toward a city to live in.
They were hungry and thirsty;
  their life was ebbing away.
In their distress they cried to the LORD,
  who rescued them in their peril,
Guided them by a direct path
  so they reached a city to live in.

Let them thank the LORD for such kindness,
    such wondrous deeds for mere mortals,
For he satisfied the thirsty,
    filled the hungry with good things.

Some lived in darkness and gloom,
    in prison, bound with chains,
Because they rebelled against God's word,
    scorned the counsel of the Most High,
Who humbled their hearts through hardship;
    they stumbled with no one to help.
In their distress they cried to the LORD,
    who saved them in their peril,
Led them forth from darkness and gloom
    and broke their chains asunder.
Let them thank the LORD for such kindness,
    such wondrous deeds for mere mortals.
For he broke down the gates of bronze
    and snapped the bars of iron.

Some fell sick from their wicked ways,
    afflicted because of their sins.
They loathed all manner of food;
    they were at the gates of death.
In their distress they cried to the LORD,
    who saved them in their peril,
Sent forth the word to heal them,
    snatched them from the grave.
Let them thank the LORD for such kindness,
    such wondrous deeds for mere mortals.
Let them offer a sacrifice in thanks,
    declare his works with shouts of joy.

Some went off to sea in ships,
    plied their trade on the deep waters.

They saw the works of the LORD,
    the wonders of God in the deep.
He spoke and roused a storm wind;
    it tossed the waves on high.
They rose up to the heavens, sank to the depths;
    their hearts trembled at the danger.
They reeled, staggered like drunkards;
    their skill was of no avail.
In their distress they cried to the LORD,
    who brought them out of their peril,
Hushed the storm to a murmur;
    the waves of the sea were stilled.
They rejoiced that the sea grew calm,
    that God brought them to the harbor they
        longed for.
Let them thank the LORD for such kindness,
    such wondrous deeds for mere mortals.
Let them praise him in the assembly of the people,
    give thanks in the council of the elders.

God changed rivers into desert,
    springs of water into thirsty ground,
Fruitful land into a salty waste,
    because of the wickedness of its people.
He changed the desert into pools of water,
    arid land into springs of water,
And settled the hungry there;
    they built a city to live in.
They sowed fields and planted vineyards,
    brought in an abundant harvest.
God blessed them, they became very many,
    and their livestock did not decrease.
But he poured out contempt on princes,
    made them wander the trackless wastes,

Where they were diminished and brought low
    through misery and cruel oppression,
While the poor were released from their affliction;
    their families increased like their flocks.
The upright saw this and rejoiced;
    all wickedness shut its mouth.
Whoever is wise will take note of these things,
    will ponder the merciful deeds of the LORD.

Psalm 108

Prayer for Victory

Morning Prayer

My heart is steadfast, God;
    my heart is steadfast.
    I will sing and chant praise.
Awake, my soul; awake, lyre and harp!
    I will wake the dawn.
I will praise you among the peoples, LORD;
    I will chant your praise among the nations.
For your love towers to the heavens;
    your faithfulness, to the skies.
Appear on high over the heavens, God;
    may your glory appear above all the earth.
Help with your right hand and answer us
    that your loved ones may escape.

God promised in the sanctuary:
    "I will exult, I will apportion Shechem;
    the valley of Succoth I will measure out.
Gilead is mine, mine is Manasseh;
    Ephraim is the helmet for my head,
    Judah, my own scepter.
Moab is my washbowl;
    upon Edom I cast my sandal;

I will triumph over Philistia."

Who will bring me to the fortified city?
　　Who will lead me into Edom?
Was it not you who rejected us, God?
　　Do you no longer march with our armies?
Give us aid against the foe;
　　worthless is human help.
We will triumph with the help of God,
　　who will trample down our foes.

Psalm 110:1-5,7

God Appoints the King Both King and Priest

Evening Prayer

The LORD says to you, my lord:
　　"Take your throne at my right hand,
　　while I make your enemies your footstool."
The scepter of your sovereign might
　　the LORD will extend from Zion.
The LORD says: "Rule over your enemies!
　　Yours is princely power from the day of your
　　　　birth.
In holy splendor before the daystar,
　　like the dew I begot you."
The LORD has sworn and will not waver:
　　"Like Melchizedek* you are a priest forever."
At your right hand is the LORD,
　　who crushes kings on the day of wrath,
Who drinks from the brook by the wayside
　　and thus holds high his head.

---

　　* "Like Melchizedek": Melchizedek was the ancient king
of Salem (Jerusalem) who blessed Abraham (Genesis 14:18-20).
Like other kings of the time, he performed priestly functions.
Hebrews 7 sees in Melchizedek a type of Christ.

Psalm 111

Praise of God for Goodness to Israel

I will praise the LORD with all my heart
    in the assembled congregation of the upright.
Great are the works of the LORD,
    to be treasured for all their delights.
Majestic and glorious is your work,
    your wise design endures forever.
You won renown for your wondrous deeds;
    gracious and merciful is the LORD.
You gave food to those who fear you,
    mindful of your covenant forever.
You showed powerful deeds to your people,
    giving them the lands of the nations.
The works of your hands are right and true,
    reliable all your decrees,
Established forever and ever,
    to be observed with loyalty and care.
You sent deliverance to your people,
    ratified your covenant forever;
    holy and awesome is your name.
The fear of the LORD is the beginning of wisdom;
    prudent are all who live by it.
    Your praise endures forever.

Psalm 112

The Blessings of the Just

Happy are those who fear the LORD,
    who greatly delight in God's commands.
Their descendants shall be mighty in the land,
    a generation upright and blessed.

Wealth and riches shall be in their homes;
  their prosperity shall endure forever.
They shine through the darkness, a light for the
    upright;
  they are gracious, merciful, and just.
All goes well for those gracious in lending,
  who conduct their affairs with justice.
They shall never be shaken;
  the just shall be remembered forever.
They shall not fear an ill report;
  their hearts are steadfast, trusting the LORD.
Their hearts are tranquil, without fear,
  till at last they look down on their foes.
Lavishly they give to the poor;
  their prosperity shall endure forever;
  their horn* shall be exalted in honor.
The wicked shall be angry to see this;
  they will gnash their teeth and waste away;
  the desires of the wicked come to nothing.

Psalm 113

Praise of God's Care of the Poor

Evening Prayer

Praise, you servants of the LORD,
  praise the name of the LORD.
Blessed be the name of the LORD
  both now and forever.
From the rising of the sun to its setting
  let the name of the LORD be praised.

High above all nations is the LORD;
  above the heavens God's glory.

---

* "Horn": the symbol for vitality and honor.

Who is like the LORD,
    our God enthroned on high,
    looking down on heaven and earth?
The LORD raises the needy from the dust,
    lifts the poor from the ash heap,
Seats them with princes,
    the princes of the people,
Gives the childless wife a home,
    the joyful mother of children.
Hallelujah!

Psalm 114

The Lord's Wonders at the Exodus

Evening Prayer

When Israel came forth from Egypt,
    the house of Jacob from an alien people,
Judah became God's holy place,
    Israel, God's domain.
The sea beheld and fled;
    the Jordan turned back.
The mountains skipped like rams;
    the hills, like lambs of the flock.
Why was it, sea, that you fled?
    Jordan, that you turned back?
You mountains, that you skipped like rams?
    You hills, like lambs of the flock?
Tremble, earth, before the Lord,
    before the God of Jacob,
Who turned rock into pools of water,
    stone into flowing springs.

Psalm 115

The Greatness of the True God

Not to us, LORD, not to us
  but to your name give glory
  because of your faithfulness and love.
Why should the nations say,
  "Where is their God?"
Our God is in heaven;
  whatever God wills is done.

Their idols are silver and gold,
  the work of human hands.
They have mouths but do not speak,
  eyes but do not see.
They have ears but do not hear,
  noses but do not smell.
They have hands but do not feel,
  feet but do not walk,
  and no sound rises from their throats.
Their makers shall be like them,
  all who trust in them.

The house of Israel trusts in the LORD,
  who is their help and shield.
The house of Aaron trusts in the LORD,
  who is their help and shield.
Those who fear the LORD trust in the LORD,
  who is their help and shield.
The LORD remembers us and will bless us,
  will bless the house of Israel,
  will bless the house of Aaron,
Will bless those who fear the LORD,
  small and great alike.

May the LORD increase your number,
   you and your descendants.
May you be blessed by the LORD,
   who made heaven and earth.
The heavens belong to the LORD,
   but the earth is given to us.
The dead do not praise the LORD,
   all those gone down into silence.
It is we who bless the LORD,
   both now and forever.
Hallelujah!

Psalm 116

Thanksgiving to God Who Saves from Death

Evening Prayer

I love the LORD, who listened
   to my voice in supplication,
Who turned an ear to me
   on the day I called.
I was caught by the cords of death;
   the snares of Sheol had seized me;
   I felt agony and dread.
Then I called on the name of the LORD,
   "O LORD, save my life!"

Gracious is the LORD and just;
   yes, our God is merciful.
The LORD protects the simple;
   I was helpless, but God saved me.
Return, my soul, to your rest;
   the LORD has been good to you.
For my soul has been freed from death,
   my eyes from tears, my feet from stumbling.
I shall walk before the LORD

in the land of the living.

I kept faith, even when I said,
    "I am greatly afflicted!"
I said in my alarm,
    "No one can be trusted!"
How can I repay the LORD
    for all the good done for me?
I will raise the cup of salvation
    and call on the name of the LORD.
I will pay my vows to the LORD
    in the presence of all his people.
Too costly in the eyes of the LORD
    is the death of his faithful.
LORD, I am your servant,
    your servant, the child of your maidservant;
    you have loosed my bonds.
I will offer a sacrifice of thanksgiving
    and call on the name of the LORD.
I will pay my vows to the LORD
    in the presence of all his people,
In the courts of the house of the LORD,
    in your midst, O Jerusalem.
Hallelujah!

Psalm 117

The Nations Called to Praise

Morning Prayer

Praise the LORD, all you nations!
    Give glory, all you peoples!
The LORD's love for us is strong;
    the LORD is faithful forever.
Hallelujah!

Psalm 118

Hymn of Thanksgiving

Give thanks to the LORD, who is good,
  whose love endures forever.
Let the house of Israel say:
  God's love endures forever.
Let the house of Aaron say,
  God's love endures forever.
Let those who fear the LORD say,
  God's love endures forever.

In danger I called on the LORD;
  the LORD answered me and set me free.
The LORD is with me; I am not afraid;
  what can mortals do against me?
The LORD is with me as my helper;
  I shall look in triumph on my foes.
Better to take refuge in the LORD
  than to put one's trust in mortals.
Better to take refuge in the LORD
  than to put one's trust in princes.

All the nations surrounded me;
  in the LORD's name I crushed them.
They surrounded me on every side;
  in the LORD's name I crushed them.
They surrounded me like bees;
  they blazed like fire among thorns;
  in the LORD's name I crushed them.
I was hard pressed and falling,
  but the LORD came to my help.
The LORD, my strength and might,
  came to me as savior.

The joyful shout of deliverance
  is heard in the tents of the victors:
"The LORD's right hand strikes with power;
  the LORD's right hand is raised;
  the LORD's right hand strikes with power."
I shall not die but live
  and declare the deeds of the LORD.
The LORD chastised me harshly,
  but did not hand me over to death.

Open the gates of victory;
  I will enter and thank the LORD.
This is the LORD's own gate,
  where the victors enter.
I thank you for you answered me;
  you have been my savior.
The stone the builders rejected
  has become the cornerstone.
By the LORD has this been done;
  it is wonderful in our eyes.
This is the day the LORD has made;
  let us rejoice in it and be glad.
LORD, grant salvation!
  LORD, grant good fortune!

Blessed is he
  who comes in the name of the LORD.
We bless you from the LORD's house.
  The LORD is God and has given us light.
Join in procession with leafy branches
  up to the horns of the altar.

You are my God, I give you thanks;
  my God, I offer you praise.

Give thanks to the LORD, who is good,
  whose love endures forever.

Psalm 121

The Lord My Guardian

I raise my eyes toward the mountains.
  From where will my help come?
My help comes from the LORD,
  the maker of heaven and earth.

God will not allow your foot to slip;
  your guardian does not sleep.
Truly, the guardian of Israel
  never slumbers nor sleeps.
The LORD is your guardian;
  the LORD is your shade
  at your right hand.
By day the sun cannot harm you,
  nor the moon by night.
The LORD will guard you from all evil,
  will always guard your life.
The LORD will guard your coming and going
  both now and forever.

Psalm 122*

A Pilgrim's Prayer for Jerusalem

Evening Prayer

I rejoiced when they said to me,
  "Let us go to the house of the LORD."
And now our feet stand

---

  * Paul VI, the first pope to visit the Holy Land since St. Peter took up residence in Rome, chose this Psalm to pray on his arrival in Jerusalem, January 4, 1964.

within your gates, Jerusalem.
Jerusalem, built as a city
    walled round about.
Here the tribes come,
    the tribes of the LORD,
As it was decreed for Israel,
    to give thanks to the name of the LORD.
Here are the thrones of justice,
    the thrones of the house of David.

For the peace of Jerusalem pray:
    "May those who love you prosper!
May peace be within your ramparts,
prosperity within your towers."

For family and friends I say,
"May peace be yours."

For the house of the LORD, our God, I pray,
"May blessings be yours."

Psalm 123

Reliance on the Lord

Evening Prayer

To you I raise my eyes,
    to you enthroned in heaven.
Yes, like the eyes of a servant
    on the hand of his master,
Like the eyes of a maid
    on the hand of her mistress,
So our eyes are on the LORD our God,
    till we are shown favor.

Show us favor, LORD, show us favor,
    for we have our fill of contempt.

We have our fill of insult from the insolent,
    of disdain from the arrogant.

Psalm 124

God, the Rescuer of the People

Evening Prayer

Had not the LORD been with us,
    let Israel say,
Had not the LORD been with us,
    when people rose against us,
They would have swallowed us alive,
    for their fury blazed against us.
The waters would have engulfed us;
    the torrent overwhelmed us;
    seething waters would have drowned us.

Blessed be the LORD, who did not leave us
    to be torn by their fangs.
We escaped with our lives
    like a bird from the fowler's snare;
    the snare was broken and we escaped.
Our help is the name of the LORD,
    the maker of heaven and earth.

Psalm 125

Israel's Protector

Evening Prayer

Like Mount Zion are they
    who trust in the LORD,
    unshakable, forever enduring.
As mountains surround Jerusalem,
    the LORD surrounds his people
    both now and forever.

The scepter of the wicked will not prevail
    in the land given to the just,
Lest the just themselves
    turn their hands to evil.

Do good, LORD, to the good,
    to those who are upright of heart.
But those who turn aside to crooked ways,
    may the LORD send down with the wicked.
Peace upon Israel!

Psalm 126

The Reversal of Zion's Fortunes

Evening Prayer

When the LORD restored the fortunes of Zion,
    then we thought we were dreaming,
Our mouths were filled with laughter;
    our tongues sang for joy.
Then it was said among the nations,
    "The LORD has done great things for them."
The LORD has done great things for us;
    Oh, how happy we were!
Restore again our fortunes, LORD,
    like the dry stream beds of the Negeb.

Those who sow in tears
    will reap with cries of joy.
Those who go forth weeping,
    carrying sacks of seed,
Will return with cries of joy,
    carrying their bundled sheaves.

Psalm 127

The Need of God's Blessing

Evening Prayer

Unless the LORD build the house,
   they labor in vain who build.
Unless the LORD guard the city,
   in vain does the guard keep watch.
It is vain for you to rise early
   and put off your rest at night,
To eat bread earned by hard toil —
   all this God gives to his beloved in sleep.

Children too are a gift from the LORD,
   the fruit of the womb, a reward.
Like arrows in the hand of a warrior
   are the children born in one's youth.
   Blessed are they whose quivers are full.
They will never be shamed
   contending with foes at the gate.*

Psalm 130

Prayer for Pardon and Mercy

Evening Prayer

Out of the depths I call to you, LORD;
   LORD, hear my cry!
May your ears be attentive
   to my cry for mercy.
If you, LORD, mark our sins,
   LORD, who can stand?
But with you is forgiveness

---

   * "At the gate": Law courts functioned in the open area near the main city gate. The more adult sons a man had, the more forceful he would appear in disputes. See Proverbs 31:23.

and so you are revered.

I wait with longing for the LORD,
  my soul waits for God's word.
My soul looks for the LORD
  more than sentinels for daybreak.
More than sentinels for daybreak,
  let Israel look for the LORD,
For with the LORD is kindness,
  with him is full redemption,
And God will redeem Israel
  from all their sins.

Psalm 131

Humble Trust in God

Evening Prayer

LORD, my heart is not proud;
  nor are my eyes haughty.
I do not busy myself with great matters,
  with things too sublime for me.
Rather, I have stilled my soul,
  hushed it like a weaned child.
Like a weaned child on its mother's lap,
  so is my soul within me.
Israel, hope in the LORD,
  now and forever.

Psalm 132

The Covenant between David and God

Evening Prayer

LORD, remember David
  and all his anxious care;
How he swore an oath to the LORD,
  vowed to the Mighty One of Jacob:

"I will not enter the house where I live,
    nor lie on the couch where I sleep;
I will give my eyes no sleep,
    my eyelids no rest,
Till I find a home for the LORD,
    a dwelling for the Mighty One of Jacob."
"We have heard of it in Ephrathah;*
    we have found it in the fields of Jaar.
Let us enter God's dwelling;
    let us worship at God's footstool."
"Arise, LORD, come to your resting place,
    you and your majestic ark.
Your priests will be clothed with justice;
    your faithful will shout for joy."
For the sake of David your servant,
    do not reject your anointed.

The LORD swore an oath to David,
    a pledge never to be broken:
    "Your own offspring I will set upon your
        throne.
If your sons observe my covenant,
    the laws I shall teach them,
Their sons, in turn,
    shall sit forever on your throne."
Yes, the LORD has chosen Zion,
    desired it for a dwelling:
"This is my resting place forever;
    here I will dwell, for I desire it.
I will bless Zion with meat;
    its poor I will fill with bread.

---

* "Ephrathah": the homeland of David. "Jaar": poetic for
Kiriath-Jearim, a town west of Jerusalem, where the ark of the
covenant remained for several generations. See 1 Samuel 7:1-2.

I will clothe its priests with blessing;
  its faithful shall shout for joy.
There I will make a horn sprout for David's line;*
  I will set a lamp for my anointed.
His foes I will clothe with shame,
  but on him my crown shall gleam."

Psalm 133

A Vision of a Blessed Community

How good it is, how pleasant,
  where the people dwell as one!
Like precious ointment† on the head,
  running down upon the beard,
Upon the beard of Aaron,
  upon the collar of his robe.
Like dew‡ of Hermon coming down
  upon the mountains of Zion.
There the LORD has lavished blessings,
  life for evermore!

Psalm 134

Exhortation to the Night Watch to Bless God

Night Prayer

Come, bless the LORD,
  all you servants of the LORD

---

  * "A horn sprout for David's line": The image of the horn, a symbol of strength, is combined with that of a "sprout," a term used for the Davidic descendant. Early Christians referred the latter designation to Christ as son of David. See Luke 1:69.

  † "Ointment": Oil was used in the consecration of the high priest. See Exodus 30:22-33.

  ‡ *"Dew": an important source of moisture in the dry climate. See Gen. 27:28. Hermon is the majestic snow-capped mountain towering above the upper Jordan Valley.

Who stand in the house of the LORD
through the long hours of night.
Lift up your hands toward the sanctuary,
and bless the LORD.
May the LORD who made heaven and earth
bless you from Zion.

Psalm 135

Praise of God, the Ruler and Benefactor of Israel

Morning Prayer

Praise the name of the LORD!
Praise, you servants of the LORD,
Who stand in the house of the LORD,
in the courts of the house of our God!
Praise the LORD; the LORD is good!
Sing to that name; it is gracious!
For the LORD has chosen Jacob,
Israel as a treasured possession.

I know that the LORD is great,
our LORD is greater than all gods.
Whatever the LORD wishes
he does in heaven and on earth,
in the seas and in all the deeps.
He raises storm clouds from the end of the earth,
makes lightning and rain,
brings forth wind from the storehouse.

He struck down Egypt's firstborn,
human and beast alike,
And sent signs and portents against you, O Egypt,
against Pharaoh and all his servants.
The Lord struck down many nations,
slew mighty kings —

Sihon, king of the Amorites,
  Og, king of Bashan,
  all the kings of Canaan —
And made their land a heritage,
  a heritage for Israel his people.
O LORD, your name is forever,
  your renown, from age to age!
For the LORD defends his people,
  shows mercy to his servants.

The idols of the nations are silver and gold,
  the work of human hands.
They have mouths but speak not;
  they have eyes but see not;
They have ears but hear not;
  no breath is in their mouths.
Their makers shall be like them,
  all who trust in them.

House of Israel, bless the LORD!
  House of Aaron, bless the LORD!
House of Levi, bless the LORD!
  You who fear the LORD, bless the LORD!
Blessed from Zion be the LORD,
  who dwells in Jerusalem!
Hallelujah!

Psalm 136

Hymn of Thanksgiving
for God's Everlasting Love

Evening Prayer

Praise the LORD, who is so good;
  God's love endures forever;
Praise the God of gods;

God's love endures forever;
Praise the Lord of lords;
    God's love endures forever;

Who alone has done great wonders,
    God's love endures forever;
Who skillfully made the heavens,
    God's love endures forever;
Who spread the earth upon the waters,
    God's love endures forever;
Who made the great lights,
    God's love endures forever;
The sun to rule the day,
    God's love endures forever;
The moon and stars to rule the night,
    God's love endures forever;

Who struck down the firstborn of Egypt,
    God's love endures forever;
And led Israel from their midst,
    God's love endures forever;
With mighty hand and outstretched arm,
    God's love endures forever;
Who split in two the Red Sea,
    God's love endures forever;
And led Israel through,
    God's love endures forever;
But swept Pharaoh and his army into the Red Sea,
    God's love endures forever;
Who led the people through the desert,
    God's love endures forever;

Who struck down great kings,
    God's love endures forever;
Slew powerful kings,

God's love endures forever;
Sihon, king of the Amorites,
   God's love endures forever;
Og, king of Bashan,
   God's love endures forever;
And made their lands a heritage,
   God's love endures forever;
A heritage for Israel, God's servant,
   God's love endures forever.

The LORD remembers us in our misery,
   God's love endures forever;
Freed us from our foes,
   God's love endures forever;
And gives food to all flesh,
   God's love endures forever.

Praise the God of heaven,
   God's love endures forever.

Psalm 137:1-6

Sorrow and Hope in Exile

Evening Prayer

By the rivers of Babylon
   we sat mourning and weeping
   when we remembered Zion.
On the poplars of that land
   we hung up our harps.
There our captors asked us
   for the words of a song;
Our tormentors, for a joyful song:
   "Sing for us a song of Zion!"
But how could we sing a song of the LORD
   in a foreign land?

If I forget you, Jerusalem,
    may my right hand wither.
May my tongue stick to my palate
    if I do not remember you,
If I do not exalt Jerusalem
    beyond all my delights.

Psalm 138

Hymn of a Grateful Heart

Evening Prayer

I thank you, LORD, with all my heart;
    before the gods* to you I sing.
I bow low toward your holy temple;
    I praise your name for your fidelity and love.
For you have exalted over all
    your name and your promise.
When I cried out, you answered;
    you strengthened my spirit.

All the kings of earth will praise you, LORD,
    when they hear the words of your mouth.
They will sing of the ways of the LORD:
    "How great is the glory of the LORD!"
The LORD is on high, but cares for the lowly
    and knows the proud from afar.
Though I walk in the midst of dangers,
    you guard my life when my enemies rage.
You stretch out your hand;
    your right hand saves me.
The LORD is with me to the end.

---

* "Before the gods": heavenly beings who were completely subordinate to Israel's God. The earthly temple represents the heavenly palace of God.

LORD, your love endures forever.
Never forsake the work of your hands!

Psalm 139:1-18, 23-24

The All-knowing and Ever-present God

LORD, you have probed me, you know me:
  you know when I sit and stand;
  you understand my thoughts from afar.
My travels and my rest you mark;
  with all my ways you are familiar.
Even before a word is on my tongue,
  LORD, you know it all.
Behind and before you encircle me
  and rest your hand upon me.
Such knowledge is beyond me,
  far too lofty for me to reach.

Where can I hide from your spirit?
  From your presence, where can I flee?
If I ascend to the heavens, you are there;
  if I lie down in Sheol, you are there too.
If I fly with the wings of dawn
  and alight beyond the sea,
Even there your hand will guide me,
  your right hand hold me fast.
If I say, "Surely darkness shall hide me,
  and night shall be my light" —
Darkness is not dark for you,
  and night shines as the day.
  Darkness and light are but one.

You formed my inmost being;
  you knit me in my mother's womb.

I praise you, so wonderfully you made me;
    wonderful are your works!
My very self you knew;
    my bones were not hidden from you,
When I was being made in secret,
    fashioned as in the depths of the earth,*
Your eyes foresaw my actions;
    in your book all are written down;
    my days were shaped before one came to be.

How precious to me are your designs, O God;
    how vast the sum of them!
Were I to count, they would outnumber the sands;
    to finish, I would need eternity.

Probe me, God, know my heart;
    try me, know my concern.
See if my way is crooked,
    then lead me in the ancient paths.

Psalm 141:1-9

Prayer for Deliverance from the Wicked

Evening Prayer

LORD, I call to you;
    come quickly to help me;
    listen to my plea when I call.
Let my prayer be incense before you;
    my uplifted hands an evening sacrifice.
Set a guard, LORD, before my mouth,
    a gatekeeper at my lips.
Do not let my heart incline to evil,

---

* "The depths of the earth": figurative language for the womb, stressing the hidden and mysterious operations that occur there.

or yield to any sin.
I will never feast upon
    the fine food of evildoers.
Let the just strike me; that is kindness;
    let them rebuke me; that is oil for my head.
All this I shall not refuse,
    but will pray despite these trials.
When their leaders are cast over the cliff,
    all will learn that my prayers were heard.
As when a farmer plows a field into broken clods,
    so their bones will be strewn at the mouth of
      Sheol.
My eyes are upon you, O GOD, my Lord;
    in you I take refuge; do not strip me of life.
Guard me from the trap they have set for me,
    from the snares of evildoers.

Psalm 142

A Prayer in Time of Trouble

Evening Prayer

With full voice I cry to the LORD;
    with full voice I beseech the LORD.
Before God I pour out my complaint,
    lay bare my distress.
My spirit is faint within me,
    but you know my path.
Along the way I walk
    they have hidden a trap for me.
I look to my right hand,
    but no friend is there.
There is no escape for me;
    no one cares for me.
I cry out to you, LORD,

I say, "You are my refuge,
my portion in the land of the living.
Listen to my cry for help,
for I am brought very low.
Rescue me from my pursuers,
for they are too strong for me.
Lead me out of my prison,
that I may give thanks to your name.
Then the just shall gather around me
because you have been good to me.

Psalm 143:1-11

A Prayer in Distress

Morning Prayer

LORD, hear my prayer;
in your faithfulness listen to my pleading;
answer me in your justice.
Do not enter into judgment with your servant;
before you no living being can be just.
The enemy has pursued me;
they have crushed my life to the ground.
They have left me in darkness
like those long dead.
My spirit is faint within me;
my heart is dismayed.
I remember the days of old;
I ponder all your deeds;
the works of your hands I recall.
I stretch out my hands to you;
I thirst for you like a parched land.
Hasten to answer me, LORD;
for my spirit fails me.
Do not hide your face from me,

lest I become like those descending to the pit.
At dawn let me hear of your kindness,
for in you I trust.
Show me the path I should walk,
for to you I entrust my life.
Rescue me, LORD, from my foes,
for in you I hope.
Teach me to do your will,
for you are my God.
May your kind spirit guide me
on ground that is level.
For your name's sake, LORD, give me life;
in your justice lead me out of distress.

Psalm 144:1-9

A Prayer for Victory and Prosperity

Blessed be the LORD, my rock,
who trains my hands for battle,
my fingers for war;
My safeguard and my fortress,
my stronghold, my deliverer,
My shield, in whom I trust,
who subdues peoples under me.

LORD, what are mortals that you notice them;
human beings, that you take thought of them?
They are but a breath;
their days are like a passing shadow.
LORD, incline your heavens and come;
touch the mountains and make them smoke.
Flash forth lightning and scatter my foes;
shoot your arrows and rout them.
Reach out your hand from on high;
deliver me from the many waters,

rescue me from the hands of foreign foes.
Their mouths speak untruth;
   their right hands are raised in lying oaths.
O God, a new song I will sing to you;
   on a ten-stringed lyre I will play for you.

Psalm 145

The Greatness and Goodness of God

Evening Prayer

I will extol you, my God and king;
   I will bless your name forever.
Every day I will bless you;
   I will praise your name forever.
Great is the LORD and worthy of high praise;
   God's grandeur is beyond understanding.
One generation praises your deeds to the next
   and proclaims your mighty works.
They speak of the splendor of your majestic glory,
   tell of your wonderful deeds.
They speak of your fearsome power,
   and attest to your great deeds.
They publish the renown of your abounding
      goodness
   and joyfully sing of your justice.
The LORD is gracious and merciful,
   slow to anger and abounding in love.
The LORD is good to all,
   compassionate to every creature.
All your works give you thanks, O LORD;
   and your faithful bless you.
They speak of the glory of your reign
   and tell of your great works,
Making known to all your power,

the glorious splendor of your rule.
Your reign is a reign for all ages,
    your dominion for all generations.
The LORD is trustworthy in every word,
    and faithful in every work.
The LORD supports all who are falling
    and raises up all who are bowed down.
The eyes of all look hopefully to you;
    you give them their food in due season.
You open wide your hand
    and satisfy the desire of every living thing.
You, LORD, are just in all your ways,
    faithful in all your works.
You, LORD, are near to all who call upon you,
    to all who call upon you in truth.
You satisfy the desire of those who fear you;
    you hear their cry and save them.
You, LORD, watch over all who love you,
    but all the wicked you destroy.
My mouth will speak your praises, LORD;
    all flesh will bless your holy name forever.

Psalm 146

Trust in God the Creator and Redeemer

Morning Prayer

Praise the LORD, my soul;
    I shall praise the LORD all my life,
    sing praise to my God while I live.

Put no trust in princes,
    in mere mortals powerless to save.
When they breathe their last, they return to the
      earth;
    that day all their planning comes to nothing.

Happy those whose help is Jacob's God,
  whose hope is in the LORD, their God,
The maker of heaven and earth,
  the seas, and all that is in them,
Who keeps faith forever,
  secures justice for the oppressed,
  gives food to the hungry.
The LORD sets prisoners free;
  the LORD gives sight to the blind.
The LORD raises up those who are bowed down;
  the LORD loves the righteous.
The LORD protects the stranger,
  sustains the orphan and the widow,
  but thwarts the way of the wicked.
The LORD shall reign forever,
  your God, Zion, through all generations!
Hallelujah!

Psalm 147

God's Word Restores Jerusalem

Morning Prayer

How good to celebrate our God in song;
  how sweet to give fitting praise.
The LORD rebuilds Jerusalem,
  gathers the dispersed of Israel,
Heals the brokenhearted,
  binds up their wounds,
Numbers all the stars,
  calls each of them by name.
Great is our Lord, vast in power,
  with wisdom beyond measure.
The LORD sustains the poor,
  but casts the wicked to the ground.

Sing to the LORD with thanksgiving;
    with the lyre celebrate our God,
Who covers the heavens with clouds,
    provides rain for the earth,
    makes grass sprout on the mountains,
Who gives animals their food
    and ravens what they cry for.
God takes no delight in the strength of horses,*
    no pleasure in the runner's stride.
Rather the LORD takes pleasure in the devout,
    those who await God's faithful care.

Glorify the LORD, Jerusalem;
    Zion, offer praise to your God,
Who has strengthened the bars of your gates,
    blessed your children within you,
Brought peace to your borders,
    and filled you with finest wheat.
The LORD sends a command to earth;
    his word runs swiftly!
Thus snow is spread like wool,
    frost is scattered like ash,
Hail is dispersed like crumbs;
    before such cold the waters freeze.
Again he sends his word and they melt;
    the wind is unleashed and the waters flow.
The LORD also proclaims his word to Jacob,
    decrees and laws to Israel.
God has not done this for other nations;
    of such laws they know nothing.
Hallelujah!

---

* Acknowledging one's dependence on God rather than claiming self-sufficiency pleases God.

Psalm 148

All Creation Summoned to Praise

Praise the LORD from the heavens;
    give praise in the heights.
Praise him all you angels;
    give praise, all you hosts.
Praise him sun and moon;
    give praise, all shining stars.
Praise him highest heavens,
    you waters above the heavens.
Let them all praise the LORD's name;
    for the LORD commanded and they were
      created,
Assigned them duties forever,
    gave them tasks that will never change.

Praise the LORD from the earth,
    you sea monsters and all deep waters;
You lightning and hail, snow and clouds,
    storm winds that fulfill his command;
You mountains and all hills,
    fruit trees and all cedars;
You animals wild and tame,
    you creatures that crawl and fly;
You kings of the earth and all peoples,
    princes and all who govern on earth;
Young men and women too,
    old and young alike.
Let them all praise the LORD's name,
    for his name alone is exalted,
    majestic above earth and heaven.
The LORD has lifted high the horn of his people;

to the glory of all the faithful,
of Israel, the people near to their God.
Hallelujah!

Psalm 149

Praise God with Song and Sword

Morning Prayer

Sing to the LORD a new song,
a hymn in the assembly of the faithful.
Let Israel be glad in their maker,
the people of Zion rejoice in their king.
Let them praise his name in festive dance,
make music with tambourine and lyre.
For the LORD takes delight in his people,
honors the poor with victory.
Let the faithful rejoice in their glory,
cry out for joy at their banquet,
With the praise of God in their mouths,
and a two-edged sword in their hands,
To bring retribution on the nations,
punishment on the peoples,
To bind their kings with chains,
shackle their nobles with irons,
To execute the judgments decreed for them —
such is the glory of all God's faithful.
Hallelujah!

Psalm 150

Final Doxology

Morning Prayer

Praise God in his holy sanctuary;
give praise in the mighty dome of heaven.
Give praise for his mighty deeds,

praise him for his great majesty.
Give praise with blasts upon the horn,
    praise him with harp and lyre.
Give praise with tambourines and dance,
    praise him with flutes and strings.
Give praise with crashing cymbals,
    praise him with sounding cymbals.
Let everything that has breath
    give praise to the LORD!
Hallelujah!

DEO GRATIAS!

OLD TESTAMENT CANTICLES

～～～∞∞∞～～～

Song of the Three Young Men
A Canticle of Creation
Daniel 3:57-88

Sunday

Invocation

Glorify the Lord, all you works of the Lord,
  praise him and highly exalt him for ever.
In the firmament of his power, glorify the Lord,
  praise him and highly exalt him for ever.

I. The Cosmic Order

Glorify the Lord, you angels and all powers of the
    Lord,
  O heavens and all waters above the heavens.
Sun and moon and stars of the sky, glorify the
    Lord,
  praise him and highly exalt him for ever.

Glorify the Lord, every shower of rain and fall of
    dew,
  all winds and fire and heat.
Winter and summer, glorify the Lord,
  praise him and highly exalt him for ever.

Glorify the Lord, O chill and cold,
  drops of dew and flakes of snow.
Frost and cold, ice and sleet, glorify the Lord,
  praise him and highly exalt him for ever.

Glorify the Lord, O nights and days,

O shining light and enfolding dark.
Storm clouds and thunderbolts, glorify the Lord,
   praise him and exalt him for ever.

II. The Earth and Its Creatures

Let the earth glorify the Lord,
   praise him and highly exalt him for ever.
Glorify the Lord, O mountains and hills, and all
      that grows upon the earth,
   praise him and highly exalt him for ever.

Glorify the Lord, O springs of water, seas, and
      streams,
   O whales and all that move in the waters.
All birds of the air, glorify the Lord,
   praise him and highly exalt him for ever.

Glorify the Lord, O beasts of the wild,
   and all you flocks and herds.
O men and women everywhere, glorify the Lord,
   praise him and highly exalt him for ever.

III. The People of God

Let the people of God glorify the Lord,
   praise him and highly exalt him for ever.
Glorify the Lord, O priests and servants of the
      Lord,
   praise him and highly exalt him for ever.

Glorify the Lord, O spirits and souls of the
      righteous,
   praise him and highly exalt him for ever.
You that are holy and humble of heart, glorify the
      Lord,

praise him and highly exalt him for ever.

Doxology

Let us glorify the Lord: Father, Son, and Holy
Spirit;
praise him and highly exalt him for ever.
In the firmament of his power, glorify the Lord,
praise him and highly exalt him for ever.

Prayer of Manasseh*

Kyrie Pantokrator

Prayer of Manasseh, 1-2, 4, 6-7, 11-15

Lent and Other Penitential Occasions

O Lord and Ruler of the hosts of heaven,
God of Abraham, Isaac, and Jacob,
and of all their righteous offspring;
You made the heavens and the earth,
with all their vast array.
All things quake with fear at your presence;
they tremble because of your power.
But your merciful promise is beyond all measure;
it surpasses all that our minds can fathom.
O Lord, you are full of compassion,
long-suffering, and abounding in mercy.
You hold back your hand;
you do not punish as we deserve.
In your great goodness, Lord,
you have promised forgiveness to sinners,
that they may repent of their sin and be saved.
And now, O Lord, I bend the knee of my heart,

---

* This prayer, which is in the Septuagint Greek Old Testament, is considered canonical Scripture by the Eastern Orthodox. It is used in the Liturgy of the Hours by the Orthodox and
by Byzantine-rite Catholics.

and make my appeal, sure of your gracious
  goodness.
I have sinned, O Lord, I have sinned,
and I know my wickedness only too well.
Therefore I make this prayer to you:
Forgive me, Lord, forgive me.
Do not let me perish in my sin,
nor condemn me to the depths of the earth.
For you, O Lord, are the God of those who repent,
and in me you will show forth your goodness.
Unworthy as I am, you will save me,
in accordance with your great mercy,
and I will praise you without ceasing
all the days of my life.
For all the powers of heaven sing your praises,
and yours is the glory to ages of ages. Amen.

The Canticle of Moses

Cantemus Domino

Exodus 15:1-6, 11-13, 17-18

Easter Season

I will sing to the LORD, for he is lofty and uplifted;
  the horse and its rider has he hurled into the
    sea.
The LORD is my strength and my refuge;
  the LORD has become my Savior.
This is my God and I will praise him,
  the God of my people and I will exalt him.
The LORD is a mighty warrior;
  LORD is his name.
The chariots of Pharaoh and his army has he
    hurled into the sea;
  the finest of those who bear armor have been

drowned in the Red Sea.
The fathomless deep has overwhelmed them;
  they sank into the depths like a stone.
Your right hand, O LORD, is glorious in might;
  your right hand, O LORD, has overthrown the
    enemy.
Who can be compared to you, O LORD, among the
    gods?
  who is like you, glorious in holiness,
  awesome in reknown, and worker of wonders?
You stretched forth your right hand;
  the earth swallowed them up.
With your constant love you led the people you
    redeemed;
  with your might you brought them in safety to
    your holy dwelling.
You will bring them in and plant them
  on the mount of your possession,
  the resting place you have made for yourself, O
    LORD,
  the sanctuary, O LORD, that your hand has
    established.
The LORD shall reign for ever and ever.

Canticle of Lady Wisdom

Wisdom 7:22–8:1

Wisdom, the fashioner of all things, taught me.
There is in her a spirit that is intelligent, holy,
unique, manifold, subtle,
mobile, clear, unpolluted,
distinct, invulnerable, loving the good, keen,
irresistible, beneficent, humane,
steadfast, sure, free from anxiety,

all-powerful, overseeing all,

and penetrating through all spirits

that are intelligent, pure, and altogether subtle.

For wisdom is more mobile than any motion;

because of her pureness she pervades and
    penetrates all things.

For she is a breath of the power of God,

and a pure emanation of the glory of the
    Almighty;

therefore nothing defiled gains entrance into her.

For she is a reflection of eternal light,

a spotless mirror of the working of God,

and an image of his goodness.

Although she is but one, she can do all things,

and while remaining in herself, she renews all
    things;

in every generation she passes into holy souls

and makes them friends of God, and prophets;

for God loves nothing so much as the person who
    lives with wisdom.

She is more beautiful than the sun,

and excels every constellation of the stars.

Compared with the light, she is found to be
    superior,

for it is succeeded by the night,

but against wisdom evil does not prevail.

She reaches mightily from one end of the earth to
    the other,

and she orders all things well.

PRAYERS FROM EASTERN CHURCHES

Prayers from the Byzantine Rite

The Byzantine rite is celebrated by Eastern Orthodox Christians and by a smaller number of Byzantine-rite Catholics. Pope John Paul II has expressed the hope for the reunion of the Catholic Church with the venerable Churches of the East, so that the Church can again, "breathe with both lungs, East and West." A necessary step along the road of reunion is an increasing appreciation of the spiritual riches of the Eastern Churches by Western Christians.

The English version of the Byzantine prayers quoted here is that used by the Catholic Melkites.

A notable characteristic of Eastern liturgies is their outspoken devotion to Mary, who is most frequently honored by the title Mother of God, or more precisely, Theotokos ("the one who gave birth to God"), which was confirmed by the Council of Ephesus in 431.

The most popular Byzantine devotion to Mary is the Acathist Hymn, probably composed in 532. Following are excerpts.

~∞∞∞~

Acathist

Blessed is our God at all times, now and always and for ever and ever. Amen.

I shall open my mouth, and it will be filled with the Spirit, and I shall sing a hymn of praise to the Mother and Queen; with great joy I shall celebrate and sing her praise.

He who sits in glory upon the throne of God, surrounded with an ethereal cloud, Jesus the supremely divine, came down, and with his mighty hand, redeemed those who cried out to Him: "Glory to your power, O Christ!"

An archangel was sent from heaven to greet the Mother of God. And as he saw you taking a body, O Lord, at the sound of his bodiless voice, he stood rapt in amazement and cried out to her in these words:

Hail, O you through whom joy will shine forth;
Hail, O you through whom the curse will
    disappear!
Hail, O Restoration of the fallen Adam;
Hail, O Redemption of the tears of Eve!
Hail, O Height above the reach of human thought;
Hail, O Depth even beyond the sight of angels!
Hail, O you who have become a kingly throne;
Hail, O you who carry Him who carries all!
Hail, O Star who manifests the Sun;
Hail, O Womb of the divine incarnation!
Hail, O you through whom creation is renewed;
Hail, O you through whom the Creator becomes a
    Babe!
Hail, O Bride and Maiden ever-pure!
Hail, O Bride and Maiden ever-pure!

Trying to grasp the meaning of this mystery, the Virgin asked the holy messenger: "How is it possible that a son be born from a virginal womb? Tell me." And he answered her with awe, crying out in these words:

Hail, O hidden Sense of the ineffable plan!
Hail, O Belief in Silence that must be!
Hail, O Forecast of the marvels of Christ;
Hail, O Fountainhead of truths concerning Him!
Hail, celestial Ladder by whom God came down;
Hail, O Bridge leading earthly ones to heaven!
Hail O Wonder, ever-thrilling to the angels;
Hail, O Wound, ever-hurting to the demons!
Hail, O you who gave birth to Light ineffably;
Hail, O you who told no one how it was done!
Hail, O you who surpass the wisdom of the wise;
Hail, O you who enlighten faithful minds!
Hail, O Bride and Maiden ever-pure!
Hail, O Bride and Maiden ever-pure!

The sons of Chaldea saw in the Virgin's hands the One whose hands had fashioned them; and acknowledging Him as the Master, although He had taken the form of a servant, they hastened to honor Him with their gifts, and cried out to the Blessed One:

Hail, O Mother of the star without setting;
Hail, O Radiance of the mystical day!
Hail, O you who quenched the flame of error;
Hail, O light of those who search the Trinity!
Hail, O you who unthroned the enemy of
    humankind;
Hail, O you who showed forth Christ, Lord, the
    Lover of humankind!

Hail, O you who cleansed us from the stain of
   pagan worship;
Hail, O you who saved us from the mire of evil
   deeds!
Hail, O you who made cease the cult of fire;
Hail, O you who dispelled the flames of passion!
Hail, O you who guide the faithful toward
   wisdom;
Hail, O you, Delight of all the nations!
Hail, O Bride and Maiden ever-pure!
Hail, O Bride and Maiden ever-pure!

Gabriel was rapt in amazement as he beheld
your virginity and the splendor of your purity, O
Mother of God, and he cried out to you: "By what
name shall I call you? I am bewildered; I am lost! I
shall greet you as I was commanded to do: 'Hail,
O Woman full of grace!' "

One of the distinctive characteristics of the
Byzantine Liturgy is the use of litanies. After the
private preparation of the gifts, the priest begins
the Liturgy as follows:

*The priest lifts the Gospel book and makes the sign of
the cross with it while singing:*
Blessed is the kingdom of the Father, and of
the Son, and of the Holy Spirit, now and always
and for ever and ever.
Then the priest or deacon begins the litany of peace:
In peace let us pray to the Lord.

R/ Lord, have mercy.

For peace from on high and the salvation of our
      souls, let us pray to the Lord.

R/ Lord, have mercy.

For peace in the whole world, the well-being of the
      holy Churches of God and the union of all, let
      us pray to the Lord.

R/ Lord, have mercy.

For this holy place and for those who enter it with
      faith, reverence and fear of God, let us pray to
      the Lord.

R/ Lord, have mercy.

For his Beatitude our Patriarch (Name), our most
      reverend bishop (Name), the reverend
      priests, the deacons in Christ, and for all the
      clergy and the people, let us pray to the Lord.

R/ Lord, have mercy.

For our public servants, for the government and
      for all who protect us, that they may be up-
      held and strengthened in every good deed,
      let us pray to the Lord.

R/ Lord, have mercy.

For this place (or monastery), for every city and
      country place and the faithful dwelling in
      them, let us pray to the Lord.

R/ Lord, have mercy.

For favorable weather, an abundance of the fruits of the earth and for peaceful times, let us pray to the Lord.

R/ Lord, have mercy.

For travelers by sea, air and land, for the sick, the suffering, for those in prison, and for their salvation, let us pray to the Lord.

R/ Lord, have mercy.

For our deliverance from all affliction, wrath, danger, and need, let us pray to the Lord.

R/ Lord, have mercy.

Help us, save us, have mercy on us and protect us, O God, by your grace.

R/ Lord, have mercy.

Let us remember our all-holy, spotless, most highly blessed and glorious Lady, the Mother of God and ever-virgin Mary with all the saints, and commend ourselves and one another and our whole life to Christ our God.

R/ To You, O Lord.

Lenten Prayer of St. Ephrem of Syria*

O Lord, Master of my life, grant that I may not be infected with the spirit of slothfulness and inquisitiveness, with the spirit of ambition and vain talking.

---

* This prayer is used daily during Great Lent by the Eastern Orthodox and Byzantine-rite Catholics.

Grant instead to me your servant the spirit of purity and humility, the spirit of patience and neighborly love.

O Lord and King, bestow upon me the grace of being aware of my sins and of not thinking evil of those of my brethren.

For you are blessed for ever and ever. Amen.

O God, be propitious to me a sinner and have mercy on me.

Yes, O Lord and King, bestow upon me the grace of being aware of my sins and of not thinking evil of those of my brethren.

Prayers from Oriental Rites

Most people think of early Christianity as spreading north and west from Palestine and taking on the Greek language and culture in the process. This is true, but it is not the whole truth. The faith also spread to the Syrian (Aramaic-speaking) Christians of the Middle East as far as present-day Iraq, and from there to India and all the way to China. In China, only a single stone monument inscribed in Syrian and Chinese remains as a reminder of a once-thriving church.

Unfortunately, these Christians, except the Maronites, were split from the universal church by early disputes, which we now realize were caused more by differences in language and culture than doctrine. This divided church was overwhelmed by the advance of Islam in the early 600s, although Christian minorities remain throughout the Middle East and in India.

Maronite Rite

The Maronite rite originated in Lebanon but has members throughout the world, including a diocese in the United States. The Maronites are the only Catholic Eastern-rite Christians who do not have an Orthodox counterpart.

~∞~

Feast of Sts. Peter and Paul

Celebrant:

Glory to you, O Word of God, giver of life and light. You founded your Church upon the apostles and instructed them to preach love and justice throughout the land. You chose Simon, son of John, and you made him a fisher of men. Then you consecrated Paul the Pharisee as apostle to the nations. Peter denied you and Paul persecuted you, but you revealed your will to them, and they accepted their vocation with joy. The fire of apostolic zeal burned in their hearts, and they became witnesses to your truth in the world. Now we petition you their intercession to protect your people and to grant us new life. Guard the flock that Peter led and that Paul encouraged. May it become a witness to your truth, guiding the world not with words, but with deeds that give life. Plant your faith and peace among us and seal your love in our hearts. Strengthen priests for your service and missionaries for the spread of your Gospel. Guide those ordained to follow in the footsteps of Peter and Paul, especially our Patriarch who shepherds the Church of Peter at Antioch, with all the bishops and priests whose faith is the faith of the apostles. And we glorify you now and forever.

Congregation:

Amen.

West Syrian Liturgy

Of the once flourishing Syrian Church, a small remnant survives in Iraq and Iran, but the largest groups are in the south of India. The West Syrian liturgy, which is used by the Syrian Orthodox and by Catholics of the Syro-Malankara rite, is a living witness to this ancient branch of Christianity. As in all the Eastern liturgies, devotion to Mary, "She who brought forth God," is most prominent and expressed in language of great tenderness.

Ode to Mary

What mind or tongue can suffice to praise the mother of God, Mary, who was greater than the chariot which Ezekiel saw; she who carried him who is worshipped in the flesh by the cherubim, second heaven who carried the sun of justice, pure fleece who received the heavenly rain, virgin mother who brought forth God who took flesh from her and through her has paid the debt of Adam and Eve.

Since she is mother of God we will call her blessed as she prophesied concerning herself, and we will say: Blessed are you who gave birth to him whose burning might the heavens cannot contain;

blessed are you who carried in your arms him who holds creation in his hand and nursed him at whose gesture the springs flow.

Therefore we beseech you, Christ our God, by her prayers look upon us with mercy. Receive our prayer and by your grace give health to the sick, relief to the afflicted, hope to the living and rest to the dead. And grant that we may be changed, that from being sinful we may become meek and gentle. Make us worthy to come to a blessed end that we may offer you praise and thanksgiving now and always and forever. Amen.

Prayer of Repentance

Lord almighty, God everlasting, creator and giver of life to all flesh, who created us in your image and gave us a law that we might walk in your sight without blame; and after we had sinned, gave us the pledge that we should rise again; now Lord, turn to your servants who have bent the necks of our souls and bodies in sorrow before you. Receive us according to your love of humankind because you do not desire the death of sinners but that they may turn from their evil way and live.

You are he who received the repentance of the Ninevites and turned aside the wrath which was threatening them. You are he who received the tears of the adulterous woman and the repentance of Zacchaeus the tax collector and the confession of Manasseh and the faith of the thief who repented on the cross. You are he who received the prodigal son who squandered his inheritance and had compassion on him. Now, O Lord, receive our repentance. Cause us to stand before you without shame. Wipe out the record of our sins and bestow on us pardon of our faults, give rest to the departed, that they and we may offer you praise and thanksgiving, now and always and forever. Amen.

~~~~~~

Chaldean Liturgy

The Chaldean liturgy is used by Chaldean Catholics and by Assyrian Christians. Most of them live in Iraq, but there is a Chaldean Catholic Diocese in the United States. The following prayers were translated from the original Aramaic by Father Jon Buffington of the Chaldean Diocese of Detroit, Michigan.

~~~~~~

Offertory Prayer

May Christ who was sacrificed for our salvation and who commanded us to make a commemoration of his death, burial and resurrection accept this offering from my hands by his grace and mercy for ever. Amen.

The priest taps the cup and plate together three times.

By your command, our Lord and our God;

By your command, our Lord and our God;

By your command, our Lord and our God, these holy, glorious, life-giving and divine mysteries are set upon the absolving altar until the second coming of our Lord from heaven. To him be glory at all times and for ever. Amen.

Lakou Mara

When the sweet fragrance of your love fills us, our Lord and our God, and our souls are enlightened by your truth, may we become worthy to witness in heaven the splendor of your beloved Son. And in your Church triumphant, full of favor and delights, we shall ever praise and glorify you, the Lord and creator of all. Amen.

~∞∞∞~

Ethiopian Rite

The Ethiopian rite is shared by the Ethiopian Orthodox and Ethiopian-rite Catholics. At the Second Vatican Council, the opening Mass for each day's sessions was celebrated on some days in one of the Eastern rites instead of the usual Roman rite. The Western bishops were most intrigued by the Ethiopian rite. The Ethiopians celebrate with obvious joy as well as solemnity. They use drums and sistra to accompany chants. The sistrum is a metal instrument shaped like a forked stick, with rods connecting the sides of the fork. On the rods are metal disks. The sound resembles that of castanets.

~∞∞∞~

Prayers of Incense before the Gospel During the Liturgy

The priest burns incense saying:
Glory and honor be to the Holy Trinity, the Father, the Son, and the Holy Spirit,

now and for ever and ever.
Amen.

Standing before the altar, he prays:

Lord our God, you accepted the sacrifice of Abraham, and in the place of Isaac you prepared a ram for his ransom. Even so, O Lord, accept from us this fragrant incense and send to us from on high the riches of your loving-kindness and your mercy, that we may be purified from the odor of our sins. Make us worthy to minister before your glorious purity, O lover of humanity, in justice and holiness all the days of our life, in joy and in rejoicing.

He walks around the altar on which rests the tabot.*

Hail Mary, you of whom we ask salvation, O holy ever-virgin parent of God, Mother of Christ and worthy of praise. Offer up our prayer on high to your beloved Son, Jesus, that he forgive our sins.

Hail Mary, you who bore for us the very light of holiness, Christ our God. O virgin pure, plead for us to our Lord that he show mercy to us and forgive our sins.

Hail Mary, O virgin pure, holy parent of God, true pleader for the human race, plead for us to Christ your Son, that he grant us forgiveness of our sins.

Hail Mary, O virgin pure, true queen. Hail, O pride of our race. Hail, you who bore for us Emmanuel. We beseech you that you remember

---

* "Tabot": a replica of the Old Testament Ark of the Covenant, which is placed on the altar. The Ethiopians also observe other Jewish customs, such as circumcision and the prohibition against eating certain foods.

us, O mediatrix, before our Lord Jesus Christ, that he forgive us our sins.

The priest comes out of the sanctuary, which is veiled, and prays:

This is the time of blessing, this is the time of incense, the time of the praise of our Savior, lover of humanity, Jesus Christ. The incense is Mary, the incense is he who was in her fragrant womb, the incense is he whom she bore. He came and saved us. O come, let us worship him and keep his commandments, that he will forgive our sins.

To Michael was given mercy, and glad tidings to Gabriel, and a heavenly gift to Mary the Virgin. To our father Peter were given the keys and apostleship to our father Paul, who was the light of the Church.

The fragrant ointment is Mary, for he who was in her womb, who is more fragrant than all incense, came and was made flesh of her. In Mary, Virgin pure, the Father was well pleased and he decked her as a tabernacle for the dwelling place of his well beloved Son.

To Moses was given the Law, the priesthood to Aaron, to Zechariah the priest was given the choice incense. They made the tabernacle of the testimony according to the word of the Lord, and the choice incense ascended in God's presence.

The seraphim worship God and the cherubim glorify him. They cry aloud saying:

Holy, holy, holy is the Lord God of Sabaoth.

You are the incense, O our Savior, for you came to
save us.

Poems and Hymns

Prayer of St. Francis of Assisi

Lord, make me an instrument of your peace.

Where there is hatred, let me sow love,

Where there is injury, pardon;

Where there is doubt, faith;

Where there is despair, hope;

Where there is darkness, light;

Where there is sadness, joy.

O divine Master, grant that I may not so much seek

To be consoled, as to console,

To be understood, as to understand,

To be loved, as to love.

For it is in giving that we receive;

In pardoning that we are pardoned;

It is in dying that we are born to eternal life.

St. Francis of Assisi, 1181-1226

The Canticle of Creation

O most high, almighty, good Lord God, to you belong

 praise, glory, honor and all blessing.

Praised be you, Lord God, with all your creatures,

 and especially our brother the sun,
 who brings us the light;

 fair is he and shines with a great splendor;
 O Lord, he signifies you to us.

Praised be you, my Lord, for our sister the moon,
 and for the stars,
 which you have set clear and
 lovely in the heavens.

Praised be you, my Lord, for our sister water,
 who is of great service to us
 and humble and precious and clean.

Praised be you, my Lord, for our brother fire,
 through whom you give us light in the
 darkness;

 he is bright and pleasant
 and mighty and strong.

Praised be you, my Lord, for our mother the earth,
 who sustains us and keeps us
 and brings forth abundant fruit,
 and flowers of many colors and grass.

Praised be you, my Lord, for all those who pardon
 one another for your love's sake,
 and endure weakness and tribulations;

 blessed are they who peaceably shall endure,
 for you, O most high, shall give them a
 crown.

Praised be you, my Lord, for our sister
 the death of the body.

Blessed are they who are found walking
 by your most holy will.

Praise and bless the Lord, and give thanks,
and serve God with great humility.

St. Francis of Assisi, 1181-1226

There's a Wideness in God's Mercy

There's a wideness in God's mercy
Like the wideness of the sea;
There's a kindness in his justice
Which is more than liberty.
There is plentiful redemption
In the blood that has been shed;
There is joy for all the members
In the sorrows of the Head.

For the love of God is broader
Than the measures of our mind,
And the heart of the Eternal
Is most wonderfully kind.
If our love were but more simple
We should take him at his word,
And our lives would be thanksgiving
For the goodness of our Lord.

Troubled souls, why will you scatter
Like a crowd of frightened sheep?
Foolish hearts, why will you wander
From a love so true and deep?
There is welcome for the sinner
And more graces for the good;
There is mercy with the Savior,
There is healing in his blood.

Frederick W. Faber, 1814-1863

Anima Christi

Soul of Christ, be my sanctification;
Body of Christ, be my salvation;
Blood of Christ, fill all my veins;
Water of Christ's side, wash out my stains;
Passion of Christ, my comfort be;
O good Jesu, listen to me;
In thy wounds I fain would hide,
Ne'er to be parted from thy side;
Guard me, should the foe assail me;
Call me when my life shall fail me;
Bid me come to thee above,
With thy saints to sing thy love,
World without end. Amen.

Early 14th century
Translated by John Henry Newman, 1801-1890

Lead, Kindly Light

Lead, kindly Light, amid th' encircling gloom,
Lead thou me on!
The night is dark, and I am far from home;
Lead thou me on!
Keep thou my feet; I do not ask to see
The distant scene; one step enough for me.

I was not ever thus, nor prayed that thou
Shouldst lead me on;
I loved to choose and see my path; but now
Lead thou me on!
I loved the garish day, and spite of fears,
Pride ruled my will; remember not past years.

So long thy power hath blest me, sure it still
Will lead me on

O'er moor and fen, o'er crag and torrent, till
The night is gone;
And with the morn those angel faces smile,
Which I have loved long since and lost awhile!

John Henry Newman, 1801-1890

In No Strange Land

O world invisible, we view thee,
O world intangible, we touch thee,
O world unknowable, we know thee,
Inapprehensible, we clutch thee!

Does the fish soar to find the ocean,
The eagle plunge to find the air —
That we ask of the stars in motion
If they have rumor of thee there?

Not where the wheeling systems darken,
And our benum'd conceiving soars! —
The drift of pinions, would we hearken,
Beats at our own clay-shuttered doors.

The angels keep their ancient places; —
Turn but a stone, and start a wing!
'Tis ye, 'tis your estrangèd faces,
That miss the many-splendored thing.

But (when so sad thou canst not sadder)
Cry — and upon thy so sore loss
Shall shine the traffic of Jacob's ladder
Pitched between Heaven and Charing Cross.
Yea, in the night, my Soul, my daughter,
Cry — clinging heaven by the hems;

And lo, Christ walking on the water,
Not of Gennesareth, but Thames!
Francis Thompson, 1859-1907

Pied Beauty

Glory be to God for dappled things —
For skies of couple-color as a brnded cow;
For rose-moles all in stipple upon trout
that swim;
Fresh firecoal chestnut-falls; finches' wings;
Landscape plotted and pieced — fold, fallow,
and plough;
And all trades, their gear and tackle and
trim.

All things counter, original, spare, strange;
Whatever is fickle, freckled (who knows
how?)
With swift, slow; sweet, sour;
adazzle, dim;
He fathers-forth whose beauty is past change:
Praise him.
Gerard Manley Hopkins, 1844-1889

God's Grandeur

The world is charged with the grandeur of God.
It will flame out, like shining from shook foil;
It gathers to a greatness, like the ooze of oil
Crushed. Why do men then now not reck his rod?

Generations, have trod, have trod, have trod;
And all is seared with trade; bleared, smeared
with toil;

And wears man's smudge and shares man's
    smell: the soil
Is bare now, nor can foot feel, being shod.

And for all this, nature is never spent;
    There lives the dearest freshness deep down
        things;
And though the last nights of the black West went
    Oh, morning, at the brown brink eastward,
        springs —
Because the Holy Ghost over the bent
    World broods with warm breast and with ah!
        bright wings.

Gerard Manley Hopkins, 1844-1889

We Lift Our Hearts to Thee

We lift our hearts to thee,
O Daystar from on high!
The sun itself is but thy shade,
Yet cheers both earth and sky.

O let thine orient beams
The night of sin disperse,
The mists of error and of vice
Which shade the universe!

How beauteous nature now!
How dark and sad before!
With joy we view the pleasing change,
And nature's God adore.

May we this life improve,
To mourn for errors past;
And live this short, revolving day
As if it were our last.

To God the Father, Son,
And Spirit, One in Three,
Be glory as it was, is now,
And shall forever be. Amen.

John Wesley, 1703-1791

How Happy Are Thy Servants, Lord

How happy are thy servants, Lord,
Who thus remember thee!
What tongue can tell our sweet accord,
Our perfect harmony?

Who thy mysterious supper share,
Here at thy table fed,
Many, and yet one we are,
One undivided bread.
One with the living bread divine
Which now by faith we eat,
Our hearts and minds and spirit join,
And all in Jesus meet.

So dear the tie where souls agree
In Jesus' dying love!
Then only can it closer be,
When all are joined above. Amen.

Charles Wesley, 1707-1788

African-American Spirituals

Go Tell It on the Mountain

Go tell it on the mountain
Over the hills and ev'rywhere;
Go tell it on the mountain
That Jesus Christ is born!

While shepherds kept their watching
O'er silent flocks by night,
Behold throughout the heavens
There shone a holy light.

The shepherds feared and trembled
When lo! above the earth
Rang out the angel chorus
That hailed the Savior's birth.

Down in a lowly manger
The humble Christ was born,
And God sent us salvation
That blessed Christmas morn.

Were You There When They Crucified My Lord?

Were you there when they crucified my Lord?
Were you there when they crucified my Lord?
O! Sometimes it causes me to tremble, tremble,
    tremble.
Were you there when they crucified my Lord?

Were you there when they nailed him to the tree?
Were you there when they nailed him to the tree?
O! Sometimes it causes me to tremble, tremble,
    tremble.
Were you there when they nailed him to the tree?

Were you there when they pierced him in the side?
Were you there when they pierced him in the
    side?
O! Sometimes it causes me to tremble, tremble,
    tremble.

Were you there when they pierced him in the
    side?

Were you there when the sun refused to shine?
Were you there when the sun refused to shine?
O! Sometimes it causes me to tremble, tremble,
    tremble.
Were you there when the sun refused to shine?

Were you there when they laid him in the tomb?
Were you there when they laid him in the tomb?
O! Sometimes it causes me to tremble, tremble,
    tremble.
Were you there when they laid him in the tomb?

Were you there when they rolled the stone away?
Were you there when they rolled the stone away?
O! Sometimes it causes me to tremble, tremble,
    tremble.
Were you there when they rolled the stone away?

No One Works like Him

He is King of kings,
He is Lord of lords.
Jesus Christ the first and last —
No one works like him.

He built his kingdom up in the air,
No one works like him.
And called his saints from everywhere.
No one works like him.

He pitched his tents on Canaan's ground.
No one works like him.
And broke the Roman kingdom down.
No one works like him.

Let Us Break Bread Together

Let us break bread together on our knees;
Let us break bread together on our knees;
When I fall on my knees
With my face to the rising sun,
O Lord, have mercy on me.

Let us drink wine together on our knees;
Let us drink wine together on our knees;
When I fall on my knees,
With my face to the rising sun,
O Lord, have mercy on me.

Let us praise God together on our knees;
Let us praise God together on our knees;
When I fall on my knees,
With my face to the rising sun,
O Lord, have mercy on me.

There Is a Balm in Gilead

There is a balm in Gilead
To make the wounded whole;
There is a balm in Gilead
To heal the sin-sick soul.

Sometimes I feel discouraged
And think my work's in vain,
But then the Holy Spirit
Revives my soul again.

If you cannot preach like Peter,
If you cannot pray like Paul,
You can tell the love of Jesus,
And say, "He died for all!"

I Want Jesus to Walk with Me

I want Jesus to walk with me;
I want Jesus to walk with me;
All along my pilgrim journey,
Lord, I want Jesus to walk with me.

In my trials, Lord, walk with me;
In my trials, Lord, walk with me;
When my heart is almost breaking,
Lord, I want Jesus to walk with me.

When I'm in trouble, Lord, walk with me;
When I'm in trouble, Lord, walk with me;
When my head is bowed in sorrow,
Lord, I want Jesus to walk with me.

Poems and Hymns from the Gaelic

King of the Friday

O King of the Friday
Whose limbs were stretched on the cross,
O Lord who did suffer
The bruises, the wounds, the loss,
We stretch ourselves
Beneath the shield of thy might,
Some fruit from the tree of thy passion
Fall on us this night!

An Ancient Litany of Our Lady

O Mary, kind gentle maid, give help to us;
O tabernacle of the Lord's body, O shrine of
    mysteries!
O queen of all who reign, O holy virgin maid,

Pray for us that through thee our wretched trans-
gression may be forgiven.

O compassionate, O forgiving one, with the grace
of the pure Spirit,

Entreat with us the true-judging King, thy fair
fragrant Child.

O branch of the plant of Jesse, from the beauteous
hazelwood,

Pray for me that I may have forgiveness for my
foul guilt.

O Mary, great beauteous diadem, who didst free
our race;

O light most beauteous, O garden of kings,

O lustrous one, O shining one, with deed of white
chastity,

O fair bright ark of gold, O holy birth from
heaven.

O mother of holiness, who didst exceed all,

Pray with me thy First-born to save me at the
judgment.

O lady victorious, long-descended, host-attended,
strong,

Entreat with us the mighty Christ, thy Father and
thy Son.

O glorious star elect, O bush in bloom,

O strong choice torch, O sun that warmest all,

O ladder of the great fence whereby each holy one
mounts,

Mayest thou be our protection towards the
glorious kingdom.

O city fair and fragrant, thee the King did choose;

The great guest was in thy bosom for thrice three
months.

O royal door elect, through which came into the
   body,
The shining choice Sun, Jesus, Son of the living
   God.
For the sake of the fair birth which was conceived
   in thy womb,
For the sake of the Only-begotten who is high
   King in every place,
For the sake of his cross, which is above every
   cross,
For the sake of his burial, who was buried in the
   rock,
For the sake of his resurrection, who arose before
   all,
For the sake of the holy household which will
   come from every place to judgment,
Be thou our protection in the kingdom of fair
   safety,
That we may go with Jesus we pray while life
   lasts.

**Composed by Columcille
(St. Columba of Iona) 521–597;
Translated from the Gaelic by
the Rev. Charles Plummer**

A Hymn to St. Michael

O Angel!
Bear, O Michael of the mighty powers,
My cause before the Lord.

Hearest thou?
Ask of the forgiving God
forgiveness for all my monstrous ill.

Delay not!
Bear my fervent longing
Before the King, the great King.

To my soul
Bring help, bring comfort,
In the hour of my departure from the earth.

In power,
To meet my waiting soul,
Come with many thousands of angels,
O Angel.

O warrior!
Against the crooked, foul, contentious world,
Come to help me in very deed.

Pour thou not
Contempt on what I say;
While I live, forsake me not.

I choose thee,
To free this soul of mine,
My reason, my sense, my flesh.

O advocate,
Triumphant, victorious in war,
O angelic slayer of anti-Christ!
O Angel.

**Composed by Maelisu O'Brolchan, 11th century
Translated from the Gaelic by
the Rev. Charles Plummer.**

St. Patrick's Breastplate

I bind this day to me for ever,
By power of faith, Christ's incarnation,
His baptism in the Jordan River,

His death on the cross for my salvation.
His bursting from the spiced tomb,
His riding up the heavenly way,
His coming at the day of doom
I bind unto myself today!

I bind unto myself today
the power of God to hold and lead:
His eye to watch, his might to stay,
His ear to hearken to my need;
The wisdom of my God to teach,
His hand to guide, his shield to ward;
The Word of God to give me speech,
His heavenly host to be my guard!

Christ be with me, Christ within me,
Christ behind me, Christ before me,
Christ beside me, Christ to win me,
Christ to comfort and restore me.
Christ beneath me, Christ above me,
Christ in quiet, Christ in danger,
Christ in hearts of all that love me,
Christ in mouth of friend and stranger.

I bind unto myself the name,
The strong name of the Trinity:
By invocation of the same,
The Three in One and One in Three;
Of whom all nature hath creation,
Eternal Father, Spirit, Word;
Praise to the Lord of my salvation —
Salvation is of Christ the Lord! Amen.

Ascribed to St. Patrick, 5th century
Translated from the Gaelic by
Mrs. C.F. Alexander

Act of Faith, Hope, and Love

My God, I believe in you,
I trust in you,
I love you above all things,
with all my heart and mind and strength.
I love you because you are supremely good and
      worth loving;
and because I love you,
I am sorry with all my heart for offending you.
Lord, have mercy on me, a sinner.
Amen.

Act of Contrition*

Lord Jesus,
    you opened the eyes of the blind,
    healed the sick,
    forgave the sinful woman,
    and after Peter's denial confirmed him in your
      love.
Listen to my prayer: Forgive all my sins,
    renew your love in my heart,
    help me live in perfect unity with my
    fellow Christians
    that I may proclaim your saving power to all
    the world.

or

Lord Jesus,
    you chose to be called the friend of sinners.

---

    * These prayers are taken from the revised Rite of Penance.

By your saving death and resurrection
    free me from my sins.
May your peace take root in my heart
    and bring forth a harvest
    of love, holiness, and truth.

Prayer for Unity*

Almighty and eternal God,
    you gather the scattered sheep
    and watch over those you have gathered.
Look kindly on all who follow Jesus, your Son.
You have marked them with the seal of one
        baptism,
    now make them one in the fullness of faith
    and unite them in the bond of love.
We ask this through Christ our Lord.
Amen.

Come, Holy Spirit†

V/ Come, Holy Spirit, fill the hearts of your
        faithful.

R/ And kindle in them the fire of your love.

V/ Send forth your Spirit and they shall be created.

R/ And you will renew the face of the earth.

Let us pray.

---

* This prayer is an adaptation of the opening prayer from
the votive Mass for Christian Unity.

† The first versicle and response are adapted from the
Alleluia verse before the Gospel of Pentecost; the second versicle and response from the third antiphon for the Office of Readings on Pentecost; the prayer is from the votive Mass of the
Holy Spirit in The Roman Missal.

Lord, by the light of the Holy Spirit
   you have taught the hearts of your faithful.
In the same Spirit
   help us to relish what is right
   and always rejoice in your consolation.
We ask this through Christ our Lord.

R/ Amen.

Prayer for the Church and for the Civil Authorities*

We pray thee, O almighty and eternal God, who through Jesus Christ hast revealed thy glory to all nations, to preserve the works of thy mercy, that thy Church, being spread through the whole world, may continue with unchanging faith in the confession of thy name.

We pray thee, who alone art good and holy, to endow with heavenly knowledge, sincere zeal, and sanctity of life, our chief bishop, (Name), the vicar of our Lord Jesus Christ, in the government of his Church; our own bishop (or archbishop), (Name); all other bishops, prelates, and pastors of the Church; and especially those who are appointed to exercise amongst us the functions of

* This prayer was composed by Archbishop John Carroll of Baltimore (1735-1815), the first Catholic bishop of the United States and cousin of Charles Carroll of Carrollton, a signer of the Declaration of Independence. The prayer was originally appointed to be read every Sunday at Mass after the sermon. In later and more hurried times, it was read only on national holidays. Because of its noble style, it is presented here unaltered, except that the present version acknowledges that women are now eligible to be governors and presidents.

the holy ministry, and conduct thy people into the ways of salvation.

We pray thee, O God of might, wisdom, and justice, through whom authority is rightly administered, laws are enacted, and judgment decreed, assist with thy Holy Spirit of counsel and fortitude the President of these United States, that his/her administration may be conducted in righteousness, and be eminently useful to thy people over whom he/she presides: by encouraging due respect for virtue and religion; by a faithful execution of the laws in justice and mercy; and by restraining vice and immorality. Let the light of thy divine wisdom direct the deliberations of Congress, and shine forth in all the proceedings and laws framed for our rule and government, so that they may tend to the preservation of peace, the promotion of national happiness, the increase of industry, sobriety, and useful knowledge; and may perpetuate to us the blessings of equal liberty.

We pray for his/her excellency, the Governor of this state, for the members of the Assembly, for all judges, magistrates, and other officers who are appointed to guard our political welfare, that they may be enabled, by thy powerful protection, to discharge the duties of their respective stations with honesty and ability.

We recommend likewise to thy unbounded mercy, all our brethren and fellow-citizens throughout the United States, that they may be blessed in the knowledge and sanctified in the observance of thy most holy law; that they may be preserved in union, and in that peace which the world cannot give; and, after enjoying the blessings of this life, be admitted to those which are eternal.

Finally, we pray thee, O Lord of mercy, to remember the souls of thy servants departed who are gone before us with the sign of faith and repose in the sleep of peace: the souls of our parents, relatives, and friends; of those who, when living, were members of this congregation, and particularly of such as are lately deceased; of all benefactors who by their donations or legacies to this church witnessed their zeal for the decency of divine worship and proved their claim to our grateful and charitable remembrance. To these, O Lord, and to all that rest in Christ, grant, we beseech thee, a place of refreshment, light and everlasting peace, through Jesus Christ, our Lord and Savior. Amen.

Litany of the Holy Name*

Lord, have mercy	Lord, have mercy
Christ, have mercy	Christ, have mercy
Lord, have mercy	Lord, have mercy
God our Father in heaven	Have mercy on us
God the Son, Redeemer of the world	Have mercy on us

* The origins of this litany, a commentary on Philippians 2:9-11, can be traced back to the 15th century, and some of the invocations, in a more elaborate form, are in the Litany of Our Blessed Savior found in 17th-century manuals. In its present form it was approved by Leo XIII (1810-1903) for use throughout the world.

God the Holy Spirit	Have mercy on us
Holy Trinity, one God	Have mercy on us
Jesus, Son of the living God	Have mercy on us
Jesus, splendor of the Father	Have mercy on us
Jesus, brightness of everlasting light	Have mercy on us
Jesus, king of glory	Have mercy on us
Jesus, dawn of justice	Have mercy on us
Jesus, Son of the Virgin Mary	Have mercy on us
Jesus, worthy of our love	Have mercy on us
Jesus, worthy of our wonder	Have mercy on us
Jesus, mighty God	Have mercy on us
Jesus, father of the world to come	Have mercy on us
Jesus, prince of peace	Have mercy on us
Jesus, all-powerful	Have mercy on us
Jesus, pattern of patience	Have mercy on us
Jesus, model of obedience	Have mercy on us
Jesus, gentle and humble of heart	Have mercy on us
Jesus, lover of chastity	Have mercy on us
Jesus, lover of us all	Have mercy on us
Jesus, God of peace	Have mercy on us
Jesus, author of life	Have mercy on us
Jesus, model of goodness	Have mercy on us
Jesus, seeker of souls	Have mercy on us
Jesus, our God	Have mercy on us
Jesus, our refuge	Have mercy on us
Jesus, father of the poor	Have mercy on us

Jesus, treasure of the faithful	Have mercy on us
Jesus, good shepherd	Have mercy on us
Jesus, the true light	Have mercy on us
Jesus, eternal wisdom	Have mercy on us
Jesus, infinite goodness	Have mercy on us
Jesus, our way and our life	Have mercy on us
Jesus, joy of angels	Have mercy on us
Jesus, king of patriarchs	Have mercy on us
Jesus, teacher of apostles	Have mercy on us
Jesus, master of evangelists	Have mercy on us
Jesus, courage of martyrs	Have mercy on us
Jesus, light of confessors	Have mercy on us
Jesus, purity of virgins	Have mercy on us
Jesus, crown of all saints	Have mercy on us

Lord, be merciful	Jesus, save your people
From all evil	Jesus, save your people
From every sin	Jesus, save your people
From the snares of the devil	Jesus, save your people
From your anger	Jesus, save your people
From the spirit of infidelity	Jesus, save your people
From everlasting death	Jesus, save your people
From neglect of your Holy Spirit	Jesus, save your people
By the mystery of your incarnation	Jesus, save your people
By your birth	Jesus, save your people
By your childhood	Jesus, save your people
By your hidden life	Jesus, save your people
By your public ministry	Jesus, save your people

By your agony and crucifixion	Jesus, save your people
By your abandonment	Jesus, save your people
By your grief and sorrow	Jesus, save your people
By your death and burial	Jesus, save your people
By your rising to new life	Jesus, save your people
By your return in glory to the Father	Jesus, save your people
By your gift of the holy Eucharist	Jesus, save your people
By your joy and glory	Jesus, save your people
Christ, hear us	Christ, hear us
Lord Jesus, hear our prayer	Lord Jesus, hear our prayer
Lamb of God, you take away the sins of the world	Have mercy on us
Lamb of God, you take away the sins of the world	Have mercy on us
Lamb of God, you take away the sins of the world	Have mercy on us

Let us pray.

Lord,
    may we who honor the holy name of Jesus
    enjoy his friendship in this life
    and be filled with eternal joy in the kingdom
    where he lives and reigns for ever and ever.

R/ Amen.

Litany of the Sacred Heart*

Lord, have mercy	Lord, have mercy
Christ, have mercy	Christ, have mercy
Lord, have mercy	Lord, have mercy

God our Father in heaven	Have mercy on us
God the Son, Redeemer of the world	Have mercy on us
God the Holy Spirit	Have mercy on us
Holy Trinity, one God	Have mercy on us

Heart of Jesus, Son of the eternal Father	Have mercy on us
Heart of Jesus, formed by the Holy Spirit in the wombof the Virgin Mother	Have mercy on us
Heart of Jesus, one with the eternal Word	Have mercy on us
Heart of Jesus, infinite in majesty	Have mercy on us
Heart of Jesus, holy temple of God	Have mercy on us
Heart of Jesus, tabernacle of the Most High	Have mercy on us
Heart of Jesus, house of God and gate of heaven	Have mercy on us
Heart of Jesus, aflame with love for us	Have mercy on us
Heart of Jesus, source of justice and love	Have mercy on us

---

* Many of the invocations in this litany can be traced to the 17th century. The litany was approved by Leo XIII (1810-1903).

Heart of Jesus, full of goodness and love	Have mercy on us
Heart of Jesus, well-spring of all virtue	Have mercy on us
Heart of Jesus, worthy of all praise	Have mercy on us
Heart of Jesus, king and center of all hearts	Have mercy on us
Heart of Jesus, treasure-house of wisdom and knowledge	Have mercy on us
Heart of Jesus, in whom there dwells the fullness of God	have mercy on us
Heart of Jesus, in whom the Father is well pleased	Have mercy on us
Heart of Jesus, fromwhose fullness we have all received	Have mercy on us
Heart of Jesus, desire of the eternal hills	Have mercy on us
Heart of Jesus, patient and full of mercy	Have mercy on us
Heart of Jesus, generous to all who turn to you	Have mercy on us
Heart of Jesus, fountain of life and holiness	Have mercy on us
Heart of Jesus, atonement for our sins	Have mercy on us
Heart of Jesus, overwhelmed with insults	Have mercy on us

Heart of Jesus, broken for our sins	Have mercy on us
Heart of Jesus, obedient even to death	Have mercy on us
Heart of Jesus, pierced by a lance	Have mercy on us
Heart of Jesus, source of all consolation	Have mercy on us
Heart of Jesus, our life and resurrection	Have mercy on us
Heart of Jesus, our peace and reconciliation	Have mercy on us
Heart of Jesus, victim for our sins	Have mercy on us
Heart of Jesus, salvation of all who trust in you	Have mercy on us
Heart of Jesus, hope of all who die in you	Have mercy on us
Heart of Jesus, delight of all the saints	Have mercy on us
Lamb of God, you take away the sins of the world	Have mercy on us
Lamb of God, you take away the sins of the world	Have mercy on us
Lamb of God, you take away the sins of the world	Have mercy on us

V/ Jesus, gentle and humble of heart.

R/ Touch our hearts and make them like your own.

Let us pray.

Father,
  we rejoice in the gifts of love
  we have received from the heart of Jesus your
    Son.
Open our hearts to share his life
  and continue to bless us with his love.
We ask this in the name of Jesus the Lord.

R/ Amen.

Act of Dedication to Christ the King*

Loving Jesus, Redeemer of the world,
  we are yours, and yours we wish to be.
To bind ourselves to you even more closely,
  we kneel before you today
  and offer ourselves to your most Sacred Heart.

R/ Praise to you, our Savior and our King.

Have mercy on all who have never known you
  and on all who reject you and refuse to obey
    you:
  gentle Lord, draw them to yourself.

R/ Praise to you, our Savior and our King.

Reign over the faithful who have never left you,
  reign over those who have squandered their
    inheritance,
  the prodigal children who now are starving:
  bring them back to their Father's house.

R/ Praise to you, our Savior and our King.

---

* Originally written and prescribed by Leo XIII (1810-1903) for the feast of the Sacred Heart. In 1925 Pius XI transferred it to the new feast of Christ the King.

Reign over those who are misled by error or divided by discord. Hasten the day when we shall be one in faith and truth, one flock with you, the one Shepherd. Give to your Church freedom and peace, and to all nations justice and order. Make the earth resound from pole to pole with a single cry: Praise to the Divine Heart that gained our salvation; glory and honor be his for ever and ever. Amen.

R/ Praise to you, our Savior and our King.

Litany of Loreto*

Lord, have mercy	Lord, have mercy
Christ, have mercy	Christ, have mercy
Lord, have mercy	Lord, have mercy
God our Father in heaven	Have mercy on us
God the Son, Redeemer of the world	Have mercy on us
God the Holy Spirit	Have mercy on us
Holy Trinity, one God	Have mercy on us
Holy Mary	Pray for us
Holy Mother of God	Pray for us
Most honored of virgins	Pray for us
Mother of Christ	Pray for us
Mother of the Church	Pray for us
Mother of divine grace	Pray for us

* A litany containing some of these invocations was in use in the 12th century. It was recorded in its present form (apart from a few additions by recent popes) at Loreto in 1558 and approved by Sixtus V (1521-1590). For about half of the invocations, the present translation uses the traditional renderings which have been in use since the 17th century.

Mother most pure	Pray for us
Mother of chaste love	Pray for us
Mother and virgin	Pray for us
Sinless Mother	Pray for us
Dearest of mothers	Pray for us
Model of motherhood	Pray for us
Mother of good counsel	Pray for us
Mother of our Creator	Pray for us
Mother of our Savior	Pray for us
Virgin most wise	Pray for us
Virgin rightly praised	Pray for us
Virgin rightly renowned	Pray for us
Virgin most powerful	Pray for us
Virgin gentle in mercy	Pray for us
Faithful Virgin	Pray for us
Mirror of justice	Pray for us
Throne of wisdom	Pray for us
Cause of our joy	Pray for us
Shrine of the Spirit	Pray for us
Glory of Israel	Pray for us
Vessel of selfless devotion	Pray for us
Mystical Rose	Pray for us
Tower of David	Pray for us
Tower of ivory	Pray for us
House of gold	Pray for us
Ark of the covenant	Pray for us
Gate of heaven	Pray for us
Morning Star	Pray for us
Health of the sick	Pray for us
Refuge of sinners	Pray for us
Comfort of the troubled	Pray for us
Help of Christians	Pray for us

Queen of angels	Pray for us
Queen of patriarchs and prophets	Pray for us
Queen of apostles and martyrs	Pray for us
Queen of confessors and virgins	Pray for us
Queen of all saints	Pray for us
Queen conceived in grace	Pray for us
Queen raised up to glory	Pray for us
Queen of the rosary	Pray for us
Queen of peace	Pray for us

Lamb of God, you take away the sins of the world	Have mercy on us
Lamb of God, you take away the sins of the world	Have mercy on us
Lamb of God, you take away the sins of the world	Have mercy on us

V/ Pray for us, holy Mother of God.
R/ That we may become worthy of the promises of Christ.

Let us pray.

Eternal God,
   let your people enjoy constant health in mind
      and body.
Through the intercession of the Virgin Mary
   free us from the sorrows of this life
   and lead us to happiness in the life to come.
Grant this through Christ our Lord.

R/ Amen.

Salve, Regina*

Hail, holy Queen, Mother of mercy,
hail, our life, our sweetness, and our hope.

To you we cry, the children of Eve;

to you we send up our sighs,

mourning and weeping in this land of exile.

Turn, then, most gracious advocate,

your eyes of mercy toward us;

lead us home at last

and show us the blessed fruit of your womb, Jesus:

O clement, O loving, O sweet Virgin Mary.

Memorare*

Remember, most loving Virgin Mary,

never was it heard

that anyone who turned to you for help

was left unaided.

Inspired by this confidence,

though burdened by my sins,

I run to your protection

for you are my mother.

Mother of the Word of God,

do not despise my words of pleading

but be merciful and hear my prayer.

Amen.

---

* One of the four anthems to Mary sung at the end of liturgical Night Prayer according to the season. It was used as a processional at the Abbey of Cluny from about 1135.

* A 16th-century abridgment of a 15th-century prayer. The idea that it was written by St. Bernard seems to have been due to its popularization by Pere Claude Bernard (1588-1641).

Ancient Prayer to the Virgin Mary*

We turn to you for protection,
holy Mother of God.
Listen to our prayers
and help us in our needs.
Save us from every danger,
glorious and blessed Virgin.

A Child's Prayer to Mary†

Mary, mother whom we bless,
full of grace and tenderness,
defend me from the devil's power
and greet me in my dying hour.

The Angelus‡

V/ The angel spoke God's message to Mary,

R/ and she conceived of the Holy Spirit.

Hail Mary . . . .**

V/ "I am the lowly servant of the Lord:

R/ let it be done to me according to your word."

---

* This prayer, first found in a Greek papyrus, ca. 300, is the oldest known prayer to Mary. It has long been known in the West by its opening words in Latin, "Sub tuum praesidium."

† This prayer is from the hymn "Memento rerum conditor."

‡ The custom of saying the "Hail Mary" three times when the bell rang in the evening goes back to the 13th century, and there are bells of that period inscribed with the angelic salutation. The prayer was formerly the post-Communion prayer for Masses of Our Lady in Advent and is now the opening prayer for the Fourth Sunday of Advent.

** For the text of the "Hail Mary," see page 21.

Hail Mary . . . .

V/ And the Word became flesh

R/ and lived among us.

Hail Mary . . . .

V/ Pray for us, holy Mother of God,

R/ that we may become worthy of the promises of
Christ.

Let us pray.

Lord, fill our hearts with your grace:
once, through the message of an angel
you revealed to us the incarnation of your Son;
now, through his suffering and death
lead us to the glory of his resurrection.

We ask this through Christ our Lord.

R/ Amen.

Regina Coeli*

Queen of heaven, rejoice, alleluia.
For Christ, your Son and Son of God,
has risen as he said, alleluia.
Pray to God for us, alleluia.

V/ Rejoice and be glad, O Virgin Mary, alleluia.

R/ For the Lord has truly risen, alleluia.

Let us pray.

---

* A 12th-century Evening Prayer anthem for the Easter
season. Since the 13th century, it has been used as the seasonal
antiphon in honor of the Blessed Virgin after Night Prayer.
Since 1743 it has replaced the Angelus in the Easter season.

God of life,
you have given joy to the world
by the resurrection of your Son, our Lord Jesus
Christ.
Through the prayers of his mother, the Virgin
Mary,
bring us to the happiness of eternal life.

We ask this through Christ our Lord.

R/ Amen.

Litany of St. Joseph*

Lord, have mercy	Lord, have mercy
Christ, have mercy	Christ, have mercy
Lord, have mercy	Lord, have mercy
God our Father in heaven	Have mercy on us
God the Son, Redeemer of the world	Have mercy on us
God the Holy Spirit	Have mercy on us
Holy Trinity, one God	Have mercy on us
Holy Mary	Pray for us
Saint Joseph	Pray for us
Noble son of the House of David	Pray for us
Light of patriarchs	Pray for us
Husband of the Mother of God	Pray for us
Guardian of the Virgin	Pray for us
Foster father of the Son of God	Pray for us
Faithful guardian of Christ	Pray for us
Head of the holy family	Pray for us
Joseph, chaste and just	Pray for us

* Approved by St. Pius X (1835-1914).

Joseph, prudent and brave	Pray for us
Joseph, obedient and loyal	Pray for us
Pattern of patience	Pray for us
Lover of poverty	Pray for us
Model of workers	Pray for us
Example to parents	Pray for us
Guardian of virgins	Pray for us
Pillar of family life	Pray for us
Comfort of the troubled	Pray for us
Hope of the sick	Pray for us
Patron of the dying	Pray for us
Terror of evil spirits	Pray for us
Protector of the Church	Pray for us

Lamb of God, you take away the sins of the world	Have mercy on us
Lamb of God, you take away the sins of the world	Have mercy on us
Lamb of God, you take away the sins of the world	Have mercy on us

V/ God made him master of his household.
R/ And put him in charge of all that he owned.

Let us pray.

Almighty God,
    in your infinite wisdom and love
    you chose Joseph to be the husband of Mary,
    the mother of your Son.
As we enjoy his protection on earth
    may we have the help of his prayers in heaven.

We ask this through Christ our Lord.

R/ Amen.

Dedication to Jesus

Lord Jesus Christ,
   take all my freedom,
    my memory, my understanding, and my will.
All that I have and cherish
   you have given me.
I surrender it all to be guided by your will.
Your grace and your love
   are wealth enough for me.
Give me these, Lord Jesus,
   and I ask for nothing more.

                    — **St. Ignatius Loyola (1491-1556)**

Hebrew and Greek Acclamations

Alleluia

From the Hebrew "Hallelujah": Praise the LORD!

St. Augustine said that when we pray it on earth, we pray in hope, in heaven we will pray in possession: "Here it is alleluia en route, there it is alleluia on arriving home." In the Western Church, alleluia is not sung during Lent, since it is considered the Easter prayer par excellence.

Amen

A Hebrew word meaning "It is true!" or "I believe!" Thus when Jesus says, "Amen, Amen I say to you," it means "Believe me!" St. Jerome retained the expression in his Latin translation of the Gospels and it has been restored in the Revised New Testament of the New American Bible. With their "Amen!" Jews and Christians commit themselves to what has been said in prayer.

Hosanna

A Hebrew expression of two words meaning "Save, we pray" (Psalm 118:25). It was transliterated as one word in Greek and then in modern languages. Psalm 118 was sung in the Temple during the Feast of Tabernacles (Booths). It became associated with messianic expectations. In the Gospels, it is used to hail Jesus on Palm Sunday. The words from Psalm 118:25-26: "Hosanna . . . Blessed is he who comes in the name of the Lord!" are acclaimed as he enters Jerusalem. The expression also occurs in the Sanctus (Holy, holy, holy) of the Mass.

Kyrie Eleison

A Greek prayer that means "Lord have mercy." It was retained in the Roman liturgy as a reminder that the Mass in Rome was originally celebrated in Greek. It has ecumenical significance because it is used in many Eastern liturgies. In addition to the Greeks, the Armenians, Copts, Ethiopians, Maronites, and Syrians sing the Kyrie.

III.

Listening to the Lord

Be still
&
know
that
I·AM·GOD

הַרְפּוּ
וּדְעוּ
כִּי
אָנֹכִי
אֱלֹהִים

PSALM 46 · 11

LISTENING TO THE LORD
MEDITATIVE OR CONTEMPLATIVE PRAYER

Elijah's Vision

1 Kings 19:9-12 RSV

Elijah came to a cave and lodged there; and behold, the word of the Lord came to him, and he said to him, "What are you doing here, Elijah?"
He said,

"I have been very jealous for the LORD, the God of
hosts;
for the people of Israel have forsaken thy
covenant,
thrown down thy altars,
and slain thy prophets with the sword;
and I, even I only, am left;
and they seek my life, to take it away."
And God said,

"Go forth and stand upon the mount before the
LORD."
And behold, the LORD passed by,
and a great and strong wind rent the mountains,
and broke in pieces the rocks before the LORD,
but the LORD was not in the wind;
and after the wind an earthquake,
but the LORD was not in the earthquake;
and after the earthquake a fire,

but the LORD was not in the fire;
and after the fire a still small voice.

Oh, that today you would hear God's voice:
Do not harden your hearts.

There is a growing desire among Christians for a deeper prayer life. Many are rediscovering the contemplative tradition of both Western and Eastern Christianity.

At the same time, Catholics in increasing numbers are reading the Scriptures. Many are finding in the Bible a source of deeper union with God.

One of the oldest Christian methods of prayer which combines Bible reading with prayer is called Lectio Divina (Divine Reading). It consists of the following elements:

LECTIO, reading

MEDITATIO, meditation

ORATIO, prayer

CONTEMPLATIO, resting in God

OPERATIO, putting the prayer into action.

LECTIO is a careful study of the Scriptures, in which the person's whole attention is engaged. The prayerful reading of the Scriptures is a practice which the earliest Christians, who were Jews, continued from their Jewish tradition.

MEDITATIO is an action of the mind probing the Scriptures and seeking to understand them in a personal way. I apply the word of God to myself.

ORATIO is a turning to God in which I ask God to forgive my failures and help me to do better in light of what I have just read.

CONTEMPLATIO can be described as a growing "awareness of God." In *New Seeds of Contemplation*, Thomas Merton describes contemplation as our spiritual life "fully awake, fully active, fully aware." It is a gift of God. We can only prepare ourselves to receive it. The rest is up to God.

OPERATIO calls us to act on our union with God. God's Spirit enlightens us by grace before we act and accompanies us as we act, directing our steps in the way of justice and peace.

Please see SUGGESTED BOOKS FOR FURTHER READING, page 386, for more information on this method of meditation.

THE ROSARY

The rosary became popular during the Middle Ages because it uses prayers which all Catholics should know and can be prayed in circumstances where it would be inconvenient or impossible to read from a book.

It is based on 15 mysteries that follow the historical sequence of the life of Jesus and Mary. It is prayed while fingering rosary beads (which take their name from the Old English word for prayer, "bede"). The usual rosary has beads for five mysteries. The rosary begins with the praying of the Apostles Creed on the cross. Before the first mystery there is a larger bead for the Lord's Prayer and three smaller beads for Hail Marys. Each mystery begins with the Lord's Prayer (on the larger bead). This is followed by 10 Hail Marys (on the smaller beads). At the end of each decade the "Glory be to the Father and to the Son and to the Holy Spirit" is prayed.

The most common way to pray the rosary is to spend a brief time calling to mind the mystery and then going on with the prayers. This may sound complicated but it is easily learned.

The repetition of a prayer over and over while fingering beads helps to free us from other thoughts and open us to God's Spirit.

Millions of people have risen to high levels of communion with God by praying the rosary. A beautiful description of this devotion is found in *The Song of Bernadette*, by Franz Werfel:

All the women and girls of Lourdes constantly carry a rosary upon their person. It is the authentic tool of their piety. The hands of poor hard-working women have not the habit of stillness. A prayer with empty hands would be no proper observance for them. But the prayer of the rosary is to them a sort of heavenly manual toil, an invisible needlework, a knitting or embroidery busily wrought of the fifty Hail Marys and the other invocations of their strand of beads. . . . The lips, one may say, murmur but automatically the words of the angel to the Virgin, yet the soul traverses the pastures of holiness. Thoughts often stray from the proper forms and lament the unreasonable price of eggs, and though one even drowses now and then over an Ave, it is no great misfortune. The deep feeling of being at home and protected remains.

~∞~

The Mysteries of the Rosary (with Suggested Scripture Readings)

The Joyful Mysteries

The Annunciation, Luke 1:26-38
The Visitation, Luke 1:39-56
The Nativity, Luke 2:1-14
The Presentation in the Temple, Luke 2:22-35
The Finding in the Temple, Luke 2:41-50

The Sorrowful Mysteries

The Agony in the Garden, Matthew 26:36-44
The Scourging at the Pillar, Mark 15:6-15
The Crowning with Thorns, John 19:1-7
Jesus Carries His Cross, Luke 23:26-32
Jesus Dies on the Cross, Luke 23:33-46

The Glorious Mysteries

The Resurrection, Mark 16:1-7
The Ascension, Acts 1:9-11
The Coming of the Holy Spirit, Acts 2:1-13
The Assumption of Our Lady into Heaven, 1
  Corinthians 15:51-57
The Coronation of Our Lady and the Glory of All
  the Saints, Revelation 7:9-12

These are only suggestions. Whatever way of praying the rosary works best for you is the one to use. The way to find what works best for you is to try. See SUGGESTED BOOKS FOR FURTHER READING, page 387, for more reading about the rosary.

THE JESUS PRAYER

The Jesus Prayer is a traditional method of prayer long popular among the Eastern Orthodox and Eastern-rite Catholics. It is growing in use by Western Christians: Catholics, Anglicans and Protestants.

It is based on the prayerful repetition of the name of Jesus. Over the years the prayer has taken various forms. Some people say, "Jesus Christ" or "Lord Jesus." The simplest form is the word "Jesus" used alone. But the most common formula is, "Lord Jesus Christ, Son of God, have mercy on me, a sinner," which is reverently repeated. Before using this prayer, one should try to find a quiet spot, sit in a comfortable but upright position and call on the Holy Spirit, keeping in mind the words of 1 Corinthians 12:3, "No one can say 'Jesus is Lord' except by the Holy Spirit."

In the Eastern monastic tradition, the Jesus prayer is associated with the use of prayer beads, like the Western rosary. The beads are given to monks and nuns at their religious profession.

Further reading on the Jesus Prayer may be found in SUGGESTED BOOKS FOR FURTHER READING, page 386. You should have guidance for this form of prayer. The recommended books will be helpful.

CHRISTIAN MEDITATION

A letter to Catholic bishops from the Vatican Congregation for the Doctrine of the Faith "On Some Aspects of Christian Meditation," issued December 14, 1989, reminds us of the following:

- The importance of bodily posture as an integral part of meditation, although it should be viewed as an aid and not as a means in itself.
- The universal acknowledgment of the need for a spiritual director.
- The need for asceticism, which all meditation traditions emphasize.
- The importance of tradition as a means of safeguarding and testing various meditation methods.
- The fact that there should not be an overemphasis on technique.
- The need for "interior watchfulness," which is not necessarily interrupted when one is engaged in contact with others.
- Please see SUGGESTED BOOKS FOR FURTHER READING, page 386, for more books on meditation.

IV.
Knowing the Lord

ΚΑΙ ΑΥΤΟΙ
ἐΖΗΓΟΥΝΤΟ
ΤΑ ἐΝ Τῌ ὁΔῷ
ΚΑΙ ὡc ἐΓΝῶCΘΗ
ΑΥΤΟῖC ἐΝ
Τῌ ΚΛΑCΕΙ
ΤΟΥ ἌΡΤΟΥ

Then they
told what
had happened
on the road
and how
the Lord
had been made known to them
in the breaking of the bread.

LUKE 24 : 35

KNOWING THE LORD

THE SACRAMENTS AND CHRISTIAN LIFE

God reveals himself to us in Jesus Christ, who made himself known to the disciples in the breaking of the bread at Emmaus. When the disciples who had the Emmaus experience met with their companions, they announced that Jesus had been made known to them in "the breaking of the bread." This came to be the ordinary name in the New Testament for the Eucharist. To "know" in biblical language means to have a deep personal relationship.

Christ makes himself known to us in all the sacraments. The New Testament uses the Greek word "mysterion," which means "hidden," to describe God's plan of salvation, which had been hidden and now is revealed in Christ.

As Christianity spread west from Palestine, most converts spoke Greek. But as the faith continued to spread westward, it entered places where Latin was the predominant language. Within a couple of hundred years the two main linguistic groups in the Church were the "Greeks" and the "Latins."

The Greek Fathers of the Church (early Church writers) adopted "mysterion" as a name for the sacraments because in them we experience the hidden, although real, presence of Christ.

The Latin Fathers of the Church used the Latin word "sacramentum" to describe the same reality. The sacramentum was the oath of allegiance which a Roman soldier took to the emperor. It is from this that we get the English word "sacrament." Here we see a difference of emphasis between Western and Eastern Christianity.

The Eastern theologians center on God. Western theologians emphasize humanity's response to God.

By combining the two points of view, we see that in the sacraments God reaches out to us in love through various signs. For our sharing in the sacraments to be fruitful, we must respond to God with loving faith.

This is one of the reasons that Pope John Paul II has said that the reunion of the Roman Catholic and the Eastern Orthodox Churches will allow the Church to "breathe again with both lungs."

THE SEVEN SACRAMENTS

The seven sacraments are these:

- Baptism
- Confirmation
- Holy Eucharist
- Penance
- Anointing of the Sick
- Holy Orders
- Matrimony

The Second Vatican Council reminded us that because the sacraments are outward signs of an inward grace, they also instruct us: "They not only presuppose faith, but by words and objects they also nourish, strengthen and express it." Over the centuries, many of the prayers and actions connected with the sacraments no longer could be understood without involved explanations.

The Jesuit liturgist Joseph Jungman said that the liturgy had become like an ancient castle whose various rooms had to be explained to the visitor.

Therefore the Council, besides reintroducing the language of the people into the Church's worship, initiated a revision of the rites of the sacraments (the words and actions used in administering them) so that their meaning might be clearer to people living in the world today.

The Sacraments of Initiation

The sacraments of initiation are the following:

- Baptism
- Confirmation
- Holy Eucharist

Following the mandate of the Second Vatican Council, the Congregation for Worship introduced its revision of the rites of the sacraments of initiation with these words:

Men and women are delivered from the power of darkness through the sacraments of Christian initiation. They die with Christ, are buried with him and rise again with him. They receive the Spirit who makes them God's adopted sons and daughters and, with all God's people, they celebrate the memorial of the Lord's death and resurrection.

The three sacraments of Christian initiation are thus closely intertwined that they may bring Christians to their full stature, enabling them to carry out their mission in the Church and in the world.

It is sometimes forgotten that the liturgical reforms of the Second Vatican Council were anticipated by Pope Pius XII's reform of the liturgy of Holy Week and the Easter Vigil in 1956. Pope Pius expressed the hope that the restored Vigil, as the preeminent occasion for adult baptisms, would be the means for all Catholics to appreciate the importance of their own baptism. He envisaged a general renewal of baptismal commitment as a cornerstone of spiritual renewal for Catholics.

The Second Vatican Council followed his leadership and ordered the reinstitution of the catechumenate, or the Rite of Christian Initiation of Adults (RCIA), as it has come to be known.

The catechumenate lasts for a period of several months, sometimes a year or two, during which time the catechumens are given instruction, experience mutual support and have time for a true process of conversion. Finally, they are enrolled for an intensive period of preparation during Lent. After their reception into the Church at the Easter Vigil, the new members begin the period known as mystagogia, in which they grow in their knowledge of Christ in the sacraments.

In this way, Lent has become again what it was originally: a special period of the spiritual journey of those who are preparing to enter the Church. It is also an invitation to all Catholics to stir up the grace of their own baptism by sharing in the various rites as they are celebrated with the congregation at Sunday Mass.

Because in most modern dioceses it is impossible for a bishop to confirm all the new Catholics at the Easter Vigil, the priest who in virtue of pastoral office or proper delegation receives them into the Church and baptizes them (if they have not been baptized previously in another Christian community) is given permission to confirm them. They then receive Holy Communion for the first time at the Easter Vigil Mass.

In many parishes, the elect (catechumens accepted for the final preparation for baptism) and candidates (previously baptized Christians accepted for reception into the Church) are enrolled together on the First Sunday of Lent.

The celebrant prays:

My brothers and sisters, in beginning this period of Lent, we look forward to celebrating at Easter the life-giving mysteries of our Lord's suffering, death, and resurrection. These elect and candidates, whom we bring with us to the Easter sacraments, will look to us for an example of Christian renewal. Let us pray to the Lord for them and for ourselves, that we may be renewed by one another's efforts and together come to share the joys of Easter.

During the season of Lent, the elect are brought before the congregation on the Third, Fourth and Fifth Sundays of Lent for the scrutinies, at which the Christian community prays for their purification and enlightenment. The following is a sample prayer for the elect during the first scrutiny:

Lord Jesus,
you are the fountain for which they thirst,
you are the Master whom they seek.
In your presence
they dare not claim to be without sin,
for you alone are the Holy One of God.

They open their hearts to you in faith,
they confess their faults
and lay bare their hidden wounds.
In your love free them from their infirmities,
heal their sickness,
quench their thirst, and give them peace.
In the power of your name,
which they call upon in faith,
stand by them now and heal them.
Rule over that spirit of evil,
conquered by your rising from the dead.
Show your elect the way of salvation in the Holy
    Spirit,
that they may come to worship the Father in truth,
for you live and reign for ever and ever.
Amen.

Baptism

During the Easter Vigil, after the Liturgy of
the Word, the elect are presented to the congregation. Then the Litany of the Saints is prayed. Our
brothers and sisters who surround the throne of
God are asked to pray for those who will join them
in the Communion of Saints.

Then the baptismal water is blessed:

Father,
you give us grace through sacramental signs,
which tell us of the wonders of your unseen
    power.
In baptism we use your gift of water,

which you have made a rich symbol of the grace
you give us in this sacrament.
At the very dawn of creation
your spirit breathed on the waters,
making them the wellspring of all holiness.
The waters of the great flood
you made a sign of the waters of baptism
that make an end of sin
and a new beginning of goodness.
Through the waters of the Red Sea
you led Israel out of slavery
to be an image of God's holy people,
set free from sin by baptism.
In the waters of the Jordan
your Son was baptized by John
and anointed with the Spirit.
Your Son willed that water and blood should flow
        from his side
as he hung upon the cross.
After his resurrection he told his disciples:
"Go out and teach all nations,
baptizing them in the name of the Father,
and of the Son,
and of the Holy Spirit."

Father,
look now with love upon your Church
and unseal for it the fountain of baptism.
By the power of the Holy Spirit
give to this water the grace of your Son,
so that in the sacrament of baptism
all those whom you have created in your likeness
may be cleansed from sin
and rise to a new birth of innocence

by water and the Holy Spirit.
We ask you, Father, with your Son,
to send the Holy Spirit upon the waters of this
     font.
May all who are buried with Christ in the death of
     baptism
rise also with him to newness of life.
We ask this through Christ our Lord.
Amen.

~∽∞∾~

After the elect renounce sin and profess their faith, they are baptized.

Baptism by immersion best symbolizes the reality that the baptized are buried with Christ and born again to newness of life. See Paul's Letter to the Romans 6:1-11.

~∽∞∾~

They are immersed three times —

or

Water is poured over their heads three times —
as the celebrant says:
I baptize you in the name of the Father,
and of the Son,
and of the Holy Spirit.

~∽∞∾~

Confirmation

After the ceremonies of baptism are concluded, the celebrant confirms the newly baptized and those who have been previously baptized and are candidates for membership in the Church.

After the celebrant speaks briefly to those to be confirmed, he invites the congregation to join in prayer for them. After a period of silence, the celebrant holds his hands outstretched over those to be confirmed. All other priests present also extend their hands as the celebrant prays:

All-powerful God, Father of our Lord Jesus Christ,
by water and the Holy Spirit,
you freed your sons and daughters from sin
and gave them new life.

Send your holy Spirit upon them
to be their helper and guide.

Grant them the spirit of wisdom and
      understanding,
the spirit of right judgment and courage,
the spirit of knowledge and reverence,
Fill them with the spirit of wonder and awe in
      your presence.
We ask this through Christ our Lord.
Amen.

Using chrism blessed by the bishop, the celebrant makes the sign of the cross on the forehead of each one to be confirmed as he says:

(Name), be sealed with the Gift of the Holy Spirit.

During the Liturgy of the Eucharist the neophytes (newly baptized and confirmed) receive Holy Communion for the first time.

Infant Baptism

Since the beginning of Christianity, the Church has baptized children as well as adults. St. Paul baptized his jailer and the man's entire household: "Then he and all his family were baptized at once" (Acts 16:33). See also Acts 16:14-15 and 1 Corinthians 1:16.

But children are to be baptized only if there is a reasonable belief that they will be brought up in the faith. The pastor has the responsibility to provide instruction for parents who wish their children to be baptized. Most parishes have special classes for them. Formerly, the rite of baptism was the same for adults and children. Since Vatican II, there is a special rite for the baptism of children which emphasizes the obligations of parents and godparents. If one of the parents is not a Catholic, he or she may remain silent while the other professes the faith. The non-Catholic parent needs only to permit the child to be reared in the faith.

The following are excerpts from the Rite of Baptism for Children:

The priest (deacon) speaks to the parents:

You have asked to have your children baptized. In doing so you are accepting the responsibility of training them in the practice of the faith. It will be your duty to bring them up to keep God's commandments as Christ taught us, by loving God and our neighbor. Do you clearly understand what you are undertaking?

Parents:

We do.

Then he addresses the godparents:

Are you ready to help these parents in their duty as Christian parents?

Godparents:

We are.

The celebrant continues:

My dear children, the Christian community welcomes you with great joy. In its name I claim you for Christ our Savior by the sign of his cross. I now trace the cross on your foreheads, and invite your parents and godparents to do the same.

He signs each child on the forehead and the parents and godparents do the same. It is a beautiful custom for parents to continue this practice each night, especially as a part of family prayer.

The actual baptism may be done by immersion or the pouring of water. (See adult rite above.)

After the child is baptized and has been clothed in the baptismal garment and received the baptismal candle, the celebrant addresses those present:

Dearly beloved, this child has been reborn in baptism. He/she is now called a child of God, for so indeed he/she is. In confirmation he/she will receive the fullness of God's Spirit. In holy Communion he/she will share the banquet of Christ's sacrifice, calling God his/her Father in the midst of the Church.

The celebrant concludes by praying for the parents:

God the Father, through his Son, the Virgin Mary's child, has brought joy to all Christian mothers as they see the hope of eternal life shine on their children. May he bless the mothers of these children. They now thank God for the gift of their children. May they be one with them in thanking him for ever in heaven, in Christ Jesus our Lord.

Amen.

God is the giver of all life, human and divine. May he bless the fathers of these children. With their wives they will be the first teachers of their children in the ways of faith. May they be the best of teachers, bearing witness to the faith by what they say and do, in Christ Jesus our Lord.

Amen.

———~◦∞◦~———

Catholics who have been baptized as infants should be confirmed at an age determined by the bishop after appropriate preparation.

HOLY EUCHARIST

The Liturgy of the Word

The Second Vatican Council said this about the Mass:

The treasures of the Bible are to be opened up more lavishly, so that richer fare may be provided for the faithful at the table of the Lord's Word. In this way a more representative portion of the holy Scriptures will be read to the people over a set cycle of years.

As a result of this decision, we now have a three-year cycle of Sunday readings and a two-year cycle of daily readings for the Mass.

There are three readings on Sundays and feast days, the first of which is generally taken from the Hebrew Scriptures (Old Testament). The second reading is from a New Testament letter or the Acts of the Apostles. The third reading is always taken from the Gospel.

To enhance your participation in the Sunday Eucharist, it is recommended that you read the Sunday readings during the previous week. If you cannot attend daily Mass, you can read the daily Scriptures at home. You will find the Sunday schedule of readings in THREE-YEAR CYCLE OF READINGS FOR SUNDAY MASS, page 317, and the weekday schedule of readings in WEEKDAY LECTIONARY, page 334.

After the readings there is a homily based on the Scripture of the day.

The homily is followed on Sundays and feasts by the Creed and the general intercessions, in which the congregation prays for the needs of the local community and the world.

Eucharistic Prayer

The Eucharistic Prayer is the center and summit of the Mass. It is a prayer of thanksgiving and sanctification. The priest invites the people to lift up their hearts to the Lord in prayer and thanks; he unites them with himself in the prayer he addresses in their name to the Father through Jesus Christ. The meaning of the prayer is that the entire congregation joins itself to Christ in acknowledging the great things God has done and in offering sacrifice.

The chief elements of the Eucharistic Prayer are these:

- Thanksgiving (expressed chiefly in the preface). The priest, in the name of the people, thanks God for the whole work of salvation or some special aspect of it according to the feast or season.

- Acclamation. Joining with the angels, the congregation sings the *Sanctus*. This "Holy, Holy, Holy" was first heard by Isaiah in his vision of heaven (Isaiah 6:3).

- Invocation of the Holy Spirit. The Church calls on God to send the Holy Spirit that our human gifts may become Christ's Body and Blood and be a

means of sanctification to those who
partake.

- Institution Narrative. In the words and
actions of Christ, that sacrifice is celebrated which Christ instituted at the
Last Supper and commanded us to
carry on in the mystery of the Eucharist.
- Memorial Prayer. In fulfilling the command of Christ, the Church keeps his
memorial by recalling his passion, resurrection and ascension. This is more
than just a remembering. That which
took place in the past becomes sacramentally present for this congregation,
and Christ's coming in glory is anticipated. "For as often as you eat this
bread and drink the cup, you proclaim
the Lord's death until he comes" (1
Corinthians 11:26).
- Offering. The Church here and now offers
the spotless victim to the Father in the
Holy Spirit. The faithful are not only to
offer the victim but also to learn to offer
themselves through Christ the Media-
tor to an ever more complete union
with the Father, so that at last God will
be all in all.
- Intercessions. The Eucharist is celebrated
in communion with the entire Church
of heaven and earth.
- Final Doxology. The praise of God is
summed up in the final doxology to

which the people respond in the great
Amen. St. Augustine said that, while
still a pagan, he was impressed by the
congregation's singing of the great
Amen, which "sounded like a clap of
thunder."

One of the reforms of the Second Vatican
Council was the increase in the number of Eucharistic Prayers. The following are excerpts from
four Eucharistic Prayers.

Eucharistic Prayer I
(The Roman Canon)

Thanksgiving

We come to you, Father,
with praise and thanksgiving,
through Jesus Christ your Son.
Through him we ask you to accept and bless
these gifts we offer you in sacrifice.

Intercessions for the Church

We offer them for your holy catholic Church,
watch over it, Lord, and guide it;
grant it peace and unity throughout the world.
We offer them for (Name) our pope,
for (Name) our bishop,
and for all who hold and teach the catholic faith
that comes to us from the apostles.

Remember, Lord, your people,
especially those for whom we now pray, (Name)
and (Name).

Remember all of us gathered here before you.
You know how firmly we believe in you
and dedicate ourselves to you.
We offer this sacrifice of praise
for ourselves and those who are dear to us.
We pray to you, our living and true God,
for our well-being and redemption.

Memorial and Offering

Father, we celebrate the memory of Christ, your
Son.
We, your people and your ministers,
recall his passion,
his resurrection from the dead,
and his ascension into glory;
and from the many gifts you have given us
we offer to you, God of glory and majesty,
this holy and perfect sacrifice:
the bread of life
and the cup of eternal salvation.
Look with favor on these offerings
and accept them as once you accepted
the gifts of your servant Abel,
the sacrifice of Abraham, our father in faith,*
and the bread and wine offered by your priest
Melchisedech.

---

* When Adolf Hitler began his persecution of the Jews,
Pope Pius XI pointed out to a group of German pilgrims to the
Vatican that, as this ancient prayer says, we are fellow children
of Abraham with the Jews. The pope said, "Spiritually, we are
all Semites."

Eucharistic Prayer II

Invocation of the Holy Spirit

Let your Spirit come upon these gifts to make
them holy,
so that they may become for us
the Body and Blood of our Lord, Jesus Christ.

Memorial Prayer

In memory of his death and resurrection,
we offer you, Father, this life-giving bread,
this saving cup.
We thank you for counting us worthy
to stand in your presence and serve you.

Eucharistic Prayer III

Invocation of the Holy Spirit

And so, Father, we bring you these gifts.
We ask you to make them holy by the power of
your Spirit,
that they may become the Body and Blood
of your Son, our Lord Jesus Christ,
at whose command we celebrate this Eucharist.

Memorial Prayer

Father, calling to mind the death your Son
endured for our salvation,
his glorious resurrection and ascension into
heaven,
and ready to greet him when he comes again,
we offer you in thanksgiving this holy and living
sacrifice.

Offering and Intercession

Look with favor on your Church's offering,
and see the victim whose death has reconciled us
　　　to yourself.
Grant that we, who are nourished by his Body and
　　　Blood,
may be filled with his Holy Spirit,
and become one body, one spirit in Christ.
May he make us an everlasting gift to you
and enable us to share in the inheritance of your
　　　saints,
with Mary, the virgin Mother of God;
with the apostles, the martyrs
and all your saints,
on whose constant intercession we rely for help.

Eucharistic Prayer IV

Intercession

Lord, remember those for whom we offer this
　　　sacrifice,
especially (Name) our pope,
(Name) our bishop, and bishops and clergy
　　　everywhere.
Remember those who take part in this offering,
those here present and all your people,
and all who seek you with a sincere heart.
Remember those who have died in the peace of
　　　Christ
and all the dead whose faith is known to you
　　　alone.
Father, in your mercy grant also to us, your
　　　children,
to enter into our heavenly inheritance

in the company of the Virgin Mary, the Mother of
God,

and your apostles and saints.

Then, in your kingdom, freed from the corruption
of sin and death,

we shall sing your glory with every creature
through Christ our Lord,

through whom you give us everything that is
good.

Eucharistic Prayer for Reconciliation II*

Priest:

The Lord be with you.

People:

And also with you.

Priest:

Lift up your hearts.

People:

We lift them up to the Lord.

Priest:

Let us give thanks to the Lord our God.

People:

It is right to give him thanks and praise.

Priest:

Father, all-powerful and ever-lasting God,

we praise and thank you through Jesus Christ our
Lord

for your presence and action in the world.

In the midst of conflict and division,

---

* In addition to the four Eucharistic Prayers in the missal,
there are other eucharistic prayers in the Sacramentary. (The
Sacramentary is the book that the priest uses at the altar and at
the presider's chair.) This Eucharistic Prayer is especially suitable as a source of private meditation and prayer.

we know it is you
who turn our minds to thoughts of peace.
Your Spirit changes our hearts:
Enemies begin to speak to one another,
those who were estranged join hands in
        friendship,
and nations seek the way of peace together.
Your Spirit is at work
when understanding puts an end to strife,
when hatred is quenched by mercy,
and vengeance gives way to forgiveness.
For this we should never cease to thank and praise
        you.
We join with all the choirs of heaven
as they sing for ever to your glory:
        All sing the Sanctus:
Holy, holy, holy Lord, God of power and might.
Heaven and earth are full of your glory.
Hosanna in the highest.
Blessed is he who comes in the name of the Lord.
Hosanna in the highest.
        Priest:
God of power and might,
we praise you through your Son, Jesus Christ,
who comes in your name.
He is the Word that brings salvation.
He is the hand you stretch out to sinners.
He is the way that leads to your peace.

God our Father,
we had wandered far from you,
but through your Son you have brought us back.
You gave him up to death
so that we might turn again to you

and find our way to one another.

Therefore we celebrate the reconciliation
Christ has gained for us.

We ask you to sanctify these gifts
by the power of your Spirit,
as we now fulfill your Son's command.

While he was at supper
on the night before he died for us,
he took bread in his hands,
and gave you thanks and praise.
He broke the bread,
gave it to his disciples, and said:

"Take this, all of you, and eat it:
This is my body which will be given up for you."

At the end of the meal he took the cup.
Again he praised you for your goodness,
gave the cup to his disciples, and said:
"Take this, all of you, and drink from it:
This is the cup of my blood,
the blood of the new and everlasting covenant.
It will be shed for you and for all
so that sins may be forgiven.
Do this in memory of me."

Let us proclaim the mystery of faith:
> *People:*
> * Christ has died,
>   Christ is risen,
>   Christ will come again.

- Dying you destroyed our death,
    rising you restored our life.
    Lord Jesus, come in glory.
- When we eat this bread and drink this
    cup,
      we proclaim your death, Lord Jesus,
      until you come in glory.
- Lord, by your cross and resurrection,
      you have set us free. You are the Savior
      of the world.

Priest:

Lord our God,
your Son has entrusted to us
this pledge of his love.
We celebrate the memory of his death and
    resurrection
and bring you the gift you have given us,
the sacrifice of reconciliation.
Therefore we ask you, Father,
to accept us, together with your Son.

Fill us with his Spirit
through our sharing in this meal.
May he take away all that divides us.
May this Spirit keep us always in communion
with (Name), our pope, (Name) our bishop,
with all the bishops and all your people.
Father, make your Church throughout the world
a sign of unity and an instrument of your peace.

You have gathered us here
around the table of your Son,
in fellowship with the Virgin Mary, Mother of
    God, and all the saints.

In that new world where the fullness of your peace
      will be revealed,
gather people of every race, language, and way of
      life
to share in the one eternal banquet
with Jesus Christ the Lord.
Through him,
with him,
in him,
in the unity of the Holy Spirit,
all glory and honor is yours,
almighty Father,
for ever and ever.
     All:
Amen.

The Communion Rite

During the Breaking of the Bread, the *Agnus
Dei* is said or sung:

Lamb of God, you take away the sins of the world:
   Have mercy on us.
Lamb of God, you take away the sins of the world:
   Have mercy on us.
Lamb of God, you take away the sins of the world:
   Grant us peace.

It was in the breaking of the bread that the
disciples at Emmaus recognized Jesus. The first
Christians gave this name to the Eucharist (Mass).

By sharing of the one Bread and the one Cup we are made one body in Christ who gives us life.

As the Council of Trent teaches, when we receive either under the species of bread or of wine, we receive Christ sacramentally whole and entire. Nevertheless, as the missal says, "The sign of Communion is more complete when given under both kinds, since the sign of the eucharistic meal appears more clearly. The intention of Christ that the new and eternal covenant be ratified in his blood is better expressed, as is the relation of the eucharistic banquet to the heavenly banquet."

Suggestions for Enriching Our Sharing in the Mass

Father Eugene Walsh, a pioneer liturgist whose life work helped the Church to prepare for the liturgical changes of the Second Vatican Council, wrote a book to help Catholics to "get more out of the Mass." *The Ministry of the Celebrating Community* is short and easy to read. It is listed on page 381 in SUGGESTED BOOKS FOR FURTHER READING.

Father Walsh says that the purpose of gathering people for the celebration of the Eucharist is "to give everyone the possibility of an experience of God." He says that two things are always at work in our relationship with God:

- God is always reaching out to us in love.
- Each of us is striving for fulfillment. We often don't realize it, but the striving is real.

We will find this fulfillment not by ourselves, but as members of a community of believers, our sisters and brothers.

Father Walsh says that the most important thing we must do is to "pay attention."

- We must pay attention to one another. Pope John XXIII expressed this idea beautifully. He said that the Mass is not a cafeteria at which each of us takes our food and eats separately. It is a banquet which we share together.

- We must pay attention to those who are leading the worship: the priest, of course, but also the readers and song leaders. We must really pay attention to the readings and the other prayers of the Mass. Even though your parish furnishes participation aids such as missalettes, it is most helpful to have a missal of your own to read at home before you come to Mass.

- We must pay attention to what is going on inside ourselves. What is God trying to tell me in this Mass? How does it relate to my daily life? How am I being strengthened, encouraged and challenged? Can I surrender my anxieties to God? How does my opened mouth or extended hand at Communion symbolize my deep need for God?

PENANCE (RECONCILIATION)

Vatican Council II says: "Those who approach the sacrament of Penance obtain pardon from God's mercy for the offense committed against him and are, at the same time, reconciled with the Church which they wounded by their sins and which by charity, by example and by prayer works for their conversion."

The Gospel of John tells us that on the night of Christ's resurrection, the disciples were gathered in fear behind locked doors. Jesus came and stood among them and said: "'Peace be with you.' After he said this, he showed them his hands and his side. Then the disciples rejoiced when they saw the Lord. Jesus said to them again, 'Peace be with you. As the Father has sent me, so I send you.' When he had said this, he breathed on them and said to them, 'Receive the Holy Spirit. If you forgive the sins of any, they are forgiven; if you retain the sins of any, they are retained.' "

The first thing we should remember about the Sacrament of Penance is that it is a gift of God. Jesus gave it to the Church as a fruit of his own death and resurrection. It would be ungrateful of us to fail to make use of it.

All the sacraments are social in nature. Even when the Sacrament of Penance is celebrated privately, it affects the whole Church, because as Pope Paul VI said, "Human beings are joined together by supernatural necessity, so that the sin of one injures others, and the holiness of one benefits others."

Communal Celebrations of Penance

To emphasize the social aspect of the sacrament, the new rite of penance provides for communal penance services. In most parishes these celebrations take place several times a year, particularly in preparation for great feasts. The people listen together to the word of God, which proclaims God's mercy and invites them to conversion. They compare their own lives with God's word and help one another by mutual prayer. They may offer each other a sign of peace as a sign of reconciliation.

Normally, they then confess their sins privately and are absolved individually by the priest. If a large number of penitents are expected, a number of priests may be available for private confession and absolution.

After all have confessed and been absolved, all together may join in praising God for his gift of reconciliation.

Church law requires that all Catholics who are conscious of having committed grave sin must be reconciled in the Sacrament of Penance before they receive Holy Communion. They must receive the Sacrament of Penance at least once a year.

Regular reception of the sacrament is also recommended to those who are not guilty of serious sin. In this way we become more deeply conformed to Christ and submissive to the voice of the Holy Spirit.

There are good psychological reasons for regular confession. We all have deep need for confiding our weaknesses to another human being. Many bartenders are secular confessors to a multitude who might be better served in the Sacrament of Penance.

It is also good for our humanity to admit regularly to another human being that we are not as sure of ourselves as we would like the world to believe. And it is especially good for us to be assured that we are forgiven and that God loves us and does not give up on us.

Private Celebration of Penance

Before entering the confessional, the penitent makes an examination of conscience. See the Appendix to the Rite of Penance published by authority of the Bishops' Committee on the Liturgy, National Conference of Catholic Bishops, in SUGGESTED BOOKS FOR FURTHER READING, page 390. See also WALKING WITH THE LORD, "GUIDELINES FOR CHRISTIAN LIVING," page 3.

The following form is recommended, but it may be shortened for pastoral reasons:

The priest greets the penitent with words of welcome.

The penitent responds and makes the Sign of the Cross.

The priest may read a short selection from the Bible.

The penitent tells the priest how long it has been since the last confession. If the penitent has committed any grave sins since the last confession, they must be confessed. It is helpful to mention one's most troublesome venial sins, but it is not necessary to give a detailed list of them.

The priest will give any necessary advice and assign a penance.

The penitent expresses sorrow. This need not be a long prayer. A prayer based on Scripture is preferred — for example, "Lord Jesus Christ, Son of God, have mercy on me, a sinner." (For other prayers of contrition, see page 24).

The priest then places his hands on the penitent's head (or extends his hand toward the penitent) and prays the words of absolution:

God, the Father of mercy, through the death and resurrection of his Son, has reconciled the world to himself and sent the Holy Spirit among us for the forgiveness of sins; through the ministry of the Church may God give you pardon and peace, and I absolve you from your sins in the name of the Father, and of the Son, and of the Holy Spirit."

The penitent answers:

Amen.

The priest then says:

Give thanks to the Lord, for he is good.

The penitent answers:

His mercy endures for ever.

The priest then dismisses the penitent, who should perform the penance as soon as possible.

Thanksgiving for God's Forgiveness (Optional)

Psalm 103

Bless the Lord, my soul;
  all my being, bless his holy name!
Bless the Lord, my soul;
  do not forget all the gifts of God,
Who pardons all your sins,
  heals all your ills,
Delivers your life from the pit,
  surrounds you with love and compassion,
Fills your days with good things;
  your youth is renewed like the eagle's.*

The Lord does righteous deeds,
  brings justice to all the oppressed.
His ways were revealed to Moses,
  mighty deeds to the people of Israel.
Merciful and gracious is the Lord,
  slow to anger, abounding in kindness.
God does not always rebuke,
  nurses no lasting anger,
Has not dealt with us as our sins merit,
  nor requited us as our deeds deserve.

As the heavens tower over the earth,
  so God's love towers over the faithful.
As far as the east is from the west,

---

  * "Your youth is renewed like the eagle's": Because of the eagle's long life, it was a symbol of perennial youth and vigor. See Isaiah 40:31.

so far have our sins been removed from us.
As a father has compassion on his children,
    so the Lord has compassion on the faithful.
For he knows how we are formed,
    remembers that we are dust.
Our days are like the grass;
    like flowers of the field we blossom.
The wind sweeps over us and we are gone;
    our place knows us no more.
But the Lord's kindness is forever,
    toward the faithful from age to age.
He favors the children's children
    of those who keep his covenant,
    who take care to fulfill its precepts.

The Lord's throne is established in heaven;
    God's royal power rules over all.
Bless the Lord, all you angels,
    mighty in strength and attentive,
    obedient to every command.
Bless the Lord, all you hosts,
    ministers who do God's will.
Bless the Lord, all creatures,
    everywhere in God's domain.
Bless the Lord, my soul.

ANOINTING OF THE SICK

The Second Vatican Council said: "By the sacred anointing of the sick and the prayer of the priests, the whole Church commends those who are ill to the suffering and glorified Lord that he may raise them up and save them. And indeed the Church exhorts them to contribute to the people of God by freely uniting themselves to the passion and death of Christ." It then cites Colossians 1:24, "I am now rejoicing in my suffering for your sake, and in my flesh I am completing what is lacking in Christ's afflictions for the sake of his body, that is, the Church." The council also stated that the sacrament of the sick is more fittingly called the Anointing of the Sick rather than Extreme Unction, because "it is not a sacrament for those only who are at the point of death."

The current liturgical directives say: "The Letter of James states that the sick are to be anointed in order to raise them up and save them (James 5:14-15). Great care and concern should be taken to see that those of the faithful whose health is seriously impaired by sickness or old age should receive this sacrament."

If there is any doubt about the seriousness of an illness, the priest should be consulted.

Elderly people may be anointed if they have become notably weakened, even if no serious illness is present.

The new liturgy of the sick also provides for an anointing of seriously ill individuals or groups at Mass. These Masses may be celebrated either in a private home or hospital or in a church.

Since all the sacraments are communal by nature, at least family members should be present and take part in the prayers of the anointing and of holy Communion if it is administered.

Ordinarily, the Anointing of the Sick is preceded by a friendly greeting, a sprinkling with holy water, and a brief instruction on the meaning of the rite. If the patient wishes to receive the Sacrament of Penance, other people should leave the room. Otherwise all present join in the penitential rite, followed by a reading from the word of God.

The priest may lead all present in a litany for the sick person. Then he says a prayer of thanksgiving over oil which has been previously blessed or he may bless the oil himself.

Prayer over Blessed Oil

Praise to you, God, the almighty Father.
You sent your Son to live among us
and bring us salvation.

R/ Blessed be God who heals us in Christ.

Praise to you, God, the only-begotten Son.
You humbled yourself to share in our humanity
and you heal our infirmities.

R/ Blessed be God who heals us in Christ.

Praise to you, God, the Holy Spirit, the Consoler.
Your unfailing power gives us strength
in our bodily weakness.

R/ Blessed be God who heals us in Christ.

God of mercy,
ease the sufferings and comfort the weakness of
    your servant (Name),
whom the Church anoints with this holy oil.

We ask this through Christ our Lord.

R/ Amen.

Laying on of Hands

The priest lays his hands on the sick person in
silence.

Anointing

The priest anoints the sick person with the blessed
oil.

He anoints the forehead, saying:

Through this holy anointing
may the Lord in his love and mercy help you
with the grace of the Holy Spirit.

R/ Amen.

Then he anoints the hands, saying:

May the Lord who frees you from sin
save you and raise you up.

R/ Amen.

This is followed by an appropriate prayer and holy
Communion, if the sick person is able to receive.

Holy Orders

The Second Vatican Council stated:

Christ the Lord, high priest taken from among men (cf. Heb. 5:1-5), made the new people "a kingdom of priests to God his Father" (Rev. 1:6; cf. 5:9-10). The baptized, by regeneration and anointing of the Holy Spirit, are consecrated to be a spiritual house and a holy priesthood, that through all the works of Christian men (and women) they may offer spiritual sacrifices and proclaim the perfection of him who has called them out of darkness into his marvelous light (cf. 1 Pet. 2:4-10). Therefore all the disciples of Christ, persevering in prayer, should present themselves as a sacrifice, living, holy and pleasing to God (cf. Rom. 12:1).

Though they differ essentially and not only in degree, the common priesthood of the faithful and the ministerial or hierarchical priesthood are nonetheless ordered to one another; each in its proper way shares in the one priesthood of Christ (*Lumen Gentium,* 10).

Ordination of a Deacon

The council restored the ancient practice of ordaining permanent deacons to assist the bishop and the priest in preaching the word, baptizing, witnessing marriages, and ministering to the sick and the needy. Married as well as single men may be ordained permanent deacons. Transitional deacons — that is, those who are candidates for the priesthood — must make a public commitment to celibacy. Otherwise, the ordination ceremony for permanent and transitional deacons is the same

∽∾∾∿∽

The ordination of a deacon takes place at a Mass on a Sunday or holy day when a large number of the faithful can attend. The deacon is ordained after the Gospel.

After the presentation of the candidate and the consent of the congregation, the bishop gives the homily, in which he explains the dignity and the duties of the deacon's calling to the congregation and the candidate.

Then he examines him on his understanding and willingness to fulfill his vocation.

The deacon then promises obedience and reverence to the bishop and his successors.

After the singing of the Litany of the Saints, during which the candidate prostrates himself before the altar, the bishop lays his hands on the candidate, who kneels in front of him.

Then the bishop sings or says the prayer of consecration:

Almighty God,
be present with us by your power.
You are the source of all honor,
you assign to each his rank,
you give to each his ministry.
You remain unchanged
but you watch over all creation and make it new
through your Son, Jesus Christ, our Lord:
he is your Word, your power, and your wisdom.
You foresee all things in your eternal providence
and make due provision for every age.
You make the Church, Christ's Body,

grow to its full stature as a new and greater
    temple.
You enrich it with every kind of grace
and perfect it with a diversity of members
to serve the whole body in a wonderful pattern of
    unity.

You established a threefold ministry of worship
    and service
for the glory of your name.
As ministers of your tabernacle you chose the sons
    of Levi
and gave them your blessing as their everlasting
    inheritance.
In the first days of your Church
under the inspiration of the Holy Spirit
the apostles of your Son appointed seven men of
    good repute
to assist them in the daily ministry,
so that they themselves might be more free for
    prayer and preaching.
By prayer and the laying on of hands
the apostles entrusted to those chosen men the
    ministry of serving at tables.

Ordination of a Priest

The ordained minister whom the average
person meets most often is the priest. The priest is
ordinarily the pastor or vicar of the parish where
Catholics participate in the Sunday Mass and the
other sacraments.

The ordination of a priest should take place at a Mass at which a large number of the faithful can attend.

The ordination takes place after the Gospel of the Mass. After the people have indicated their acceptance of the candidate, the bishop addresses the people and the candidate:

This man, your relative and friend, is now to be raised to the order of priests. Consider carefully the position to which he is to be promoted in the Church.

It is true that God has made his entire people a royal priesthood in Christ. But our High Priest, Jesus Christ, also chose some of his followers to carry out publicly in the Church a priestly ministry in his name on behalf of mankind. He was sent by the Father, and he in turn sent the apostles into the world; through them and their successors, the bishops, he continues his work as Teacher, Priest, and Shepherd. Priests are co-workers of the order of bishops. They are joined to the bishops in the priestly office and are called to serve God's people.

Our brother has seriously considered this step and is now to be ordained to the priesthood in the presbyteral order. He is to serve Christ the Teacher, Priest and Shepherd in his ministry which is to make his own body, the Church, grow into the people of God, a holy temple.

He is called to share in the priesthood of the bishops and to be molded into the likeness of Christ, the supreme and eternal Priest. By consecration he will be made a true priest of the New Testament, to preach the Gospel, sustain God's people, and celebrate the liturgy, above all, the Lord's sacrifice.

The bishop then addresses the candidate:

My son, you are now to be advanced to the order of the presbyterate. You must apply your energies to the duty of teaching in the name of Christ, the chief Teacher. Share with all mankind the word of God you have received with joy. Meditate on the law of God, believe what you read, teach what you believe, and put into practice what you teach.

Let the doctrine you teach be true nourishment for the people of God. Let the example of your life attract the followers of Christ, so that by word and action you may build up the house which is God's Church.

In the same way you must carry out your mission of sanctifying in the power of Christ. Your ministry will perfect the spiritual sacrifice of the faithful by uniting it to Christ's sacrifice, which is offered sacramentally through your hands. Know what you are doing and imitate the mystery you celebrate. In the memorial of the Lord's death and resurrection, make every effort to die to sin and to walk in the new life of Christ.

When you baptize, you will bring men and women into the people of God. In the Sacrament of Penance, you will forgive sins in the name of Christ and the Church. With holy oil you will relieve and console the sick. You will celebrate the liturgy and offer thanks and praise to God throughout the day, praying not only for the people of God but for the whole world. Remember that you are chosen from among God's people and appointed to act for them in relation to God. Do your part in the work of Christ the Priest with genuine joy and love, and attend to the concerns of Christ before your own.

Finally, conscious of sharing in the work of Christ, the Head and Shepherd of the Church, and united with the bishop and subject to him, seek to bring the faithful together in a unified family and to lead them effectively, through Christ and the Holy Spirit, to God the Father. Always remember the example of the Good Shepherd who came not to be served but to serve, and to seek out and rescue those who were lost.

The bishop then questions the candidate about his intentions and asks him to promise respect and obedience to him and his successor. Then the Litany of Saints is prayed while the candidate prostrates himself before the altar.

At the conclusion of the litany, the bishop prays:

Hear us, Lord our God,

and pour out upon this servant of yours

the blessing of the Holy Spirit

and the grace of the priesthood.

In your sight we offer this man for ordination:

support him with your unfailing love.

We ask this through Christ our Lord.

Amen.

The candidate goes to the bishop and kneels before him. The bishop lays his hands on the candidate's head, in silence.

Next, all the priests present lay their hands upon the candidate in silence. After the laying on of hands, the priests remain on either side of the bishop until the prayer of consecration is completed.

The bishop then says the prayer of consecration over the candidate:

Come to our help,
Lord, Holy Father, almighty and eternal God;
you are the source of every honor and dignity,
of all progress and stability.
You watch over the growing human family
by your gift of wisdom and pattern of order.
When you had appointed high priests to rule your
     people,
you chose other men next to them in rank and
     dignity
to be with them and to help them in their task;
and so there grew up
the ranks of priests and the offices of Levites,
established by sacred rites.

In the desert
you extended the spirit of Moses to seventy wise
     men
who helped him to rule the great company of his
     people.
You shared among the sons of Aaron
the fullness of their father's power,
to provide worthy priests in sufficient number
for the increasing rites of sacrifice and worship.
With the same loving care
you gave companions to your Son's apostles
to help in teaching the faith:
they preached the Gospel to the whole world.

Lord,
grant to us such fellow workers,
for we are weak and our need is greater.

Almighty Father,
grant to this servant of yours
the dignity of the priesthood.
Renew within him the Spirit of holiness.
As a co-worker with the order of bishops,
may he be faithful to the ministry
that he receives from you, Lord God,
and be to others a model of right conduct.

May he be faithful in working with the order of
      bishops
so that the words of the Gospel may reach the
      ends of the earth
and the family of nations,
made one in Christ,
may become God's one, holy people.

We ask this through our Lord Jesus Christ, your
      Son,
who lives and reigns with you and the Holy Spirit,
one God, for ever and ever.
Amen.

*The newly ordained priest joins the other priests
present in concelebrating the Mass with the bishop.*

~∞∞∞~

Ordination of a Bishop

Together with the pope and under his
authority, bishops have been sent to continue
through the ages the work of Christ, the eternal
High Priest. Christ gave the Apostles and their
successors the power and command to teach all
nations and to make all people holy in the truth.

Priests and deacons cooperate with the bishops and extend their ministry

---

The ordination of a bishop should take place on a Sunday or holy day when a large number of the faithful can attend, unless pastoral reasons suggest another day, such as the feast of an apostle.

The principal consecrator should be assisted by at least two other consecrating bishops, but it is fitting for all the bishops present together with the principal consecrator to ordain the bishop-elect.

The ordination of the bishop takes place after the Gospel.

While all stand, the "Veni Creator Spiritus" or another appropriate hymn is sung.

After the reading of the Apostolic Letter from the Holy See, the people give their consent by saying, "Thanks be to God," or in some other way, according to local custom.

Then the principal consecrator addresses the clergy, people and the bishop-elect. He may use these words:

Consider carefully the position in the Church to which our brother is about to be raised. Our Lord Jesus Christ, who was sent by the Father to redeem the human race, in turn sent twelve apostles into the world. These men were filled with the power of the Holy Spirit to preach the Gospel and gather every race and people into a single flock to be guided and governed in the way of holiness. Because this service was to continue to the end of time, the apostles selected others to help them. By the laying on of hands which confers the sacrament of orders in its fullness, the apostles passed on the gift of the Holy Spirit which they themselves had received from Christ. In that way, by a succession of bishops unbroken from one generation to the next, the powers conferred in the beginning were handed down, and the work of the Savior lives in our time.

In the person of the bishop, with his priests around him, Jesus Christ, the Lord, who became High Priest forever, is present among you. Through the ministry of the bishop, Christ himself continues to proclaim the Gospel and to confer the mysteries of faith on those who believe. Through the fatherly action of the bishop, Christ adds new members to his body. Through the bishop's wisdom and prudence, Christ guides you in your earthly pilgrimage toward eternal happiness.

Gladly and gratefully, therefore, receive our brother whom we are about to accept into the college of bishops by the laying on of hands. Respect him as a minister of Christ and a steward of the mysteries of God. He has been entrusted with the task of witnessing to the truth of the Gospel and fostering a spirit of justice and holiness. Remember the words of Christ spoken to the apostles: "Whoever listens to you listens to me; whoever rejects you rejects me, and those who reject me reject the one who sent me."

The principal consecrator then addresses the bishop-elect:

You, dear brother, have been chosen by the Lord. Remember that you are chosen from among men to act for men and women in relation to God. The title of bishop is one not of honor but of function, and therefore a bishop should strive to serve rather than to rule. Such is the counsel of the Master: The greater should behave as if he were the least, and the leader as if he were the one who serves. Proclaim the message whether it is welcome or unwelcome; correct error with unfailing patience and teaching. Pray and offer sacrifice for the people committed to your care and so draw every kind of grace for them from the overflowing holiness of Christ.

As a steward of the mysteries of Christ in the Church entrusted to you, be a faithful overseer and guardian. Since you are chosen by the Father to rule over his family, always be mindful of the Good Shepherd, who knows his sheep and is known by them and who did not hesitate to lay down his life for them.

As a father and brother, love all those whom God places in your care. Love the priests and deacons who share with you the ministry of Christ. Love the poor and infirm, strangers and the homeless. Encourage the faithful to work with you in your apostolic task; listen willingly to what they have to say. Never relax your concern for those who do not yet belong to the one fold of Christ; they are commended to you in the Lord. Never forget that in the Catholic Church, made one by the bond of Christian love, you are incorporated into the college of bishops. You should, therefore, have a constant concern for all the churches and gladly come to the aid and support of churches in need. Attend to the whole flock in which the Holy Spirit appoints you an overseer of the Church of God — in the name of the Father, whose image you personify in the Church — and in the name of his Son, Jesus Christ, whose role of Teacher, Priest and Shepherd you undertake — and in the name of the Holy Spirit who gives life to the Church of Christ and supports our weakness with his strength.

The principal consecrator then questions the bishop-elect on his resolve to uphold the faith and to discharge his duties faithfully.

Then he invites the people to pray, all kneeling, except during the Easter season.

The bishop-elect prostrates himself while the Litany of the Saints is prayed.

The principal consecrator then lays his hands on the head of the bishop-elect, in silence. After him, all the bishops present do the same.

Then the principal consecrator places the open Book of the Gospels on the head of the bishop-elect; two deacons, standing at either side of the bishop-elect, hold the Book of the Gospels above his head until the prayer of consecration is completed.

Next, the principal consecrator, with his hands extended over the bishop-elect, sings or says the prayer of consecration:

God the Father of our Lord Jesus Christ,
Father of mercies and God of all consolation,
you dwell in heaven,
you look with compassion on all that is humble.
You know all things before they come to be;
by your gracious word
you have established the plan of your Church.

From the beginning
you chose the descendants of Abraham to be your
holy nation.

You established rulers and priests,
and did not leave your sanctuary without
　　　ministers to serve you.
From the creation of the world
you have been pleased to be glorified
by those whom you have chosen.
　　　The following part of the prayer is recited by all the
consecrating bishops with hands joined:
So now pour out upon this chosen one
that power which is from you,
the governing Spirit
whom you gave to your beloved Son, Jesus Christ,
the Spirit given by him to the holy apostles,
who founded the Church in every place to be your
　　　temple
for the unceasing glory and praise of your name.
　　　Then the principal consecrator continues alone:
Father, you know all hearts.
You have chosen your servant for the office of
　　　bishop.
May he be a shepherd to your holy flock,
and a high priest blameless in your sight,
ministering to you night and day;
may he always gain the blessing of your favor
and offer the gifts of your holy Church.
Through the Spirit who gives the grace of high
　　　priesthood
grant him the power to forgive sins as you have
　　　commanded,
to assign ministries as you have decreed,
and to loose every bond by the authority which
you gave to your apostles.

May he be pleasing to you by his gentleness and
        purity of heart,
presenting a fragrant offering to you,
through Jesus Christ, your Son,
through whom glory and power and honor are
        yours
with the Holy Spirit
in your holy Church,
now and for ever.
Amen.

*After the prayer of consecration, the Book of Gospels
is removed from the head of the new bishop.*

*The principal consecrator anoints the head of the
new bishop with Chrism, saying:*

God has brought you to share the high priesthood
        of Christ,
May he pour out on you the oil of mystical
        anointing
and enrich you with spiritual blessings.

*After washing his hands, the principal consecrator
hands the Book of the Gospels to the newly ordained
bishop, saying:*

Receive the Gospel and preach the word of
God with unfailing patience and sound teaching.

*Then he places the ring on the ring finger of the new
bishop's right hand, saying:*

Take this ring, the seal of your fidelity.
With faith and love protect the bride of God, his
        holy Church.

*He places the miter on the new bishop's head in
silence.*

*Lastly, he gives the pastoral staff to the new bishop,
and says:*

Take this staff as a sign of your pastoral office:

keep watch over the whole flock
in which the Holy Spirit has appointed you
to shepherd the Church of God.

After the new bishop receives the kiss of peace from all the bishops present, the Mass continues as usual.

MATRIMONY

The Second Vatican Council said: "In virtue of the sacrament of matrimony by which they signify and share the mystery of the unity and faithful love between Christ and the Church, Christian married couples help one another to attain holiness in their married life and in the rearing of their children."

The council also said: "Married love is an eminently human love because it is an affection between two persons rooted in the will and it embraces the good of the whole person; it can enrich the sentiments of the spirit and their physical expression with a unique dignity and ennoble them as the special elements and signs of the friendship proper to marriage. The Lord, wishing to bestow special gifts of grace and divine love on it, has restored, perfected, and elevated it. A love like that, bringing together the human and divine, leads the partners to free and mutual giving of self, experienced in tenderness and action, and permeates their whole lives; besides, this love is actually developed and increased by the exercise of it."

Because of the importance of marriage and the many challenges that married couples face in the modern world, the Church requires that couples who are planning to marry be properly prepared.

Every Catholic should make himself or herself aware of diocesan regulations for marriage preparation, which may in a given diocese take up to six months, or even longer.

Couples will also be invited to plan the actual wedding ceremony.

Among the books available for this purpose, one that many people have found helpful is *Together for Life*, by Joseph M. Champlin, a priest of the Diocese of Syracuse, New York. It is available in two paperback editions: for marriages within Mass or outside of Mass. It is listed in SUGGESTED BOOKS FOR FURTHER READING, page 385.

There are many choices available for prayers and Scripture readings. In my experience, some people have difficulty choosing a reading from the Old Testament unless they have some understanding of the biblical mind. Many young people are influenced by a "creeping fundamentalism." Also some translations do not take into consideration the changing meaning of the English word "man." One reading, for example, Genesis 1:26-28, 31a, gives a different impression when translated, "Let us make man in our image" (traditional) or "Let us make humankind in our image" NRSV ("human beings" REB and GNB).

In my view, no one has translated the wisdom books of the Bible as well as Monsignor Ronald Knox. Here is his translation of the Song of Songs 2:8-10, 14, 16a; 8:6-7a, one of the Old Testament readings suggested for weddings:

A Reading from the Song of Songs

The voice I love!
See how he comes,
how he speeds over the mountains,
how he spurns the hills!
Gazelle nor fawn was ever so fleet of foot
as my heart's love.

And now he is standing
on the other side of this very wall;
now he is looking in
through each window in turn,
peering through every chink.

I can hear my true love
calling to me:
Rise up,
rise up quickly, dear heart,
so gentle, so beautiful,
rise up and come with me.

Rouse thee and come,
so beautiful,
so well beloved,
still hiding thyself
as a dove hides in cleft rock
or crannied wall.
Shew me but thy face,
let me but hear thy voice,
that voice sweet as thy face is fair.

All mine, my true love,
and I all his.
He said to me:

Hold me close to thy heart,
close as locket
or bracelet fits;
not death itself
is so strong as love.
The torch that lights it
is a blaze of fire

Yes, love is a fire
no waters avail to quench,
no floods to drown.

     Although there are many excellent readings from the New Testament on marriage and Christian love, many couples choose 1 Corinthians 12:31-13:8a.

     There is no clear favorite Gospel passage, but many couples choose Matthew 19:3-6, which asserts the indissolubility of marriage.

     The favorite nuptial blessing, in my experience, is the first, which says, in paragraphs 4 through 6:

Look with love upon this woman, your daughter,
now joined to her husband in marriage.
She asks your blessing.
Give her the grace of love and peace.

May she always follow the example of the holy
     women
whose praises are sung in the Scriptures.

May her husband put his trust in her
and recognize that she is his equal

and the heir with him to the life of grace.
May he always honor her and love her
as Christ loves his bride, the Church.

~⚬⚬⚬~

THE DEATH OF A CHRISTIAN

Commendation of the Dying

Even if a Christian has received the Anointing of the Sick, the Church's ordained minister should still be called when the time of death approaches.

The Church's ritual for the sick and dying says: "The presence of a priest or deacon shows more clearly that the Christian dies in the communion of the Church. He should assist the dying person and those present in the recitation of the prayers of commendation and, following death, he should lead those present in the prayer after death."

If a priest or deacon is unable to be present, a lay person may lead the prayers. It is fitting that some passages from Scripture be read. The following Psalms may be found in the Psalter section of this book: 23, 25, 91, 121.

Favorite prayers from TALKING WITH THE LORD also may be read, including the litanies.

When the moment of death seems near, some of the following prayers may be said:

Go forth, Christian soul, from this world
in the name of God the almighty Father,
who created you,
in the name of Jesus Christ, Son of the living God,
who suffered for you,
in the name of the Holy Spirit,

who was poured out upon you,
go forth, faithful Christian.

May you live in peace this day,
may your home be with God in Zion,
with Mary, the virgin Mother of God,
with Joseph, and all the angels and saints.

I commend you, my dear brother/sister,
to almighty God,
and entrust you to your Creator.
May you return to him
who formed you from the dust of the earth.
May holy Mary, the angels, and all the saints
come to meet you as you go forth from this life.
May Christ who was crucified for you
bring you freedom and peace.
May Christ who died for you
admit you into his garden of paradise.
May Christ the true Shepherd,
acknowledge you as one of his flock.
May he forgive all your sins,
and set you among those he has chosen.
May you see your Redeemer face to face,
and enjoy the vision of God for ever.
Amen.

Welcome your servant, Lord, into the place of sal-
    vation which because of your mercy she/he
    rightly hoped for.

Amen. /or/ Lord, save your people.

Deliver your servant, Lord, from every distress.

Amen. /or/ Lord, save your people.

Deliver your servant, Lord, as you delivered Noah
from the flood.

Amen. /or/ Lord, save your people.

Deliver your servant, Lord, as you delivered
Abraham from Ur of the Chaldees.

Amen. /or/ Lord, save your people.

Deliver your servant, Lord, as you delivered Job
from his sufferings.

Amen. /or/ Lord, save your people.

Deliver your servant, Lord, as you delivered
Moses from the hand of the Pharaoh.

Amen. /or/ Lord, save your people.

Deliver your servant, Lord, as you delivered
Daniel from the den of lions.

Amen. /or/ Lord, save your people.

Deliver your servant, Lord, as you delivered the
three young men from the fiery furnace.

Amen. /or/ Lord, save your people.

Deliver your servant, Lord, as you delivered
Susanna from her false accusers.

Amen. /or/ Lord, save your people.

Deliver your servant, Lord, as you delivered David
from the attacks of Saul and Goliath.

Amen. /or/ Lord, save your people.

Deliver your servant, Lord, as you saved Peter and
   Paul from prison.

Amen. /or/ Lord, save your people.

Deliver your servant, Lord, through Jesus our Savior, who suffered death for us and gave us
   eternal life.

Amen. /or/ Lord, save your people.

Lord Jesus Christ, Savior of the world,
we pray for your servant (Name),
and commend him/her to your mercy.
For his/her sake you came down from heaven;
receive him/her now into the joy of your kingdom.

For though he/she has sinned,
he/she has not denied the Father, the Son and the
   Holy Spirit,
but has believed in God
and has worshiped his/her Creator.
Amen.

Hail, holy queen, mother of mercy,
hail, our life, our sweetness, and our hope.
To you we cry, the children of Eve;
to you we send up our sighs,
mourning and weeping in this land of exile.
Turn, then, most gracious advocate,
your eyes of mercy toward us;
lead us home at last
and show us the blessed fruit of your womb, Jesus;
O clement, O loving, O sweet Virgin Mary.

Prayers after Death

When death has occurred, one or more of the following prayers may be said.

∽◦◦◦∽

Saints of God, come to his/her aid!
Come to meet him/her, angels of the Lord.

R/ Receive his/her soul and present him/her to
   God the Most High.

May Christ, who called you, take you to himself;
may angels lead you to Abraham's side.

R/ Receive his/her soul and present him/her to
   God the Most High.

Eternal rest grant to him/her, O Lord,
and let perpetual light shine upon him/her for
   ever.

R/ Receive his/her soul and present him/her to
   God the Most High.

Psalm 130

Out of the depths I call to you, LORD;
   Lord, hear my cry!
May your ears be attentive
   to my cry for mercy.
If you, LORD, mark our sins,
   Lord, who can stand?
But with you is forgiveness
   and so you are revered.

I wait with longing for the LORD,
   my soul waits for his word.

My soul looks for the Lord
　　more than sentinels for daybreak.
More than sentinels for daybreak,
　　let Israel look for the LORD.
For with the LORD is kindness,
　　with him is full redemption.
And God will redeem Israel
　　from all their sins.

Let us pray.

God of love,
welcome into your presence
your son/daughter (Name), whom you have
　　called from this life.
Release him/her from all his/her sins,
bless him/her with eternal light and peace,
raise him/her up to live for ever with all your
　　saints
in the glory of the resurrection.

We ask this through Christ our Lord.

Let us pray.

God of mercy,
hear our prayers and be merciful
to your son/daughter (Name), whom you have
　　called from this life.
Welcome him/her into the company of your
　　saints,
in the kingdom of light and peace.
We ask this through Christ our Lord.
Amen.

Loving and merciful God,

we entrust our brother/sister to your mercy.

You loved him/her greatly in this life;
now that he/she is freed from all its cares,
give him/her happiness and peace for ever.

The old order has passed away;
welcome him/her now into paradise
where there will be no more sorrow,
no more weeping or pain,
but only peace and joy
with Jesus, your Son,
and the Holy Spirit
for ever and ever.
Amen.

Lord Jesus, our Redeemer,
you willingly gave yourself up to death
so that all people might be saved
and pass from death into a new life.
Listen to our prayers,
look with love on your people
who mourn and pray for their brother/sister
        (Name).

Lord Jesus, holy and compassionate,
forgive (Name) his/her sins.
By dying you opened the gates of life
for those who believe in you;
do not let our brother/sister be parted from you,
but by your glorious power
give him/her light, joy, and peace in heaven
where you live for ever and ever.
Amen.

It is fitting to make the sign of the cross on the forehead of the deceased at the conclusion of these prayers.

Prayers for the Dead

If a priest is called to attend a person who has already died, he may not give the Sacrament of Penance or anointing. Since it is not certain exactly when the soul leaves the body, however, the priest may give conditional absolution and anointing to someone who has apparently died.

In any case, the following beautiful prayers may be led by a priest or deacon. In the absence of an ordained minister, a lay person may lead the prayers.

A

In this moment of sorrow,
the Lord is in our midst
and comforts us with these words:
Blessed are the sorrowful; they shall be consoled.

B

Praised be God, the Father of our Lord Jesus
　　　　Christ,
the Father of mercies,
and the God of all consolation!
He comforts us in all our afflictions
and thus enables us to comfort those who are in
　　　　trouble
with the same consolation
we have received from him.

Let us pray.

Almighty and eternal God,
hear our prayers for your son/daughter (Name),
whom you have called from this life to yourself.
Grant him/her light, happiness, and peace.
Let him/her pass in safety through the gates of
    death,
and live for ever with all your saints
in the light you promised to Abraham
and to all his descendants in faith.

Guard him/her from all harm
and on that great day of resurrection and reward
raise him/her up with all your saints.
Pardon his/her sins
and give him/her eternal life in your kingdom.

We ask this through Christ our Lord.
Amen.

Other prayers and readings may be used from the Prayers after Death in the previous section.

The Lord's Prayer

The Lord's Prayer is appropriate to pray after death, and it may be introduced in these or similar words:

A

With God there is mercy and fullness of redemption; let us pray as Jesus taught us:

B

Let us pray for the coming of God's kingdom as Jesus taught us:

Our Father . . .*

Lord Jesus, our Redeemer,
you willingly gave yourself up to death
so that all people might be saved
and pass from death into a new life.
Listen to our prayers,
look with love on your people
who mourn and pray for their brother/sister
      (Name).

Lord Jesus, holy and compassionate,
forgive (Name) his/her sins.
By dying you opened the gates of life
for those who believe in you;
do not let our brother/sister be parted from you,
but by your glorious power
give him/her light, joy, and peace in heaven
where you live for ever and ever.
Amen.
    It is fitting to make the sign of the cross on the fore-
head of the deceased at the conclusion of these prayers.

Suggested Texts for the Mass of Christian Burial

The family or friends of the deceased may wish to choose the Scripture readings for the Mass of Christian Burial.

The pastoral minister making the funeral arrangements may have a book to assist in making

---

* See page 21 for the traditional version of the Lord's Prayer and page 22 for a contemporary version.

choices. Many people find the following readings appropriate.

Old Testament

Isaiah 25:6-9 (God will swallow up death for ever)

Isaiah 61:1-3 (To comfort those who mourn)

Lamentations 3:17-26 (God is good to those who wait)

Wisdom 3:1-5,9 (The souls of the just are in God's hands)

Job 19:22-27a (I know that my Redeemer lives)

2 Maccabees 12:43-46 (It is good to pray for the dead)

New Testament

Romans 5:5-11 (We shall be saved by Christ's death)

Romans 8:14-23 (We groan while we wait for redemption)

1 Corinthians 15:20-23 (All will be brought to life in Christ)

2 Corinthians 4:14-5:1 (Eternal reality unseen)

1 John 3:1-2 (We shall be like God)

Revelation 7:9-17 (God will wipe away every tear)

Revelation 21:2-7 (Behold, I make all things new)

Gospel

Matthew 5:1-12a (Your reward will be great in heaven)

Matthew 11:25-30 (I will give you rest)

Matthew 25:31-46 (Come, you who are blessed by my Father)

Luke 7:11-17 (Young man, I tell you, arise)

Luke 23:33, 39-43 (Today you will be with me in Paradise)

Luke 24:13-35 (It was necessary that the Messiah suffer and so enter into his glory)

John 6:37-40 (I will raise them up)

John 6:51-58 (All who eat this bread will live for ever)

John 11:21-27 (I am the resurrection and the life)

John 11:32-45 (Lazarus, come out!)

Reading the BIBLE

Your word
is a lamp
for my feet,
a light
on my path;

PSALM 119 · 105

READING THE BIBLE

THE CHRISTIAN AND THE SCRIPTURES

Both Jews and Christians consider regular Bible reading important. St. Jerome (345-420), the greatest biblical scholar of the early Church, wrote: "To be ignorant of Scripture is not to know Jesus Christ." Like the other Church Fathers, Jerome saw all of Scripture as preparing for Christ or flowing from his teaching. The Church gradually developed a liturgical year in which readings appropriate to each season are read in a systematic way.

In this section are listed the Bible readings for the three-year cycle for Sunday Mass (see page 317) and the two-year cycle for weekday Mass (see page 334). The purpose of these readings is to give you a good cross section of the Bible. You will find it helpful to read the Scripture of the day before attending Mass. If you cannot attend daily Mass, the readings will help you pray with the Church.

You will find another list of readings for Morning and Evening Prayer (see page 355). These additional readings will help you become familiar with the rest of the Bible.

In private prayer, you can, of course, adapt the schedule of readings to your daily schedule. Whatever plan you use, you will find your prayer life deeply enriched by regular Bible reading.

It is important that those unfamiliar with the Scriptures have a study Bible that gives them an adequate background for their reading. Until comparatively recently, we knew little about the world in which our spiritual forebears lived. Practically nothing was known of the world of the ancient Hebrews except what the Bible itself told us.

The Bible is not a book. It is a library containing many different kinds of literature. Formerly, the reader of the Bible was like a person who enters a library in which the various kinds of literature were not labeled. The Bible is composed of history (of a special kind, different from our modern concept of history), edifying fiction, poetry and apocalypse, to name only some of the literary types.

Within the last century, the literature of the Hebrews' neighbors has been deciphered and analyzed. Scholars can now compare the Bible with the religious writings of the Hebrews' neighbors to recognize the similarities and the differences. The fascinating results are now available to the average reader.

See SUGGESTED BOOKS FOR FURTHER READING for recommended Bibles and commentaries. As a basic book for Catholics, *The Catholic Study Bible* is highly recommended. Do not be put off by the abundance of resources available. Start reading one good study Bible, and you will soon be encouraged by your increased understanding of what God is saying to you. "Your word is a lamp for my feet, a light for my path," Psalm 119.

Three-Year Cycle of Readings for Sunday Mass

Guide: The figure 1. refers to Reading I. The figure 2. refers to Reading II. The figure 3. refers to the Gospel.

Year A: 1993, 1996, 1999, 2002, 2005, 2008, 2011, 2014

Year B: 1994, 1997, 2000, 2003, 2006, 2009, 2012, 2015

Year C: 1995, 1998, 2001, 2004, 2007, 2010, 2013, 2016

Year A

Advent Season

1st Sunday of Advent
1. Isaiah 2:1-5
2. Romans 13:11-14
3. Matthew 24:37-44

2nd Sunday of Advent
1. Isaiah 11:1-10
2. Romans 15:4-9
3. Matthew 3:1-12

3rd Sunday of Advent
1. Isaiah 35:1-6a, 10
2. James 5:7-10
3. Matthew 11:2-11

4th Sunday of Advent
1. Isaiah 7:1-14.
2. Romans 1:1-7
3. Matthew 1:18-24

Christmas Season

Christmas Vigil
1. Isaiah 62:1-5
2. Acts 13:16-17, 22-25
3. Matthew 1:1-25

Christmas (at Midnight)
1. Isaiah 9:1-6
2. Titus 2:11-14
3. Luke 2:1-14

Christmas (at Dawn)
1. Isaiah 62:11-12
2. Titus 3:4-7
3. Luke 2:15-20

Christmas Day
1. Isaiah 52:7-10
2. Hebrews 1:1-6
3. John 1:1-18

Sunday after Christmas (Holy Family)
1. Sirach 3:2-6.12-14
2. Colossians 3:12-21
3. Matthew 2:13-15, 19-23

January 1 (Solemnity of Mary, Mother of God)
1. Numbers 6:22-27
2. Galatians 4:4-7
3. Luke 2:16-21

2nd Sunday after Christmas
1. Sirach 24:1-2, 8-12
2. Ephesians 1:3-6, 15-18
3. John 1:1-18

Epiphany
1. Isaiah 60:1-6
2. Ephesians 3:2-3a, 5-6
3. Matthew 2:1-12

Sunday after Epiphany (Baptism of the Lord)
1. Isaiah 42:1-4, 6-7
2. Acts 10:34-38
3. Matthew 3:13-17

Lenten Season

Ash Wednesday
1. Joel 2:12-18
2. 2 Corinthians 5:20–6:2
3. Matthew 6:1-6, 16-18

1st Sunday of Lent
1. Genesis 2:7-9; 3:1-7
2. Romans 5:12-19
3. Matthew 4:1-11

2nd Sunday of Lent
1. Genesis 12:1-4a
2. 2 Timothy 1:8b-10
3. Matthew 4:1-11

3rd Sunday of Lent
1. Exodus 17:3-7
2. Romans 5:1-2, 5-8
3. John 4:5-42

4th Sunday of Lent
1. 1 Samuel 16:1b, 6-7, 10-13b
2. Ephesians 5:8-14
3. John 9:1-41

5th Sunday of Lent
1. Ezekiel 37:12-14
2. Romans 8:8-11
3. John 11:1-45

Passion Sunday (Palm Sunday)
Procession: Matthew 21:1-11
1. Isaiah 50:4-7
2. Philippians 2:6-11
3. Matthew 26:14-27, 66

Easter Triduum and Easter Season

Mass of Lord's Supper
1. Exodus 12:1-8, 11-14
2. 1 Corinthians 11:23-26
3. John 13:1-15

Good Friday
1. Isaiah 52:13–53:12
2. Hebrews 4:14-16; 5:7-9
3. John 18:1-19:42

Easter Vigil
1. Genesis 1:1–2:2
   Genesis 22:1-18
   Exodus 14:15–15:1
   Isaiah 54:5-14
   Isaiah 55:1-11
   Baruch 3:9-15, 33–4:4
   Ezekiel 36:16-28
2. Romans 6:3-11
3. Matthew 28:1-10

Easter Sunday
1. Acts 10:34a, 37-43
2. Colossians 3:1-4
   or 1 Corinthians 5:6b-8
3. John 20:1-9
   or Matthew 28:1-10
   Evening: 3. Luke 24:13-35

2nd Sunday of Easter
1. Acts 2:42-47
2. 1 Peter 1:3-9
3. John 20:19-31

3rd Sunday of Easter
1. Acts 2:14, 22-28
2. 1 Peter 1:17-21
3. Luke 24:13-35

4th Sunday of Easter
1. Acts 2:14a, 36-41
2. 1 Peter 2:20b-25
3. John 10:1-10

5th Sunday of Easter
1. Acts 6:1-7
2. 1 Peter 2:4-9
3. John 14:1-12

6th Sunday of Easter
1. Acts 8:5-8, 14-17
2. 1 Peter 3:15-18
3. John 14:15-21

Ascension of Our Lord
1. Acts 1:1-11
2. Ephesians 1:17-23
3. Matthew 28:16-20

7th Sunday of Easter
1. Acts 1:12-14
2. 1 Peter 4:13-16
3. John 17:1-11a

Pentecost Vigil
1. Genesis 11:1-9
   or Exodus 19:3-8a, 16-20b
   or Ezekiel 37:1-14
   or Joel 3:1-5
2. Romans 8:22-27
3. John 7:37-39

Pentecost Mass
1. Acts 2:1-11
2. 1 Corinthians 12:3b-7, 12-13
3. John 20:19-23

Solemnities of the Lord during Ordinary Time

Trinity Sunday (Sunday after Pentecost)
1. Exodus 34:4b-6, 8-9
2. 2 Corinthians 13:11-13
3. John 20:1-9

or Matthew 28:1-10

Evening: 3. Luke 24:13-35

Corpus Christi
1. Deuteronomy 8:2-3, 14b-16a
2. 1 Corinthians 10:16-17
3. John 6:51-58

Sacred Heart of Jesus
1. Deuteronomy 7:6-11
2. 1 John 4:7-16
3. Matthew 11:25-30

Ordinary Time

1st Sunday (See Baptism of the Lord, page 318)

2nd Sunday
1. Isaiah 49:3, 5-6
2. 1 Corinthians 1:1-3
3. John 1:29-34

3rd Sunday
1. Isaiah 8:23b-9:3
2. 1 Corinthians 1:10-13, 17
3. Matthew 4:12-23

4th Sunday
1. Zephaniah 2:3; 3:12-13
2. 1 Corinthians 1:26-31
3. Matthew 5:1-12a

5th Sunday
1. Isaiah 58:7-10
2. 1 Corinthians 2:1-5
3. Matthew 5:13-16

6th Sunday
1. Sirach 15:15-20
2. 1 Corinthians 2:6-10
3. Matthew 5:17-37

7th Sunday
1. Leviticus 19:1-2, 17-18
2. 1 Corinthians 3:16-23
3. Matthew 5:38-48

8th Sunday
1. Isaiah 49:14-15
2. 1 Corinthians 4:1-5
3. Matthew 6:24-34

9th Sunday
1. Deuteronomy 11:18, 26-28
2. Romans 3:21-25a, 28
3. Matthew 7:21-27

10th Sunday
1. Hosea 6:3-6
2. Romans 4:18-25
3. Matthew 9:9-13

11th Sunday
1. Exodus 19:2-6a
2. Romans 5:6-11
3. Matthew 9:36–10:8

12th Sunday
1. Jeremiah 20:10-13
2. Romans 5:12-15
3. Matthew 10:26-33

13th Sunday
1. 2 Kings 4:8-11, 14-16a
2. Romans 6:3-4, 8-11
3. Matthew 10:37-42

14th Sunday
1. Zechariah 9:9-10
2. Romans 8:9, 11-13
3. Matthew 11:25-30

15th Sunday
1. Isaiah 55:10-11
2. Romans 8:18-23
3. Matthew 13:1-23

16th Sunday
1. Wisdom 12:13, 16-19
2. Romans 8:26-27
3. Matthew 13:24-43

17th Sunday
1. 1 Kings 3:5, 7-12
2. Romans 8:28-30
3. Matthew 13:44-52

18th Sunday
1. Isaiah 55:1-3
2. Romans 8:35, 37-39
3. Matthew 14:13-21

19th Sunday
1. 1 Kings 19:9a, 11-13a
2. Romans 9:1-5
3. Matthew 14:22-33

20th Sunday
1. Isaiah 56:1, 6-7
2. Romans 11:13-15, 29-32
3. Matthew 15:21-28

21st Sunday
1. Isaiah 22:19-23
2. Romans 11:33-36
3. Matthew 16:13-20

22nd Sunday
1. Jeremiah 20:7-9
2. Romans 12:1-2
3. Matthew 16:21-27

23rd Sunday
1. Ezekiel 33:7-9
2. Romans 13:8-10
3. Matthew 18:15-20

24th Sunday
1. Sirach 27:30–28:7
2. Romans 14:7-9
3. Matthew 18:21-35

25th Sunday
1. Isaiah 55:6-9
2. Philippians 1:20c-24, 27a
3. Matthew 20:1-16a

26th Sunday
1. Ezekiel 18:25-28
2. Philippians 2:1-11
3. Matthew 21:28-32

27th Sunday
1. Isaiah 5:1-7
2. Philippians 4:6-9
3. Matthew 21:33-43

28th Sunday
1. Isaiah 25:6-10a
2. Philippians 4:12-14, 19-20
3. Matthew 22:1-14

29th Sunday
1. Isaiah 45:1, 4-6
2. 1 Thessalonians 1:1-5b
3. Matthew 22:15-21

30th Sunday
1. Exodus 22:20-26
2. 1 Thessalonians 1:5c-10
3. Matthew 22:34-40

31st Sunday
1. Malachi 1:14b–2:2b, 8-10
2. 1 Thessalonians 2:7b-9, 13
3. Matthew 23:1-12

32nd Sunday
1. Wisdom 6:12-16
2. 1 Thessalonians 4:13-18
3. Matthew 25:1-13

33rd Sunday
1. Proverbs 31:10-13, 19-20, 30-31
2. 1 Thessalonians 5:1-6
3. Matthew 25:14-30

34th Sunday (Christ the King)
1. Ezekiel 34:11-12, 15-17
2. 1 Corinthians 15:20-26, 28
3. Matthew 25:31-46

Year B

Advent Season

1st Sunday of Advent
1. Isaiah 63:16b-17, 19b; 64:2b-7
2. 1 Corinthians 1:3-9
3. Mark 13:33-37

2nd Sunday of Advent
1. Isaiah 40:1-5, 9-11
2. 2 Peter 3:8-14
3. Mark 1:1-8

3rd Sunday of Advent
1. Isaiah 61:1-2a, 10-11
2. 1 Thessalonians 5:16-24
3. John 1:6-8, 19-28

4th Sunday of Advent
1. 2 Samuel 7:1-5, 8b-11, 16
2. Romans 16:25-27
3. Luke 1:26-38

Christmas Season

Christmas Vigil
1. Isaiah 62:1-5
2. Acts 13:16-17, 22-25
3. Matthew 1:1-25

Christmas (at Midnight)
1. Isaiah 9:1-6
2. Titus 2:11-14
3. Luke 2:1-14

Christmas (at Dawn)
1. Isaiah 62:11-12
2. Titus 3:4-7
3. Luke 2:15-20

Christmas Day
1. Isaiah 52:7-10
2. Hebrews 1:1-6
3. John 1:1-18

Sunday after Christmas (Holy Family)
1. Genesis 15:1-6; 21:1-3
2. Hebrews 11:8, 11-12, 17-19
3. Luke 2:22-40

January 1 (Solemnity of Mary, Mother of God)
1. Numbers 6:22-27
2. Galatians 4:4-7
3. Luke 2:16-21

2nd Sunday after Christmas
1. Sirach 24:1-2, 8-12
2. Ephesians 1:3-6, 15-18
3. John 1:1-18

Epiphany
1. Isaiah 60:1-6
2. Ephesians 3:2-3a, 5-6
3. Matthew 2:1-12

Sunday after Epiphany (Baptism of the Lord)
1. Isaiah 42:1-4, 6-7
2. Acts 10:34-38
3. Mark 1:6b-11

Lenten Season

Ash Wednesday
1. Joel 2:12-18
2. 2 Corinthians 5:20—6:2
3. Matthew 1:6b-11

1st Sunday of Lent
1. Genesis 9:8-15
2. 1 Peter 3:18-22
3. Mark 1:12-15

2nd Sunday of Lent
1. Genesis 22:1-2, 9a, 10-13, 15-18
2. Romans 8:31b-34
3. Mark 9:2-10

3rd Sunday of Lent
1. Exodus 20:1-17
2. 1 Corinthians 1:22-25
3. John 2:13-25

4th Sunday of Lent
1. 2 Chronicles 36:14-16, 19-23
2. Ephesians 2:4-10
3. John 3:14-21

5th Sunday of Lent
1. Jeremiah 31:31-34
2. Hebrews 5:7-9
3. John 12:20-33

Passion Sunday (Palm Sunday)
Procession: Mark 11:1-10 or John 12:12-16
1. Isaiah 50:4-7
2. Philippians 2:6-11
3. Mark 14:1—15:47

Easter Triduum and Easter Season

Mass of Lord's Supper
1. Exodus 12:1-8, 11-14
2. 1 Corinthians 11:23-26
3. John 13:1-15

Good Friday
1. Isaiah 52:13–53:12
2. Hebrews 4:14-16; 5:7-9
3. John 18:1–19:42

Easter Vigil
1. Genesis 1:1–2:2
   Genesis 22:1-18
   Exodus 14:15–15:1
   Isaiah 54:5-14
   Isaiah 55:1-11
   Baruch 3:9-15, 33–4:4
   Ezekiel 36:16-28
2. Romans 6:3-11
3. Mark 16:1-8

Easter Sunday
1. Acts 10:34a, 37-43
2. Colossians 3:1-4
   or 1 Corinthians 5:6b-8
3. John 20:1-9
   or Mark 16:1-8

2nd Sunday of Easter
1. Acts 4:32-35
2. 1 John 5:1-6
3. John 20:19-31

3rd Sunday of Easter
1. Acts 3:13-15, 17-19
2. 1 John 2:1-5a
3. Luke 24:35-48

4th Sunday of Easter
1. Acts 4:8-12
2. 1 John 3:1-2
3. John 10:11-18

5th Sunday of Easter
1. Acts 9:26-31
2. 1 John 3:18-24
3. John 15:1-8

6th Sunday of Easter
1. Acts 10:25-26, 34-35, 44-48
2. 1 John 4:7-10
3. John 15:9-17

Ascension of Our Lord
1. Acts 1:1-11
2. Ephesians 1:17-23 or 4:1-13
3. Mark 16:15-20

7th Sunday of Easter
1. Acts 1:15-17, 20a, 20c-26
2. 1 John 4:11-16
3. John 17:11b-19

Pentecost Vigil
1. Genesis 11:1-9
   or Exodus 19:3-8a, 16-20b
   or Ezekiel 37:1-14
   or Joel 3:1-5
2. Romans 8:22-27
   or Galatians 5:16-25
3. John 7:37-39
   or John 15:26-27; 16:12-15

Pentecost Mass
1. Acts 2:1-11
2. 1 Corinthians 12:3b-7, 12-13
3. John 20:19-23

Solemnities of the Lord during Ordinary Time

Trinity Sunday (Sunday after Pentecost)
1. Deuteronomy 4:32-34, 39-40
2. Romans 8:14-17
3. Matthew 28:16-20

Corpus Christi
1. Exodus 24:3-8
2. Hebrews 9:11-15
3. Mark 14:12-16, 22-26

Sacred Heart of Jesus
1. Hosea 11:1, 3-4, 8c-9
2. Ephesians 3:8-12, 14-19
3. John 19:31-37

Ordinary Time

1st Sunday (See Baptism of the Lord, page 323)

2nd Sunday
1. 1 Samuel 3:3b-10, 19
2. 1 Corinthians 6:13c-15a, 17-20
3. John 1:35-42

3rd Sunday
1. Jonah 3:1–5:10
2. 1 Corinthians 7:29-31
3. Mark 1:14-20

4th Sunday
1. Deuteronomy 18:15-20
2. 1 Corinthians 7:32-35
3. Mark 1:21-28

5th Sunday
1. Job 7:1-4, 6-7
2. 1 Corinthians 9:16-19, 22-23
3. Mark 1:29-39

6th Sunday
1. Leviticus 13:1-2, 45-46
2. 1 Corinthians 10:31–11:1
3. Mark 1:40-45

7th Sunday
1. Isaiah 43:18-19, 21-22, 24b-25
2. 2 Corinthians 1:18-22
3. Mark 2:1-12

8th Sunday
1. Hosea 2:16b, 17b, 21-22
2. 2 Corinthians 3:1b-6
3. Mark 2:18-22

9th Sunday
1. Deuteronomy 5:12-15
2. 2 Corinthians 4:6-11
3. Mark 2:23–3:6

10th Sunday
1. Genesis 3:9-15
2. 2 Corinthians 4:13–5:1
3. Mark 3:20-35

11th Sunday
1. Ezekiel 17:22-24
2. 2 Corinthians 5:6-10
3. Mark 4:26-34

12th Sunday
1. Job 38:1, 8-11
2. 2 Corinthians 5:6-10
3. Mark 4:35-41

13th Sunday
1. Wisdom 1:13-15; 2:23-24
2. 2 Corinthians 8:7, 9, 13-15
3. Mark 5:21-43

14th Sunday
1. Ezekiel 2:2-5
2. 2 Corinthians 12:7-10
3. Mark 6:1-6

15th Sunday
1. Amos 7:12-15
2. Ephesians 1:3-14
3. Mark 6:7-13

16th Sunday
1. Jeremiah 23:1-6
2. Ephesians 2:13-18
3. Mark 6:30-34

17th Sunday
1. 2 Kings 4:42-44
2. Ephesians 4:1-6
3. John 6:1-15

18th Sunday
1. Exodus 16:2-4, 12-15
2. Ephesians 4:17, 20-24
3. John 6:24-35

19th Sunday
1. 1 Kings 19:4-8
2. Ephesians 4:30–5:2
3. John 6:41-51

20th Sunday
1. Proverbs 9:1-6
2. Ephesians 5:15-20
3. John 6:51-58

21st Sunday
1. Joshua 24:1-2a, 15-17, 18b
2. Ephesians 5:21-32
3. John 6:60-69

22nd Sunday
1. Deuteronomy 4:1-2, 6-8
2. James 1:17-18, 21b-22, 27
3. Mark 7:1-8, 14-15, 21-23

23rd Sunday
1. Isaiah 35:4-7a
2. James 2:1-5
3. Mark 7:31-37

24th Sunday
1. Isaiah 50:5-9a
2. James 2:14-18
3. Mark 8:27-35

25th Sunday
1. Wisdom 2:12, 17-20
2. James 3:16–4:3
3. Mark 9:30-37

26th Sunday
1. Numbers 11:25-29
2. James 5:1-6
3. Mark 9:38-43, 45, 47-48

27th Sunday
1. Genesis 2:18-24
2. Hebrews 2:9-11
3. Mark 10:2-16

28th Sunday
1. Wisdom 7:7-11
2. Hebrews 4:12-13
3. Mark 10:17-30

29th Sunday
1. Isaiah 53:10-11
2. Hebrews 4:14-16
3. Mark 10:35-45

30th Sunday
1. Jeremiah 31:7-9
2. Hebrews 5:1-6
3. Mark 10:46-53

31st Sunday
1. Deuteronomy 6:2-6
2. Hebrews 7:23-28
3. Mark 12:28b-34

32nd Sunday
1. 1 Kings 17:10-16
2. Hebrews 9:24-28
3. Mark 12:38-44

33rd Sunday
1. Daniel 12:1-3
2. Hebrews 10:11-14, 18
3. Mark 13:24-32

34th Sunday (Christ the King)
1. Daniel 7:13-14
2. Revelation 1:5-8
3. John 18:33b-37

Year C

Advent Season

1st Sunday of Advent
1. Jeremiah 33:14-16
2. 1 Thessalonians 3:12–4:2
3. Luke 21:25-28, 34-36

2nd Sunday of Advent
1. Baruch 5:1-9
2. Philippians 1:4-6, 8-11
3. Luke 3:1-6

3rd Sunday of Advent
1. Zephaniah 3:14-18a
2. Philippians 4:4-7
3. Luke 3:10-18

4th Sunday of Advent
1. Micah 5:1-4a
2. Hebrews 10:5-10
3. Luke 1:39-45

Christmas Season

Christmas Vigil
1. Isaiah 62:1-6
2. Acts 13:16-17, 22-25
3. Matthew 1:1-25

Christmas (at Midnight)
1. Isaiah 9:1-6
2. Titus 2:11-14
3. Luke 2:1-14

Christmas (at Dawn)
1. Isaiah 62:11-12
2. Titus 3:4-7
3. Luke 2:15-20

Christmas Day
1. Isaiah 52:7-10
2. Hebrews 1:1-6
3. John 1:1-18

Sunday after Christmas (Holy Family)
1. 1 Samuel 1:19b-22, 24-28
2. 1 John 3:1-2, 21-24
3. Luke 2:41-52

January 1 (Solemnity of Mary, Mother of God)
1. Numbers 6:22-27
2. Galatians 4:4-7
3. Luke 2:16-21

2nd Sunday after Christmas
1. Sirach 24:1-2, 8-12
2. Ephesians 1:3-6, 15-18
3. John 1:1-18

Epiphany
1. Isaiah 60:1-6
2. Ephesians 3:2-3a, 5-6
3. Matthew 2:1-12

Sunday after Epiphany (Baptism of the Lord)
1. Isaiah 42:1-4, 6-7
2. Acts 10:34-38
3. Luke 3:15-16, 21-22

Lenten Season

Ash Wednesday
1. Joel 2:12-18
2. 2 Corinthians 5:20–6:2
3. Matthew 6:1-6, 16-18

1st Sunday of Lent
1. Deuteronomy 26:4-10
2. Romans 10:8-13
3. Luke 4:1-13

2nd Sunday of Lent
1. Genesis 15:5-12, 17-18
2. Philippians 3:17–4:1
3. Luke 9:28b-36

3rd Sunday of Lent
1. Exodus 3:1-8a, 13-15
2. 1 Corinthians 10:1-6, 10-12
3. Luke 13:1-9

4th Sunday of Lent
1. Joshua 5:9a, 10-12
2. 2 Corinthians 5:17-12
3. Luke 15:1-3, 11-32

5th Sunday of Lent
1. Isaiah 43:16-21
2. Philippians 3:8-14
3. John 8:1-11

Passion Sunday (Palm Sunday)
Procession: Luke 19:28-40
1. Isaiah 50:4-7
2. Philippians 2:6-11
3. Luke 22:14–23:56

Easter Triduum and Easter Season

Mass of Lord's Supper
1. Exodus 12:1-8, 11-14
2. 1 Corinthians 11:23-26
3. John 13:1-15

Good Friday
1. Isaiah 52:13–53:12
2. Hebrews 4:14-16; 5:7-9
3. John 18:1–19:42

Easter Vigil
1. Genesis 1:1–2:2
   Genesis 22:1-18
   Exodus 14:15–15:1
   Isaiah 54:5-14
   Isaiah 55:1-11
   Baruch 3:9-15, 32–4:4
   Ezekiel 36:16-28
2. Romans 6:3-11
3. Luke 24:1-12

Easter Sunday
1. Acts 10:34a, 37-43
2. Colossians 3:1-4
or 1 Corinthians 5:6b-8
3. John 20:1-9
or Luke 24:1-12
Evening: 3. Luke 24:13-35

2nd Sunday of Easter
1. Acts 5:12-16
2. Revelation 1:9-11a, 12-13, 17-19
3. John 20:19-31

3rd Sunday of Easter
1. Acts 5:27b-32, 40b-41
2. Revelation 5:11-14
3. John 21:1-19

4th Sunday of Easter
1. Acts 13:14, 43-52
2. Revelation 7:9, 14b-17
3. John 10:27-30

5th Sunday of Easter
1. Acts 14:21-27
2. Revelation 21:1-5a
3. John 13:31-33a, 34-35

6th Sunday of Easter
1. Acts 15:1-2, 22-29
2. Revelation 21:10-14, 22-23
3. John 14:23-29

Ascension of Our Lord
1. Acts 1:1-11
2. Ephesians 1:17-23
or Hebrews 9:24-28; 10:19-23
3. Luke 24:46-53

7th Sunday of Easter
1. Acts 7:55-60
2. Revelation 22:12-14, 16-17, 20
3. John 17:20-26

Pentecost Vigil
1. Genesis 11:1-9
or Exodus 19:3-8a, 16-20b
or Ezekiel 37:1-14
or Joel 3:1-5
2. Romans 8:22-27
3. John 7:37-39

Pentecost Mass
1. Acts 2:1-11
2. 1 Corinthians 12:3b-7, 12-13
or Romans 8:8-27
3. John 20:19-23

Solemnities of the Lord during Ordinary Time

Trinity Sunday (Sunday after Pentecost)

1. Proverbs 8:22-31
2. Romans 5:1-5
3. John 16:12-15

Corpus Christi

1. Genesis 14:18-20
2. 1 Corinthians 11:23-26
3. Luke 9:11b-17

Sacred Heart of Jesus

1. Ezekiel 34:11-16
2. Romans 5:5-11
3. Luke 15:3-7

Ordinary Time

1st Sunday (See Baptism of the Lord, page 328)

2nd Sunday

1. Isaiah 62:1-5
2. 1 Corinthians 12:4-11
3. John 2:1-12

3rd Sunday

1. Nehemiah 8:1-4a, 5-6, 8-10
2. 1 Corinthians 12:12-30
3. Luke 1:1-4; 4:14-21

4th Sunday

1. Jeremiah 1:4-5, 17-19
2. 1 Corinthians 12:31–13:13
3. Luke 4:21-30

5th Sunday

1. Isaiah 6:1-2a, 3-8
2. 1 Corinthians 15:1-11
3. Luke 5:1-11

6th Sunday

1. Jeremiah 17:5-8
2. 1 Corinthians 15:12, 16-20
3. Luke 6:17, 20-26

7th Sunday

1. 1 Samuel 26:2, 7-9, 12-13, 22-23
2. 1 Corinthians 15:45-49
3. Luke 6:27-38

8th Sunday

1. Sirach 27:4-7
2. 1 Corinthians 15:54-58
3. Luke 6:39-45

9th Sunday

1. 1 Kings 8:41-43
2. Galatians 1:1-2, 6-10
3. Luke 7:1-10

10th Sunday

1. 1 Kings 17:17-24
2. Galatians 1:11-19
3. Luke 7:11-17

11th Sunday
1. 2 Samuel 12:7-10, 13
2. Galatians 2:16, 19-21
3. Luke 9:18-24

12th Sunday
1. Zechariah 12:10-11
2. Galatians 3:26-29
3. Luke 9:18-24

13th Sunday
1. 1 Kings 19:16b, 19-21
2. Galatians 5:1, 13-18
3. Luke 9:51-62

14th Sunday
1. Isaiah 66:10-14c
2. Galatians 6:14-18
3. Luke 10:1-12, 17-20

15th Sunday
1. Deuteronomy 30:10-14
2. Colossians 1:15-20
3. Luke 10:25-37

16th Sunday
1. Genesis 18:1-10a
2. Colossians 1:24-28
3. Luke 10:38-42

17th Sunday
1. Genesis 18:20-32
2. Colossians 3:1-5, 9-11
3. Luke 11:1-13

18th Sunday
1. Ecclesiastes 1:2; 2:21-23
2. Colossians 3:1-5, 9-11
3. Luke 12:13-31

19th Sunday
1. Jeremiah 38:4-6.8-10
2. Hebrews 12:1-4
3. Luke 12:49-53

20th Sunday
1. Proverbs 9:1-6
2. Ephesians 5:15-20
3. John 6:51-58

21st Sunday
1. Isaiah 66:18-21
2. Hebrews 12:5-7, 11-13
3. Luke 13:22-30

22nd Sunday
1. Sirach 3:17-18, 20, 28-29
2. Hebrews 12:18-19, 22-24a
3. Luke 14:1, 7-14

23rd Sunday
1. Wisdom 9:13-18b
2. Philemon 9b-10, 12-17
3. Luke 14:25-33

24th Sunday
1. Exodus 32:7-11, 13-14
2. 1 Timothy 1:12-17
3. Luke 15:1-32

25th Sunday
1. Amos 8:4-7
2. 1 Timothy 2:1-8
3. Luke 16:1-13

26th Sunday
1. Amos 6:1a, 4-7
2. 1 Timothy 6:11-16
3. Luke 16:19-31

27th Sunday
1. Hebrews 1:2-3 ;2:2-4
2. 2 Timothy 1:6-8, 13-14
3. Luke 17:5-10

28th Sunday
1. 2 Kings 5:14-17
2. 2 Timothy 2:8-13
3. Luke 17:11-19

29th Sunday
1. Exodus 17:8-13
2. 2 Timothy 3:14–4:2
3. Luke 18:1-8

30th Sunday
1. Sirach 35:12-14, 16-18
2. 2 Timothy 4:6-8, 16-18
3. Luke 18:9-14

31st Sunday
1. Wisdom 11:23–12:2
2. 2 Thessalonians 1:11–2:2
3. Luke 19:1-10

32nd Sunday
1. 2 Maccabees 7:1-2, 9-14
2. 2 Thessalonians 2:16–3:5
3. Luke 20:27-38

33rd Sunday
1. Malachi 3:19-20a
2. 2 Thessalonians 3:7-12
3. Luke 21:5-19

34th Sunday (Christ the King)
1. 2 Samuel 5:1-3
2. Colossians 1:12-20
3. Luke 23:35-43

Readings for Major Feasts of the Year

February 2: Presentation of the Lord
1. Malachi 3:1-4
2. Hebrews 2:14-18
3. Luke 2:22-40

March 19: Joseph, Husband of Mary
1. 2 Samuel 7:4-5a, 12-14a, 16
2. Romans 4:13, 16-18, 22
3. Matthew 1:16, 18-21, 24a

or Luke 2:41-51a

March 25: Annunciation
1. Isaiah 7:10-14
2. Hebrews 10:4-10
3. Luke 1:26-28

June 24: John the Baptist Vigil
1. Jeremiah 1:4-10
2. 1 Peter 1:8-12
3. Luke 1:5-17

John the Baptist Mass
1. Isaiah 49:1-6
2. Acts 13:22-26
3. Luke 1:57-66, 80

June 29: Peter and Paul Vigil
1. Acts 3:1-10
2. Galatians 1:11-20
3. John 21:15-19

Peter and Paul Mass
1. Acts 12:1-11
2. 2 Timothy 4:6-8, 17-18
3. Matthew 16:13-19

**August 6: Transfigura-
tion**
1. Daniel 7:9-10, 13-14
2. 2 Peter 1:16-19
3. (A) Matthew 7:1-9
   (B) Mark 9:2-10
   (C) Luke 9:28b-36

**August 15: Assumption
Vigil**
1. 1 Chronicles 15:3–
   4.15; 16:1-2
2. 1 Corinthians 15:54-57
3. Luke 11:27-28

Assumption Mass
1. Revelation 11:19a;
   12:1-6a, 10ab
2. 1 Corinthians 15:20-26
3. Luke 1:39-56

**September 14: Triumph
of the Cross**
1. Numbers 21:4-9
2. Philippians 2:6-11
3. John 3:13-17

November 1: All Saints
1. Revelation 7:2-4, 9-14
2. 1 John 3:1-3
3. Matthew 5:1-12a

**November 2: All Souls
First Mass**
1. Job 19:1, 23-27
2. 1 Corinthians 15:51-57
3. John 6:37-40

All Souls Second Mass
1. Wisdom 3:1-9
2. Philippians 3:20-21
3. John 11:17-27

All Souls Third Mass
1. 2 Maccabees 12:43-46
2. Revelation 14:13
3. John 14:1-6
(Other readings may be
   chosen.)

**November 9: Dedication
of St. John Lateran**
1. 2 Chronicles 5:6-10,
   13–6:2
2. 1 Corinthians 3:9-13,
   16-17
3. Luke 19:1-10
(Other readings may be
   chosen.)

**December 8: Immaculate
Conception**
1. Genesis 3:9-15, 20
2. Ephesians 1:3-6, 11-12
3. Luke 1:26-38

WEEKDAY LECTIONARY

Advent Season

1st Week of Advent

M	Isaiah 2:1-5	Matthew 8:5-11
	(Year A*: Isaiah 4:2-6)	
Tu	Isaiah 11:1-10	Luke 10:21-24
W	Isaiah 25:6-10a	Matthew 15:29-37
Th	Isaiah 26:1-6	Matthew 7:21, 24-27
F	Isaiah 29:17-24	Matthew 9:27-31
Sa	Isaiah 30:19-21	Matthew 9:35–10:1, 6-8

2nd Week of Advent

M	Isaiah 35:1-10	Luke 5:17-26
Tu	Isaiah 40:1-11	Matthew 18:12-14
W	Isaiah 40:25-31	Matthew 11:28-30
Th	Isaiah 41:13-20	Matthew 11:11-15
F	Isaiah 48:17-19	Matthew 11:16-19
Sa	Sirach 48:1-4, 9-11	Matthew 17:10-13

3rd Week of Advent

M	Numbers 24:2-7, 15-17a	Matthew 21:23-27
Tu	Zephaniah 3:1-2, 9-13	Matthew 21:28-32
W	Isaiah 45:6b-8, 18, 21b-25	Luke 7:18b-23
Th	Isaiah 54:1-10	Luke 7:24-30
F	Isaiah 56:1-3a, 6-8	John 5:33-36

From December 17 to December 24

17	Genesis 49:2, 8-10	Matthew 1:1-17
18	Jeremiah 23:5-8	Matthew 1:18-24
19	Judges 13:2-7, 24-25a	Luke 1:5-25
20	Isaiah 7:10-14	Luke 1:26-38
21	Song of Songs 2:8-14	Luke 1:39-45
	or Zephaniah 3:14-18a	

---

* See page 317 for definitions of Years A, B and C.

22	1 Samuel 1:24-28	Luke 1:46-56
23	Malachi 3:1-4, 23-24	Luke 1:57-66
24	2 Samuel 7:1-5, 8b-11, 16	Luke 1:67-79

Christmas Season

Octave of Christmas

2nd Day (St. Stephen)

Acts 6:8-10; 7:54-59   Matthew 10:17-22

3rd Day (St. John)

1 John 1:1-4   John 20:2-8

4th Day (Holy Innocents)

1 John 1:5–2:2   Matthew 2:13-18

5th Day

1 John 2:3-11   Luke 2:22-35

6th Day

1 John 2;12-17   Luke 2:36-40

7th Day

1 John 2:18-21   John 1:1-18

January 2

1 John 2:22-28   John 1:19-28

January 3

1 John 2:29–3:6   John 1:29-34

January 4

1 John 3:7-10   John 1:35-42

January 5

1 John 3:11-21   John 1:43-51

January 6 (if Epiphany is not celebrated)*

1 John 5:5-13	Mark 1:6b-11

Week after Epiphany

M	1 John 3:22–4:6	Matthew 4:12-17, 23-25
Tu	1 John 4:7-10	Mark 6:34-44
W	1 John 4:11-18	Mark 6:45-52
Th	1 John 4:19–5:4	Luke 4:14-22a
F	1 John 5:5-13	Luke 5:12-16
Sa	1 John 5:14-21	John 3:22-30

Lenten Season

Ash Wednesday

	Joel 2:12-18	Matthew 6:1-6, 16-18
	2 Corinthians 5:20–6:2	
Th	Deuteronomy 30:15-20	Luke 9:22-25
F	Isaiah 58:1-9a	Matthew 9:14-15
Sa	Isaiah 58:9b-14	Luke 5:27-32

1st Week of Lent

M	Leviticus 19:1-2, 11-18	Matthew 25:31-46
Tu	Isaiah 55:10-11	Matthew 6:7-15
W	Jonah 3:1-10	Luke 11:29-32
Th	Esther C:12, 14-16, 23-25	Matthew 7:7-12
F	Ezekiel 18:21-28	Matthew 5:20-26
Sa	Deuteronomy 26:16-19	Matthew 5:43-48

2nd Week of Lent

M	Daniel 9:4b-10	Luke 6:36-38
Tu	Isaiah 1:10, 16-20	Matthew 23:1-12
W	Jeremiah 18:18-20	Matthew 20:17-28
Th	Jeremiah 17:5-10	Luke 16:19-31
F	Genesis 37:3-4, 12-13a, 17b-28	Matthew 21:33-43, 45-46

---

* Readings may vary slightly depending on when Epiphany is celebrated.

| Sa | Micah 7:14-15, 18-20 | Luke 15:1-3, 11-32 |

3rd Week of Lent

M	2 Kings 5:1-15a	Luke 4:24-30
Tu	Daniel 3:25, 34-43	Matthew 18:21-35
W	Deuteronomy 4:1, 5-9	Matthew 5:17-19
Th	Jeremiah 7:23-28	Luke 11:14-23
F	Hosea 14:2-10	Mark 12:28b-34
Sa	Hosea 6:1-6	Luke 18:19-24

4th Week of Lent

M	Isaiah 65:17-21	John 4:43-54
Tu	Ezekiel 47:1-9, 12	John 5:1-3a, 5-16
W	Isaiah 49:8-15	John 5:17-30
Th	Exodus 32:7-14	John 5:31-47
F	Wisdom 2:1a, 12-22	John 7:1-2, 10, 25-30
Sa	Jeremiah 11:18-20	John 7:40-53

5th Week of Lent

M	Daniel 13:1-9, 15-17, 19-30, 33-62	John 8:1-11 (Year C: John 8:12-20)
Tu	Numbers 21:4-9	John 8:21-30
W	Daniel 3:14-20, 91-92, 95	John 8:31-42
Th	Genesis 17:3-9	John 8:51-59
F	Jeremiah 20:10-13	John 10:31-42
Sa	Ezekiel 37:21-28	John 11:45-56

Holy Week

M	Isaiah 42:1-7	John 12:1-11
Tu	Isaiah 49:1-6	John 13:21-33, 36-38
W	Isaiah 50:4-9a	Matthew 26:14-25

Thursday Chrism Mass

| Isaiah 61:1-3a, 6a, 8b-9 | Luke 4:16-21 |
| Revelation 1:5-8 | |

Easter Season

Octave of Easter

M	Acts 2:14, 22-32	Matthew 28:8-15
Tu	Acts 2:36-41	John 20:11-18
W	Acts 3:1-10	Luke 24:13-35
Th	Acts 3:11-26	Luke 24:35-48
F	Acts 4:1-12	John 21:1-14
Sa	Acts 4:13-21	Mark 16:9-15

2nd Week of Easter

M	Acts 4:23-31	John 3:1-8
Tu	Acts 4:32-37	John 3:7-15
W	Acts 5:17-26	John 3:16-21
Th	Acts 5:27-33	John 3:31-36
F	Acts 5:34-42	John 6:1-15
Sa	Acts 6:1-7	John 6:16-21

3rd Week of Easter

M	Acts 6:8-15	John 6:22-29
Tu	Acts 7:51–8:1a	John 6:30-35
W	Acts 8:1-8	John 6:35-40
Th	Acts 8:26-40	John 6:44-51
F	Acts 9:1-20	John 6:52-59
Sa	Acts 9:31-42	John 6:60-69

4th Week of Easter

M	Acts 11:1-18	John 10:1-10
		(Year A: John 10:11-18)
Tu	Acts 11:19-26	John 10:22-30
W	Acts 12:24–13:5a	John 12:44-50
Th	Acts 13:13-25	John 13:16-20
F	Acts 13:26-33	John 14:1-6
Sa	Acts 13:44-52	John 14:7-14

5th Week of Easter

M	Acts 14:5-18	John 14:21-26
Tu	Acts 14:19-28	John 14:27-31a

W	Acts 15:1-6	John 15:1-8
Th	Acts 15:7-21	John 15:9-11
F	Acts 15:22-31	John 15:12-17
Sa	Acts 16:1-10	John 15:18-21

6th Week of Easter

M	Acts 16:11-15	John 15:26–16:4a
Tu	Acts 16:22-34	John 16:5-11
W	Acts 17:15, 22–18:1	John 16:12-15
Th	Acts 18:1-8	John 16:16-20
F	Acts 18:9-18	John 16:20-23a
Sa	Acts 18:23-28	John 16:23b-28

7th Week of Easter

M	Acts 19:1-8	John 16:29-33
Tu	Acts 20:17-27	John 17:1-11a
W	Acts 20:28-38	John 17:11b-19
Th	Acts 22:30, 23:6-11	John 17:20-26
F	Acts 25:13-21	John 21:15-19
Sa	Acts 28:16-20, 30-31	John 21:20-25

Ordinary Time

Guide: Year I refers to odd-numbered years, starting with the preceding Advent. Year II refers to even-numbered years, starting with the preceding Advent.

	YEAR I	YEAR II

1st Week

M	Hebrews 1:1-6	1 Samuel 1:1-8
	Mark 1:14-20	Mark 1:14-20
Tu	Hebrews 2:5-12	1 Samuel 1:9-20
	Mark 1:21-28	Mark 1:21-28
W	Hebrews 2:14-18	1 Samuel 3:1-10, 19-20
	Mark 1:29-39	Mark 1:29-39

	YEAR I	YEAR II
Th	Hebrews 3:7-14	1 Samuel 4:1-11
	Mark 1:40-45	Mark 1:40-45
F	Hebrews 4:1-5, 11	1 Samuel 8:4-7, 10-22a
	Mark 2:1-12	Mark 2:1-12
Sa	Hebrews 4:12-16	1 Samuel 9:1-14, 17-19; 10:1a
	Mark 2:13-17	Mark 2:13-17

2nd Week

	YEAR I	YEAR II
M	Hebrews 5:1-10	1 Samuel 15:16-23
	Mark 2:18-22	Mark 2:18-22
Tu	Hebrews 6:10-20	1 Samuel 16:1-13
	Mark 2:23-28	Mark 2:23-28
W	Hebrews 7:1-3, 15-17	1 Samuel 17:32-33, 37, 40-51
	Mark 3:1-6	Mark 3:1-6
Th	Hebrews 7:25–8:6	1 Samuel 18:6-9; 19:1-7
	Mark 3:7-12	Mark 3:7-12
F	Hebrews 8:6-13	1 Samuel 24:3-21
	Mark 3:13-19	Mark 3:13-19
Sa	Hebrews 9:2-3, 11-14	2 Samuel 1:1-4, 11-12, 19, 23-27
	Mark 3:20-21	Mark 3:20-21

3rd Week

	YEAR I	YEAR II
M	Hebrews 9:15, 24-28	2 Samuel 5:1-7, 10
	Mark 3:22-30	Mark 3:22-30
Tu	Hebrews 10:1-10	2 Samuel 6:12b-15, 17-19
	Mark 3:31-35	Mark 3:31-35
W	Hebrews 10:11-18	2 Samuel 7:4-17
	Mark 4:1-20	Mark 4:1-20
Th	Hebrews 10:19-25	2 Samuel 7:18-19, 24-29
	Mark 4:21-25	Mark 4:21-25
F	Hebrews 10:32-39	2 Samuel 11:1-4a, 5-10a, 13-17
	Mark 4:26-34	Mark 4:26-34

	YEAR I	**YEAR II**
Sa	Hebrews 11:1-2, 8-9 Mark 4:35-41	2 Samuel 12:1-7a, 10-17 Mark 4:35-41

4th Week

	YEAR I	**YEAR II**
M	Hebrews 11:32-40 Mark 5:1-20	2 Samuel 15:13-14, 30; 16:5-13a Mark 5:1-20
Tu	Hebrews 12:1-4 Mark 5:21-43	2 Samuel 18:9-10, 14b, 24-25a, 30–19:3 Mark 5:21-43
W	Hebrews 12:4-7, 11-15 Mark 6:1-6	2 Samuel 24:2, 9-17 Mark 6:1-6
Th	Hebrews 12:18-19, 21-24 Mark 6:7-13	1 Kings 2:1-4, 10-12 Mark 6:7-13
F	Hebrews 13:1-8 Mark 6:14-29	Sirach 47:2-11 Mark 6:14-29
Sa	Hebrews 13:15-17, 20-21 Mark 6:30-34	1 Kings 3:4-13 Mark 6:30-34

5th Week

	YEAR I	**YEAR II**
M	Genesis 1:1-19 Mark 6:53-56	1 Kings 8:1-7, 9-13 Mark 6:53-56
Tu	Genesis 1:20–2:4a Mark 7:1-13	1 Kings 8:22-23, 27-30 Mark 7:1-13
W	Genesis 2:4b-9, 15-17 Mark 7:14-23	1 Kings 10:1-10 Mark 7:14-23
Th	Genesis 2:18-25 Mark 7:24-30	1 Kings 11:4-13 Mark 7:24-30
F	Genesis 3:1-8 Mark 7:31-37	1 Kings 11:29-32; 12:19 Mark 7:31-37
Sa	Genesis 3:9-24 Mark 8:1-10	1 Kings 12:26-32; 13:33-34 Mark 8:1-10

6th Week

	YEAR I	**YEAR II**
M	Genesis 4:1-15, 25 Mark 8:11-13	James 1:1-11 Mark 8:11-13

	YEAR I	YEAR II
Tu	Genesis 6:5-8; 7:1-5, 10	James 1:12-18
	Mark 8:14-21	Mark 8:14-21
W	Genesis 8:6-13, 20-22	James 1:19-27
	Mark 8:22-26	Mark 8:22-26
Th	Genesis 9:1-13	James 2:1-9
	Mark 8:27-33	Mark 8:27-33
F	Genesis 11:1-9	James 2:14-24, 26
	Mark 8:34–9:1	Mark 8:34–9:1
Sa	Hebrews 11:1-7	James 3:1-10
	Mark 9:2-13	Mark 9:2-13

7th Week

M	Sirach 1:1-10	James 3:13-18
	Mark 9:14-29	Mark 9:14-29
Tu	Sirach 2:1-11	James 4:1-10
	Mark 9:30-37	Mark 9:30-37
W	Sirach 4:11-19	James 4:13-17
	Mark 9:38-40	Mark 9:38-40
Th	Sirach 5:1-8	James 5:1-6
	Mark 9:41-50	Mark 9:41-50
F	Sirach 6:5-17	James 5:9-12
	Mark 10:1-12	Mark 10:1-12
Sa	Sirach 17:1-15	James 5:13-20
	Mark 10:13-16	Mark 10:13-16

8th Week

M	Sirach 17:19-27	1 Peter 1:3-9
	Mark 10:17-27	Mark 10:17-27
Tu	Sirach 35:1-12	1 Peter 1:10-16
	Mark 10:28-31	Mark 10:28-31
W	Sirach 36:1, 5-6, 10-17	1 Peter 1:18-25
	Mark 10:32-45	Mark 10:32-45
Th	Sirach 42:15-25	1 Peter 2:2-5, 9-12
	Mark 10:46-52	Mark 10:46-52
F	Sirach 44:1, 9-13	1 Peter 4:7-13
	Mark 11:11-26	Mark 11:11-26

	Year I	Year II
Sa	Sirach 51:12b-20	Jude 17:20b-25
	Mark 11:27-33	Mark 11:27-33

9th Week

	Year I	Year II
M	Tobit 1:1a-2; 2:1-9	2 Peter 1:2-7
	Mark 12:1-12	Mark 12:1-12
Tu	Tobit 2:9-14	2 Peter 3:12-15a, 17-18
	Mark 12:13-17	Mark 12:13-17
W	Tobit 3:1-11, 16	2 Timothy 1:1-3, 6-12
	Mark 12:18-27	Mark 12:18-27
Th	Tobit 6:10-11; 7:1, 9-17; 8:4-7	2 Timothy 2:8-15
	Mark 12:28b-34	Mark 12:28b-34
F	Tobit 11:5-17	2 Timothy 3:10-17
	Mark 12:35-37	Mark 12:35-37
Sa	Tobit 12:1, 5-15, 20	2 Timothy 4:1-8
	Mark 12:38-44	Mark 12:38-44

10th Week

	Year I	Year II
M	2 Corinthians 1:1-7	1 Kings 17:1-6
	Matthew 5:1-12	Matthew 5:1-12
Tu	2 Corinthians 1:18-22	1 Kings 17:7-16
	Matthew 5:13-16	Matthew 5:13-16
W	2 Corinthians 3:4-11	1 Kings 18:20-39
	Matthew 5:17-19	Matthew 5:17-19
Th	2 Corinthians 3:15–4:1, 3-6	1 Kings 18:41-46
	Matthew 5:20-26	Matthew 5:20-26
F	2 Corinthians 4:7-15	1 Kings 19:9a, 11-16
	Matthew 5:27-32	Matthew 5:27-32
Sa	2 Corinthians 5:14-21	1 Kings 19:19-21
	Matthew 5:33-37	Matthew 5:33-37

11th Week

	Year I	Year II
M	2 Corinthians 6:1-10	1 Kings 21:1-16
	Matthew 5:38-4	Matthew 5:38-42

	YEAR I	YEAR II
Tu	2 Corinthians 8:1-9	1 Kings 21:17-29
	Matthew 5:43-48	Matthew 5:43-48
W	2 Corinthians 9:6-11	1 Kings 2:1, 6-14
	Matthew 6:1-6, 16-18	Matthew 6:1-6, 16-18
Th	2 Corinthians 11:1-11	Sirach 48:1-15
	Matthew 6:7-15	Matthew 6:7-15
F	2 Corinthians 11:18, 21b-30	2 Kings 11:1-4, 9-18, 20
	Matthew 6:19-23	Matthew 6:19-23
Sa	2 Corinthians 12:1-10	2 Chronicles 24:17-25
	Matthew 6:24-34	Matthew 6:24-34

12th Week

	YEAR I	YEAR II
M	Genesis 12:1-9	2 Kings 17:5-8, 13-15a, 18
	Matthew 7:1-5	Matthew 7:1-5
Tu	Genesis 13:2, 5-8	2 Kings 19:9b-11, 14-21, 31-35a, 36
	Matthew 7:6, 12-14	Matthew 7:6, 12-14
W	Genesis 15:1-12, 17-18	2 Kings 22:8-13; 23:1-3
	Matthew 7:15-20	Matthew 7:15-20
Th	Genesis 16:1-12, 15-16	2 Kings 24:8-17
	Matthew 7:21-29	Matthew 7:21-29
F	Genesis 17:1, 9-10, 15-22	2 Kings 25:1-12
	Matthew 8:1-4	Matthew 8:1-4
Sa	Genesis 18:1-15	Lamentations 2:2, 10-14, 18-19
	Matthew 8:5-17	Matthew 8:5-17

13th Week

	YEAR I	YEAR II
M	Genesis 18:16-33	Amos 2:6-10, 13-16
	Matthew 8:18-22	Matthew 8:18-22
Tu	Genesis 19:15-29	Amos 3:1-8; 4:11-12
	Matthew 8:23-27	Matthew 8:23-27
W	Genesis 21:5, 8-20	Amos 5:14-15, 21-24
	Matthew 8:28-34	Matthew 8:28-34
Th	Genesis 22:1-19	Amos 7:10-17
	Matthew 9:1-8	Matthew 9:1-8

	YEAR I	YEAR II
F	Genesis 23:1-4, 19; 24:1-8, 62-67	Amos 8:4-6, 9-12
	Matthew 9:9-13	Matthew 9:9-13
Sa	Genesis 27:1-5, 15-29	Amos 9:11-15
	Matthew 9:14-17	Matthew 9:14-17

14th Week

	YEAR I	YEAR II
M	Genesis 28:10-22a	Hosea 2:16, 17b-18, 21-22
	Matthew 9:18-26	Matthew 9:18-26
Tu	Genesis 32:22-33	Hosea 8:4-7, 11-13
	Matthew 9:32-38	Matthew 9:32-38
W	Genesis 41:51-57; 42:5-7a, 17-24a	Hosea 10:1-3, 7-8, 12
	Matthew 10:1-7	Matthew 10:1-7
Th	Genesis 44:18-21, 23b-29; 45:1-5	Hosea 11:1, 3-4, 8c-9
	Matthew 10:7-15	Matthew 10:7-15
F	Genesis 46:1-7, 28-30	Hosea 14:2-10
	Matthew 10:16-23	Matthew 10:16-23
Sa	Genesis 49:29-33; 50:15-24	Isaiah 6:1-8
	Matthew 10:24-33	Matthew 10:24-33

15th Week

	YEAR I	YEAR II
M	Exodus 1:8-14, 22	Isaiah 1:10-17
	Matthew 10:34–11:1	Matthew 10:34–11:1
Tu	Exodus 2:1-15a	Isaiah 7:1-9
	Matthew 11:20-24	Matthew 11:20-24
W	Exodus 3:1-6, 9-12	Isaiah 10:5-7, 13-16
	Matthew 11:25-27	Matthew 11:25-27
Th	Exodus 3:13-20	Isaiah 26:7-9, 12, 16-19
	Matthew 11:28-30	Matthew 11:28-30
F	Exodus 20:1-17	Jeremiah 3:14-17
	Matthew 13:18-23	Matthew 13:18-23
Sa	Exodus 24:3-8	Jeremiah 7:1-11
	Matthew 13:24-30	Matthew 13:24-30

16th Week

M	Exodus 14:5-18	Micah 6:1-4, 6-8
	Matthew 12:38-42	Matthew 12:38-42
Tu	Exodus 14:21–15:1	Micah 7:14-15, 18-20
	Matthew 12:46-50	Matthew 12:46-50
W	Exodus 16:1-5, 9-15	Jeremiah 1:1, 4-10
	Matthew 13:1-9	Matthew 13:1-9
Th	Exodus 19:1-2, 9-11, 16-20b	Jeremiah 2:1-3, 7-8, 12-13
	Matthew 13:10-17	Matthew 13:10-17
F	Exodus 20:1-17	Jeremiah 3:14-17
	Matthew 13:18-23	Matthew 13:18-23
Sa	Exodus 24:3-8	Jeremiah 7:1-11
	Matthew 13:24-30	Matthew 13:24-30

17th Week

M	Exodus 32:15-24, 30-34	Jeremiah 13:1-11
	Matthew 13:31-35	Matthew 13:31-35
Tu	Exodus 33:7-11; 34:5b-9, 28	Jeremiah 14:17-22
	Matthew 13:36-43	Matthew 13:36-43
W	Exodus 34:29-34	Jeremiah 15:10, 16-21
	Matthew 13:44-46	Matthew 13:44-46
Th	Exodus 40:16-21, 34-38	Jeremiah 18:1-6
	Matthew 13:47-53	Matthew 13:47-53
F	Leviticus 23:1, 4-11, 15-16, 27, 34b-37	Jeremiah 26:1-9
	Matthew 13:54-58	Matthew 13:54-58
Sa	Leviticus 25:1, 8-17	Jeremiah 26:11-16, 24
	Matthew 14:1-12	Matthew 14:1-12

18th Week

M	Numbers 11:4b-15	Jeremiah 28:1-17
	Matthew 14:31-2	Matthew 14:31-2
	or Matthew 14:22-36	or Matthew 14:22-36

	YEAR I	YEAR II
Tu	Numbers 12:1-13	Jeremiah 30:1-2, 12-15, 18-22
	Matthew 14:22-36 or Matthew 15:1-2, 10-14	Matthew 14:22-36 or Matthew 15:1-2, 10-14
W	Numbers 13:1-2a, 13:25–14:1, 26-29, 34-35	Jeremiah 31:1-7
	Matthew 15:21-28	Matthew 15:21-28
Th	Numbers 20:1-13	Jeremiah 31:31-34
	Matthew 16:13-23	Matthew 16:13-23
F	Deuteronomy 4:32-40	Nahum 2:1, 3; 3:1-3, 6-7
	Matthew 16:24-28	Matthew 16:24-28
Sa	Deuteronomy 6:4-13	Hebrews 1:12–2:4
	Matthew 17:14-20	Matthew 17:14-20

19th Week

	YEAR I	YEAR II
M	Deuteronomy 10:12-22	Ezekiel 1:2-5, 24-28c
	Matthew 17:22-27	Matthew 17:22-27
Tu	Deuteronomy 31:1-8	Ezekiel 2:8–3:4
	Matthew 18:1-5, 10, 12-14	Matthew 18:1-5, 10, 12-14
W	Deuteronomy 34:1-12	Ezekiel 9:1-7, 10, 18-22
	Matthew 18:15-20	Matthew 18:15-20
Th	Joshua 3:7-10a, 11, 13-17	Ezekiel 12:1-12
	Matthew 18:21–19:1	Matthew 18:21–19:1
F	Joshua 24:1-13	Ezekiel 16:1-15, 60, 63
	Matthew 19:3-12	Matthew 19:3-12
Sa	Joshua 24:14-29	Ezekiel 18:1-10, 13b, 30-32
	Matthew 19:13-15	Matthew 19:13-15

20th Week

	YEAR I	YEAR II
M	Judges 2:11-19	Ezekiel 24:15-24
	Matthew 19:16-22	Matthew 19:16-22

	YEAR I	YEAR II
Tu	Judges 6:11-24a	Ezekiel 28:1-10
	Matthew 19:23-30	Matthew 19:23-30
W	Judges 9:6-15	Ezekiel 34:1-11
	Matthew 20:1-16a	Matthew 20:1-16a
Th	Judges 11:29-39a	Ezekiel 36:23-28
	Matthew 22:1-14	Matthew 22:1-14
F	Ruth 1:1, 3-6, 14b-16, 22	Ezekiel 37:1-14
	Matthew 22:34-40	Matthew 22:34-40
Sa	Ruth 2:1-3, 8-11; 4:13-17	Ezekiel 43:1-7a
	Matthew 23:1-12	Matthew 23:1-12

21st Week

	YEAR I	YEAR II
M	1 Thessalonians 1:2b-5, 8b-10	2 Thessalonians 1:1-5, 11b-12
	Matthew 23:13-22	Matthew 23:13-22
Tu	1 Thessalonians 2:1-8	2 Thessalonians 2:1-3a, 13-17
	Matthew 23:23-26	Matthew 23:23-26
W	1 Thessalonians 2:9-13	2 Thessalonians 3:6-10, 16-18
	Matthew 23:27-32	Matthew 23:27-32
Th	1 Thessalonians 3:7-13	1 Corinthians 1:1-9
	Matthew 24:42-51	Matthew 24:42-51
F	1 Thessalonians 4:1-8	1 Corinthians 1:17-25
	Matthew 25:1-13	Matthew 25:1-13
Sa	1 Thessalonians 4:9-12	1 Corinthians 1:26-31
	Matthew 25:14-30	Matthew 25:14-30

22nd Week

	YEAR I	YEAR II
M	1 Thessalonians 4:13-18	1 Corinthians 2:1-5
	Luke 4:16-30	Luke 4:16-30
Tu	1 Thessalonians 5:1-6, 9-11	1 Corinthians 2:10b-16
	Luke 4:31-37	Luke 4:31-37
W	Colossians 1:1-8	1 Corinthians 3:1-9
	Luke 4:38-44	Luke 4:38-44

	YEAR I	YEAR II
Th	Colossians 1:9-14 Luke 5:1-11	1 Corinthians 3:18-23 Luke 5:1-11
F	Colossians 1:15-20 Luke 5:33-39	1 Corinthians 4:1-5 Luke 5:33-39
Sa	Colossians 1:21-23 Luke 6:1-5	1 Corinthians 4:9-15 Luke 6:1-5

23rd Week

	YEAR I	YEAR II
M	Colossians 1:24—2:3 Luke 6:6-11	1 Corinthians 5:1-8 Luke 6:6-11
Tu	Colossians 2:6-15 Luke 6:12-19	1 Corinthians 6:1-11 Luke 6:12-19
W	Colossians 3:1-11 Luke 6:20-26	1 Corinthians 7:25-31 Luke 6:20-26
Th	Colossians 3:12-17 Luke 6:27-38	1 Corinthians 8:1b-7, 11-13 Luke 6:27-38
F	1 Timothy 1:1-2, 12-14 Luke 6:39-42	1 Corinthians 9:16-19, 22b-27 Luke 6:39-42
Sa	1 Timothy 1:15-17 Luke 6:43-49	1 Corinthians 10:14-22a Luke 6:43-49

24th Week

	YEAR I	YEAR II
M	1 Timothy 2:1-8 Luke 7:1-10	1 Corinthians 11:17-26, 33 Luke 7:1-10
Tu	1 Timothy 3:1-13 Luke 7:11-17	1 Corinthians 12:12-14, 27-31a Luke 7:11-17
W	1 Timothy 3:14-16 Luke 7:31-35	1 Corinthians 12:31—13:13 Luke 7:31-35
Th	1 Timothy 4:12-16 Luke 7:36-50	1 Corinthians 15:1-11 Luke 7:36-50
F	1 Timothy 6:2c-12 Luke 8:1-3	1 Corinthians 15:12-20 Luke 8:1-3

	YEAR I	**YEAR II**
Sa	1 Timothy 6:13-16	1 Corinthians 15:36-37, 42-49
	Luke 8:4-15	Luke 8:4-15

25th Week

	YEAR I	**YEAR II**
M	Ezra 1:1-6	Proverbs 3:27-34
	Luke 8:16-18	Luke 8:16-18
Tu	Ezra 6:7-8, 12b, 14-20	Proverbs 21:1-6, 10-13
	Luke 8:19-21	Luke 8:19-21
W	Ezra 9:5-9	Proverbs 30:5-9
	Luke 9:1-6	Luke 9:1-6
Th	Haggai 1:1-8	Ecclesiastes 1:2-11
	Luke 9:7-9	Luke 9:7-9
F	Haggai 1:15b–2:9	Ecclesiastes 3:1-11
	Luke 9:18-22	Luke 9:18-22
Sa	Zechariah 2:5-9a; 14-15a	Ecclesiastes 11:9–12:8
	Luke 9:43b-45	Luke 9:43b-45

26th Week

	YEAR I	**YEAR II**
M	Zechariah 8:1-8	Job 1:6-22
	Luke 9:46-50	Luke 9:46-50
Tu	Zechariah 8:20-23	Job 3:1-3, 11-17, 20-23
	Luke 9:51-56	Luke 9:51-56
W	Nehemiah 2:1-8	Job 9:1-12, 14-16
	Luke 9:57-62	Luke 9:57-62
Th	Nehemiah 8:1-4a, 5-6, 7b-12	Job 19:12-27
	Luke 10:1-12	Luke 10:1-12
F	Baruch 1:15-22	Job 38:1, 12-21; 40:3-5
	Luke 10:13-16	Luke 10:13-16
Sa	Baruch 4:5-12, 27-29	Job 42:1-3, 5-6, 12-17
	Luke 10:17-24	Luke 10:17-24

27th Week

	YEAR I	**YEAR II**
M	Jonah 1:1–2:1, 11	Galatians 1:6-12
	Luke 10:25-37	Luke 10:25-37

	YEAR I	YEAR II
Tu	Jonah 3:1-10	Galatians 1:13-24
	Luke 10:38-42	Luke 10:38-42
W	Jonah 4:1-11	Galatians 2:1-2, 7-14
	Luke 11:1-4	Luke 11:1-4
Th	Malachi 3:13-20a	Galatians 3:1-5
	Luke 11:5-13	Luke 11:5-13
F	Joel 1:13-15; 2:1-2	Galatians 3:7-14
	Luke 11:15-26	Luke 11:15-26
Sa	Joel 4:12-21	Galatians 3:22-29
	Luke 11:27-28	Luke 11:27-28

28th Week

	YEAR I	YEAR II
M	Romans 1:1-7	Galatians 4:22-24, 26-27
	Luke 11:29-32	Luke 11:29-32
Tu	Romans 1:16-25	Galatians 5:1-6
	Luke 11:37-41	Luke 11:37-41
W	Romans 2:1-11	Galatians 5:18-25
	Luke 11:42-46	Luke 11:42-46
Th	Romans 3:21-29	Ephesians 1:3-10
	Luke 11:47-54	Luke 11:47-54
F	Romans 4:1-8	Ephesians 1:11-14
	Luke 12:1-7	Luke 12:1-7
Sa	Romans 4:13, 16-18	Ephesians 1:15-23
	Luke 12:8-12	Luke 12:8-12

29th Week

	YEAR I	YEAR II
M	Romans 4:20-25	Ephesians 2:1-10
	Luke 12:13-21	Luke 12:13-21
Tu	Romans 5:12, 15b, 17-19, 20b-21	Ephesians 2:12-22
	Luke 12:35-38	Luke 12:35-38
W	Romans 6:12-18	Ephesians 3:2-12
	Luke 12:39-48	Luke 12:39-48
Th	Romans 6:19-23	Ephesians 3:14-21
	Luke 12:49-53	Luke 12:49-53

	YEAR I	YEAR II
F	Romans 7:18-25a Luke 12:54-59	Ephesians 4:1-6 Luke 12:54-59
Sa	Romans 8:1-11 Luke 13:1-9	Ephesians 4:7-16 Luke 13:1-9

30th Week

	YEAR I	YEAR II
M	Romans 8:12-17 Luke 13:10-17	Ephesians 4:32–5:8 Luke 13:10-17
Tu	Romans 8:18-25 Luke 13:18-21	Ephesians 5:21-33 Luke 13:18-21
W	Romans 8:26-30 Luke 13:22-30	Ephesians 6:1-9 Luke 13:22-30
Th	Romans 3:31b-39 Luke 13:31-35	Ephesians 6:10-20 Luke 13:31-35
F	Romans 9:1-5 Luke 14:1-6	Philippians 1:1-11 Luke 14:1-6
Sa	Romans 11:1-2a, 11-12, 25-29 Luke 14:1, 7-11	Philippians 1:18b-26 Luke 14:1, 7-11

31st Week

	YEAR I	YEAR II
M	Romans 11:29-36 Luke 14:12-14	Philippians 2:1-4 Luke 14:12-14
Tu	Romans 12:5-16a Luke 14:15-24	Philippians 2:5-11 Luke 14:15-24
W	Romans 13:8-10 Luke 14:25-33	Philippians 2:12-18 Luke 14:25-33
Th	Romans 14:7-12 Luke 15:1-10	Philippians 3:3-8a Luke 15:1-10
F	Romans 15:14-21 Luke 16:1-8	Philippians 3:17–4:1 Luke 16:1-8
Sa	Romans 16:3-9, 16, 22-27 Luke 16:9-15	Philippians 4:10-19 Luke 16:9-15

32nd Week

M	Wisdom 1:1-7	Titus 1:1-9
	Luke 17:1-6	Luke 17:1-6
Tu	Wisdom 2:23–3:9	Titus 2:1-8, 11-14
	Luke 17:7-10	Luke 17:7-10
W	Wisdom 6:1-11	Titus 3:1-7
	Luke 17:11-19	Luke 17:11-19
Th	Wisdom 7:22–8:1	Philemon 7-20
	Luke 17:20-25	Luke 17:20-2
F	Wisdom 13:1-9	2 John 4-9
	Luke 17:26-37	Luke 17:26-37
Sa	Wisdom 18:14-16; 19:6-9	3 John 5-8
	Luke 18:1-8	Luke 18:1-8

33rd Week

M	1 Maccabees 1:10-15, 41-43, 54, 57, 62, 64	Revelation 1:1-4; 2:1-5a
	Luke 18:35-43	Luke 18:35-43
Tu	2 Maccabees 6:18-31	Revelation 3:1-6, 14-22
	Luke 19:1-10	Luke 19:1-10
W	2 Maccabees 7:1, 20-31	Revelation 4:1-11
	Luke 19:11-28	Luke 19:11-28
Th	1 Maccabees 2:15-29	Revelation 5:1-10
	Luke 19:41-44	Luke 19:41-44
F	1 Maccabees 4:36-37, 52-59	Revelation 10:8-11
	Luke 19:45-48	Luke 19:45-48
Sa	Maccabees 6:1-13	Revelation 11:4-12
	Luke 20:27-40	Luke 20:27-40

34th Week

M	Daniel 1:1-6, 8-20	Revelation 14:1-3, 4b-5
	Luke 21:1-4	Luke 21:1-4
Tu	Daniel 2:31-45	Revelation 14:14-19
	Luke 21:5-11	Luke 21:5-11

W	Daniel 5:1-6, 13-14, 16-17, 23-28	Revelation 15:1-4
	Luke 21:12-19	Luke 21:12-19
Th	Daniel 6:11-28	Revelation 18:1-2, 21-23; 19:1-3, 9a
	Luke 21:20-28	Luke 21:20-28
F	Daniel 7:2-14	Revelation 20:1-4, 11–21:2
	Luke 21:29-33	Luke 21:29-33
Sa	Daniel 7:15-27	Revelation 22:1-7
	Luke 21:34-36	Luke 21:34-36

Two-Year Cycle
of Biblical Passages
for Liturgy of the Hours
Advent Season

1st Week of Advent

	Year I	Year II
Su	Isaiah 6:1-13	Isaiah 1:1-18
M	Isaiah 7:1-17	Isaiah 11:21-27; 2:1-5
Tu	Isaiah 78:1-18	Isaiah 112:6-22; 4:2-6
W	Isaiah 8:23; 9:1-6	Isaiah 5:1-7
Th	Isaiah 10:5-22	Isaiah 16:1-5; 17:4-8
F	Isaiah 11:10-16	Isaiah 19:16-25
Sa	Isaiah 13:1-22	Isaiah 21:6-12

2nd Week of Advent

	Year I	Year II
Su	Isaiah 14:1-21	Isaiah 22:8-23
M	Isaiah 34:1-17	Isaiah 24:1-18
Tu	Isaiah 35:1-10	Isaiah 24:19-23; 25:1-5
W	Ruth 1:1-22	Isaiah 25:6-12; 26:1-6
Th	Ruth 2:1-13	Isaiah 26:7-21
F	Ruth 2:14-23	Isaiah 27:1-13
Sa	Ruth 3:1-18	Isaiah 29:1-8

3rd Week of Advent

	Year I	Year II
Su	Ruth 4:1-22	Isaiah 29:13-24
M	1 Chronicles 17:1-15	Isaiah 30:18-26
Tu	Micah 4:1-7	Isaiah 30:27-33; 31:4-9
W	Micah 4:14; 5:1-7	Isaiah 31:1-3; 32:1-8
Th	Micah 7:7-13	Isaiah 32:15-20; 33:1-6
F	Micah 7:14-20	Isaiah 33:7-24

Year I	Year II

From December 17 to December 24

	Year I	Year II
17	Isaiah 40:1-11	Isaiah 45:1-13
18	Isaiah 40:12-18, 21-31	Isaiah 46:1-3
19	Isaiah 41:8-20	Isaiah 47:1-15
20	Isaiah 41:21-29	Isaiah 48:1-11
21	Isaiah 42:10-25	Isaiah 48:12-21; 49:9-13
22	Isaiah 43:1-13	Isaiah 49:14-26; 50:1
23	Isaiah 43:18-28	Isaiah 51:1-11
24	Isaiah 44:1-8, 21-23	Isaiah 51:17-23; 52:2, 7-10

Christmas

Isaiah 11:1-10	Isaiah 11:1-10

Holy Family

Ephesians 5:21; 6:1-4	Ephesians 5:21; 6:1-4

December 29 to December 31

	Year I	Year II
29	Colossians 1:1-14	Song of Songs 1:1-8
30	Colossians 1:15-29; 2:1-3	Song of Songs 1:9-17; 2:1-7
31	Colossians 2:4-15	Song of Songs 2:8-17; 3:1-5

January 1, Mary, Mother of God

Hebrews 2:9-17	Hebrews 2:9-17

Octave of Christmas

	Year I	Year II
2	Colossians 2:16-23; 3:1-4	Song of Songs 4:1-16; 5:1
3	Colossians 3:5-7	Song of Songs 5:2-16; 6:1-2
4	Colossians 3:18-25; 4:10	Song of Songs 6:3-11; 7:1-10
5	Colossians 4:2-18	Song of Songs 7:11-14; 8:1-7

	YEAR I	YEAR II
6	Isaiah 42:1-8	Isaiah 49:1-9
7	Isaiah 61:1-11	Isaiah 54:1-1

Epiphany

Isaiah 60:1-22   Isaiah 60:1-22

The following readings are used the day after the feast of the Epiphany until the feast of the Baptism of the Lord.

M	Isaiah 61:1-11	Isaiah 54:1-17
Tu	Isaiah 62:1-12	Isaiah 55:1-13
W	Isaiah 63:7-19; 64:1	Isaiah 56:1-8
Th	Isaiah 64:1-12	Isaiah 59:15-21
F	Baruch 65:13-25	Isaiah 4:5-29
Sa	Baruch 66:10-14, 18-23	Isaiah 4:30-37; 5:1-9

Baptism of the Lord

Isaiah 42:1-9; 49:1-9   Isaiah 42:1-9; 49:1-9

Lenten Season

Ash Wednesday

Isaiah 58:1-14   Isaiah 58:1-14

Thursday after Ash Wednesday

Deuteronomy 1:1, 6-18   Exodus 1:1-22

Friday after Ash Wednesday

Deuteronomy 4:1-8, 32-40   Exodus 2:1-24

Saturday after Ash Wednesday

Deuteronomy 5:1-22   Exodus 3:1-22

1st Week of Lent

Su	Deuteronomy 6:4-25	Exodus 5:1-23; 6:1
M	Deuteronomy 7:6-15; 8:1-6	Exodus 6:2-13

	YEAR I	YEAR II
Tu	Deuteronomy 9:7-21, 25-29	Exodus 6:29-30; 7:1-25
W	Deuteronomy 10:12-22; 11:7, 26-28	Exodus 10:21-29; 11:1-10
Th	Deuteronomy 12:1-14	Exodus 12:1-20
F	Deuteronomy 15:1-18	Exodus 12:21-36
Sa	Deuteronomy 16:1-17	Exodus 12:37-49; 13:11-16

2nd Week of Lent

Su	Deuteronomy 18:1-22	Exodus 13:17-22; 14:1-9
M	Deuteronomy 24:1-22; 25:1-4	Exodus 14:10-31
Tu	Deuteronomy 26:1-19	Exodus 16:1-18, 35
W	Deuteronomy 29:1-5, 9-28	Exodus 17:1-16
Th	Deuteronomy 30:1-20	Exodus 18:13-27
F	Deuteronomy 31:1-15, 23	Exodus 19:1-19; 20:18-21
Sa	Deuteronomy 32:48-52; 34:1-12	Exodus 20:1-17

3rd Week of Lent

Su	Hebrews 1:1-14; 2:1-4	Exodus 22:20-30; 23:1-9
M	Hebrews 2:5-18	Exodus 24:1-18
Tu	Hebrews 3:1-19	Exodus 32:1-6, 15-34
W	Hebrews 4:1-13	Exodus 33:7-11, 18-23; 34:5-9, 29-35
Th	Hebrews 4:14-16; 5:1-10	Exodus 34:10-29
F	Hebrews 5:11-14; 6:1-8	Exodus 35:30-35; 36:1; 37:1-9
Sa	Hebrews 6:9-20	Exodus 40:16-38

	YEAR I	YEAR II

4th Week of Lent

Su	Hebrews 7:1-11	Leviticus 8:1-17; 9:22-24
M	Hebrews 7:11-28	Leviticus 16:1-28
Tu	Hebrews 8:1-13	Leviticus 19:1-18, 31-37
W	Hebrews 9:1-14	Leviticus 26:3-17, 38-45
Th	Hebrews 9:15-28	Numbers 3:1-13; 8:5-11
F	Hebrews 10:1-10	Numbers 9:15-23; 10:10, 33-36
Sa	Hebrews 10:11-25	Hebrews 11:4-6, 10-33

5th Week of Lent

Su	Hebrews 10:25-39	Numbers 12:1-15
M	Hebrews 11:1-19	Numbers 12:16; 13:3, 17-33
Tu	Hebrews 11:20-31	Numbers 14:1-25
W	Hebrews 11:32-40	Numbers 16:1-11, 16-24, 28-35
Th	Hebrews 12:1-13	Numbers 20:1-13; 21:4-9
F	Hebrews 12:14-29	Numbers 22:1-8, 20-35
Sa	Hebrews 13:1-25	Numbers 24:1-19

6th Week of Lent

Su	Isaiah 50:4-11; 51:1-3	Jeremiah 22:1-8; 23:1-8
M	Isaiah 52:13-15; 53:1-12	Jeremiah 26:1-15
Tu	Lamentations 1:1-12, 18-20	Jeremiah 8:13-23; 9:1-8
W	Lamentations 2:1-10	Jeremiah 11:18; 12:1-13
Th	Lamentations 2:11-22	Jeremiah 15:10-21
F	Lamentations 3:1-35	Jeremiah 16:1-15
Sa	Lamentations 5:1-22	Jeremiah 20:7-18

Easter Sunday

Lessons from the Easter Vigil (See cycle of Sunday readings for Year A, page 319; Year B, page 324; and Year C, page 329.)

Easter Season

Octave of Easter

M	1 Peter 1:1-21	Acts 1:1-26
Tu	1 Peter 1:22-23; 2:1-10	Acts 2:1-21
W	1 Peter 2:11-25	Acts 2:22-41
Th	1 Peter 3:1-17	Acts 2:42-47; 3:1-11
F	1 Peter 3:18-22; 4:1-11	Acts 3:12-26; 4:1-4
Sa	1 Peter 4:12-19; 5:1-14	Acts 4:5-31

2nd Week of Easter

Su	Colossians 3:1-17	Colossians 3:1-17
M	Revelation 1:1-20	Acts 4:32-37; 5:1-16
Tu	Revelation 2:1-11	Acts 5:17-42
W	Revelation 2:18-29	Acts 6:1-15
Th	Revelation 3:1-22	Acts 7:1-16
F	Revelation 4:1-11	Acts 7:17-43
Sa	Revelation 5:1-14	Acts 7:44–8:3

3rd Week of Easter

Su	Revelation 6:1-17	Acts 8:4-25
M	Revelation 7:1-17	Acts 8:26-40
Tu	Revelation 8:1-13	Acts 9:1-22
W	Revelation 9:1-12	Acts 9:23-43
Th	Revelation 9:13-21	Acts 10:1-33
F	Revelation 10:1-11	Acts 10:34-48; 11:4-18
Sa	Revelation 11:1-19	Acts 11:19-30

4th Week of Easter

Su	Revelation 12:1-18	Acts 12:1-23
M	Revelation 13:1-18	Acts 12:24-25; 13:1-14

Tu	Revelation 14:1-13	Acts 13:14-43
W	Revelation 14:14-20; 15:1-4	Acts 13:44-52; 14:1-7
Th	Revelation 15:5-8; 16:1-21	Acts 14:8-28; 15:1-4
F	Revelation 17:1-18	Acts 15:5-35
Sa	Revelation 18:1-20	Acts 16:36-41; 16:1-15

5th Week of Easter

Su	Revelation 18:21-24; 19:1-10	Acts 16:16-40
M	Revelation 19:11-21	Acts 17:19-34
Tu	Revelation 20:1-15	Acts 17:19-34
W	Revelation 21:1-8	Acts 18:1-28
Th	Revelation 21:9-27	Acts 19:1-20
F	Revelation 22:1-9	Acts 19:21-40
Sa	Revelation 22:10-21	Acts 20:1-16

6th Week of Easter

Su	1 John 1:1-10	Acts 20:17-38
M	1 John 2:1-11	Acts 21:1-26
Tu	1 John 2:12-17	Acts 21:1-26
W	1 John 2:18-29	Acts 21:40; 22:1-21

Ascension Thursday

	Ephesians 4:1-24	Ephesians 4:1-24
F	1 John 3:1-10	Acts 22:22-30; 23:1-11
Sa	1 John 3:11-17	Acts 23:12-35

7th Week of Easter

Su	1 John 3:18-24	Acts 24:1-27
M	1 John 4:1-10	Acts 25:1-127
Tu	1 John 4:11-21	Acts 26:1-32
W	1 John 5:1-12	Acts 27:1-20
Th	1 John 5:13-23	Acts 27:21-44
F	2 John	Acts 28:1-14
Sa	3 John	Acts 28:15-31

YEAR I	YEAR II

Pentecost Sunday

Romans 8:5-27	Romans 8:5-27

Ordinary Time

1st Week

M	Romans 1:1-17	Genesis 1:31; 2:1-4
Tu	Romans 1:18-32	Genesis 2:4-25
W	Romans 2:1-16	Genesis 3:1-24
Th	Romans 2:17-29	Genesis 4:1-24
F	Romans 3:1-20	Genesis 6:5-22; 7:17-24
Sa	Romans 3:21-31	Genesis 8:1-22

2nd Week

Su	Romans 4:1-25	Genesis 9:1-17
M	Romans 5:1-11	Genesis 11:1-26
Tu	Romans 5:12-21	Genesis 12:1-9; 13:2-18
W	Romans 6:1-11	Genesis 14:1-24
Th	Romans 6:12-23	Genesis 15:1-21
F	Romans 7:1-13	Genesis 16:1-16
Sa	Romans 7:14-25	Genesis 17:1-27

3rd Week

Su	Romans 8:1-17	Genesis 18:1-33
M	Romans 8:18-39	Genesis 19:1-17, 23-29
Tu	Romans 9:1-18	Genesis 21:1-21
W	Romans 9:19-33	Genesis 22:1-19
Th	Romans 10:1-21	Genesis 24:1-27
F	Romans 11:1-12	Genesis 24:33-41, 49-67
Sa	Romans 11:13-24	Genesis 25:7-11, 19-34

4th Week

Su	Romans 11:25-36	Genesis 27:1-29
M	Romans 12:1-21	Genesis 27:30-45
Tu	Romans 13:1-14	Genesis 28:10-22; 29:1-14

	YEAR I	YEAR II
W	Romans 14:1-23	Genesis 31:1-20
Th	Romans 15:1-13	Genesis 32:4-31
F	Romans 15:14-33	Genesis 35:1-29
Sa	Romans 16:1-27	Genesis 37:2-4, 12-36

5th Week

Su	1 Corinthians 1:1-17	Genesis 39:1-23
M	1 Corinthians 1:18-31	Genesis 41:1-17, 25-43
Tu	1 Corinthians 2:1-16	Genesis 41:56-57; 42:1-26
W	1 Corinthians 3:1-23	Genesis 43:1-11, 13-17, 26-34
Th	1 Corinthians 4:1-21	Genesis 44:1-20, 30-34
F	1 Corinthians 5:1-13	Genesis 45:1-15, 21-28; 46:1-6
Sa	1 Corinthians 6:1-11	Genesis 49:1-28, 33

6th Week

Su	1 Corinthians 6:12-20	1 Thessalonians 1:1-10; 2:1-12
M	1 Corinthians 7:1-24	1 Thessalonians 2:13-20; 3:1-13
Tu	1 Corinthians 7:25-40	1 Thessalonians 4:1-18
W	1 Corinthians 8:1-13	1 Thessalonians 5:1-28
Th	1 Corinthians 9:1-18	2 Thessalonians 1:1-12
F	1 Corinthians 9:19-27	2 Thessalonians 2:1-17
Sa	1 Corinthians 10:1-13	2 Thessalonians 3:1-18

7th Week

Su	1 Corinthians 10:14-33; 11:1	2 Corinthians 1:1-14
M	1 Corinthians 11:2-16	2 Corinthians 1:15-24; 2:1-11
Tu	1 Corinthians 11:17-34	2 Corinthians 2:12-17; 3:1-6
W	1 Corinthians 12:1-11	2 Corinthians 3:7-18; 4:1-4

	YEAR I	YEAR II
Th	1 Corinthians 12:12-31	2 Corinthians 4:5-18
F	1 Corinthians 12:31; 13:1-13	2 Corinthians 5:1-21
Sa	1 Corinthians 14:1-19	2 Corinthians 6:1-18; 7:1

8th Week

Su	1 Corinthians 14:20-40	2 Corinthians 7:2-16
M	1 Corinthians 15:1-19	2 Corinthians 8:1-24
Tu	1 Corinthians 15:20-34	2 Corinthians 9:1-15
W	1 Corinthians 15:35-58	2 Corinthians 10:1-18; 11:1-16
Th	1 Corinthians 16:1-24	2 Corinthians 11:7-29
F	James 1:1-18	2 Corinthians 11:30-33; 12:1-13
Sa	James 1:19-27	2 Corinthians 12:14-21; 13:1-13

9th Week

Su	James 2:1-13	Galatians 1:1-12
M	James 2:14-26	Galatians 1:13-24; 2:1-10
Tu	James 3:1-12	Galatians 2:11-21; 3:1-14
W	James 3:13-18	Galatians 3:15-29; 4:1-7
Th	James 4:1-12	Galatians 4:8-31; 5:1
F	James 4:13-17; 5:1-11	Galatians 5:1-25
Sa	James 5:12-20	Galatians 5:25-26; 6:1-18

10th Week

Su	Sirach 46:1-10	Philippians 1:1-11
M	Joshua 1:1-18	Philippians 1:12-26
Tu	Joshua 2:1-24	Philippians 1:27-30; 2:1-11
W	Joshua 3:1-17; 4:14-19; 5:10-12	Philippians 2:12-30
Th	Joshua 5:13-15; 6:1-21	Philippians 3:1-16
F	Joshua 7:4-26	Philippians 3:17-21; 4:1-9
Sa	Joshua 10:1-14; 11:15-20	Philippians 4:10-23

11th Week

Su	Joshua 24:1-7, 13-28	Isaiah 44:21-28; 45:1-3
M	Judges 2:6-23; 3:1-4	Ezra 1:1-8; 2:68-70; 3:1-8
Tu	Judges 4:1-24 or 5:1-31	Ezra 4:1-5, 24; 5:1-5
W	Judges 6:1-6, 11-24	Haggai 1:1-15; 2:1-10
Th	Judges 6:33-35; 7:1-8, 16-22	Haggai 2:11-23
F	Judges 8:22-23, 30-32; 9:1-15	Zechariah 1:10-17; 2:1-4
Sa	Judges 11:1-9, 29-40	Zechariah 2:5-17

12th Week

Su	Judges 13:1-25	Zechariah 3:1-10; 4:1-14
M	Judges 16:4-6, 16-31	Zechariah 8:1-17, 20-23
Tu	1 Samuel 1:1-19	Ezra 6:1-5, 14-22
W	1 Samuel 1:20-28; 2:11-21	Ezra 7:6-28
Th	1 Samuel 2:22-36	Ezra 9:1-9, 15; 10:1-5
F	1 Samuel 3:1-21	Nehemiah 1:1-11; 2:1-8
Sa	1 Samuel 4:1-18	Nehemiah 2:9-20

13th Week

Su	1 Samuel 5:1-6; 6:1-4, 10-12, 19-21; 7:1	Nehemiah 3:33-38; 43:1-17
M	1 Samuel 7:15-17; 8:1-22	Nehemiah 5:1-19
Tu	1 Samuel 9:1-6, 14-27; 10:1	Nehemiah 7:72; 8:1-18
W	1 Samuel 11:1-15	Nehemiah 9:1-2, 5-21
Th	1 Samuel 12:1-25	Nehemiah 9:22-37
F	1 Samuel 15:1-23	Nehemiah 12:27-47
Sa	1 Samuel 16:1-13	Isaiah 59:1-14

14th Week

Su	1 Samuel 17:1-10, 23-26, 40-51	Proverbs 1:1-7, 20-33

	YEAR I	YEAR II
M	1 Samuel 17:57-58; 18:9, 20-30	Proverbs 3:1-20
Tu	1 Samuel 19:8-10; 20:1-17	Proverbs 8:1-5, 12-36
W	1 Samuel 21:1-10; 22:1-5	Proverbs 9:1-18
Th	1 Samuel 25:14-24, 28-39	Proverbs 10:6-32
F	1 Samuel 26:2-25	Proverbs 15:8-9, 16-17, 25-26, 29-30; 16:1-9; 17:5
Sa	1 Samuel 28:3-25	Proverbs 31:10-31

15th Week

	YEAR I	YEAR II
Su	1 Samuel 31:1-4	Job 1:1-22
M	2 Samuel 1:1-16; 2:1-11; 3:1-5	Job 2:1-13
Tu	2 Samuel 4:2-12; 5:1-7	Job 3:1-26
W	2 Samuel 6:1-23	Job 4:1-21
Th	2 Samuel 7:1-25	Job 5:1-27
F	2 Samuel 11:1-17, 26-27	Job 6:1-30
Sa	2 Samuel 12:1-25	Job 7:1-21

16th Week

	YEAR I	YEAR II
Su	2 Samuel 15:7-14, 24-30; 16:5-14	Job 11:1-20
M	2 Samuel 18:6-17, 24-32; 19:1-4	Job 12:1-25
Tu	2 Samuel 24:1-4, 10, 18, 24-25	Job 13:13-28; 14:1-6
W	2 Samuel 22:2-19	Job 18:1-21
Th	1 Kings 1:11-35; 2:10-12	Job 19:1-29
F	1 Kings 3:5-28	Job 22:1-30
Sa	1 Kings 8:1-21	Job 23:1-17; 24:1-12

17th Week

	YEAR I	YEAR II
Su	1 Kings 8:22-34, 54-61	Job 28:1-28
M	1 Kings 19:1-13	Job 29:1-10; 30:1, 9-23

	YEAR I	YEAR II
Tu	1 Kings 11:1-4, 26-43	Job 31:2-23, 35-37
W	1 Kings 12:1-19	Job 32:1-6; 33:1-22
Th	1 Kings 12:20-33	Job 38:1-30; 40:1-5
F	1 Kings 16:29-34; 17:1-16	Job 40:6-24; 42:1-6
Sa	1 Kings 18:16-40	Job 42:7-17

18th Week

	YEAR I	YEAR II
Su	1 Kings 19:1-9, 11-21	Obadiah 1:21
M	1 Kings 21:1-21, 27-29	Joel 1:13-20; 2:1-11
Tu	1 Kings 22:1-9, 15-23, 29, 34-38	Joel 2:12-27
W	2 Chronicles 20:1-9, 13-24	Joel 3:1-5; 4:1-8
Th	2 Kings 2:1-15	Joel 4:1-21
F	2 Kings 3:5-27	Malachi 1:1-14; 2:13-16
Sa	2 Kings 4:8-37	Malachi 3:1-21

19th Week

	YEAR I	YEAR II
Su	2 Kings 4:38-44; 6:1-7	Jonah 1:1-16; 2:1-11
M	2 Kings 5:1-19	Jonah 3:1-19; 4:1-11
Tu	2 Kings 6:8-23	Zechariah 9:1-17; 10:1-2
W	2 Kings 6:24-25, 32-33; 7:1-16	Zechariah 10:3-12; 11:1-13
Th	2 Kings 9:1-16, 22-27	Zechariah 11:4-17; 12:1-8
F	2 Kings 11:1-20	Zechariah 12:9-14; 13:1-9
Sa	2 Kings 13:10-25	Zechariah 14:1-21

20th Week

	YEAR I	YEAR II
Su	Ephesians 1:1-14	Ecclesiastes 1:1-18
M	Ephesians 1:15-23	Ecclesiastes 2:1-26
Tu	Ephesians 2:1-10	Ecclesiastes 3:1-22
W	Ephesians 2:11-22	Ecclesiastes 5:9-19; 6:1-8
Th	Ephesians 3:1-13	Ecclesiastes 7:1-29; 8:1
F	Ephesians 3:14-21	Ecclesiastes 8:5-17; 9:1-10
Sa	Ephesians 4:1-16	Ecclesiastes 11:7-10; 12:1-14

| | Year I | Year II |

21st Week

Su	Ephesians 4:17-24	Titus 1:1-16
M	Ephesians 4:25-32; 5:1	Titus 2:1-15; 3:1-2
Tu	Ephesians 5:8-20	Titus 3:3-15
W	Ephesians 5:21-33	1 Timothy 1:1-20
Th	Ephesians 6:1-9	1 Timothy 2:1-15
F	Ephesians 6:10-24	1 Timothy 3:1-16
Sa	Philemon 1-25	1 Timothy 4:1-16; 5:1-2

22nd Week

Su	2 Kings 14:1-27	1 Timothy 5:3-25
M	Amos 1:1-15; 2:1-3	1 Timothy 6:1-10
Tu	Amos 2:4-16	1 Timothy 6:11-21
W	Amos 3:1-15	2 Timothy 1:1-18
Th	Amos 4:1-13	2 Timothy 2:1-21
F	Amos 5:1-17	2 Timothy 2:22-26; 3:1-17
Sa	Amos 5:18-27; 6:1-14	2 Timothy 4:1-22

23rd Week

Su	Amos 7:1-17	2 Peter 1:1-11
M	Amos 8:1-14	2 Peter 1:12-21
Tu	Amos 9:1-15	2 Peter 2:1-8
W	Hosea 1:1-8; 3:1-5	2 Peter 2:9-22
Th	Hosea 2:4-25	2 Peter 3:1-10
F	Hosea 4:1-10; 5:1-7	2 Peter 3:11-18
Sa	Hosea 5:15; 6:1-11; 7:1-2	Jude 1-25

24th Week

Su	Hosea 8:1-14	Esther 1:1-17; 2:5-10, 16-17
M	Hosea 9:1-14	Esther 3:1-11
Tu	Hosea 10:1-15	Esther 4:1-15
W	Hosea 11:1-11	Esther 40:12-30
Th	Hosea 13:1-15; 14:1	Esther 5:1-14; 7:1-10

	YEAR I	**YEAR II**
F	Hosea 14:2-10	Baruch 1:13-22; 2:1-5; 3:1-8
Sa	2 Kings 15:1-5, 32-35; 16:1-8	Baruch 3:9-15, 24-38; 4:1-4

25th Week

	YEAR I	**YEAR II**
Su	Isaiah 6:1-13	Tobit 1:1-22
M	Isaiah 3:1-15	Tobit 2:1-14; 3:1-6
Tu	Isaiah 5:8-13, 17-24	Tobit 3:7-17
W	Isaiah 7:1-17	Tobit 4:1-6, 20-21; 5:1-22
Th	Isaiah 9:7-10; 10:1-4	Tobit 6:1-18
F	Isaiah 28:1-6, 14-22	Tobit 7:9-17; 8:1-14
Sa	Micah 1:1-9; 2:1-11	Tobit 10:8-14; 11:1-18

26th Week

	YEAR I	**YEAR II**
Su	Micah 3:1-12	Judith 2:1-6; 3:7; 4:1-2, 9-15
M	Micah 6:1-16	Judith 5:1-24
Tu	2 Kings 17:1-18	Judith 6:1-8, 10; 7:1-4
W	2 Kings 17:24-41	Judith 8:1, 9-14, 28-36; 9:1-14
Th	2 Chronicles 29:1-2; 30:1-16	Judith 10:1-5, 11-16; 11:1-6, 18-21
F	Isaiah 20:1-6	Judith 12:1-20; 13:1-3
Sa	2 Kings 20:1-19	Judith 13:4-20

27th Week

	YEAR I	**YEAR II**
Su	Isaiah 22:1-14	Sirach 1:1-29
M	Isaiah 30:1-18	Sirach 2:1-18
Tu	2 Kings 18:17-36	Sirach 3:1-16
W	2 Kings 18:37; 19:1-19, 35-37	Sirach 3:17-30; 4:1-10
Th	Isaiah 37:21-35	Sirach 5:1-17; 6:1-4
F	2 Kings 21:1-18, 23; 22:1	Sirach 6:5-37
Sa	Zephaniah 1:1-7, 14-18; 2:1-3	Sirach 7:18-36

	YEAR I	YEAR II

28th Week

Su	Zephaniah 3:8-20	Sirach 10:6-18
M	Jeremiah 1:1-19	Sirach 11:12-28
Tu	Jeremiah 2:1-13, 20-25	Sirach 14:20-27; 15:1-10
W	Jeremiah 3:1-5, 19-25; 4:1-14	Sirach 15:11-20
Th	Jeremiah 4:5-8, 13-28	Sirach 316:24-28; 17:1-14
F	Jeremiah 7:1-20	Sirach 17:15-27
Sa	Jeremiah 9:1-11, 16-21	Sirach 24:1-22

29th Week

Su	2 Kings 22:8, 10-19; 23:4, 21-23	Sirach 26:1-4, 9-18
M	Nahum 1:1-8; 3:1-7, 12-15	Sirach 27:22-30; 28:1-7
Tu	2 Chronicles 35:20-26; 36:1-12	Sirach 29:1-13; 31:1-4
W	Habakkuk 1:1-17; 2:1-4	Sirach 35:1-18
Th	Habakkuk 2:5-20	Sirach 38:24-34; 39:1-11
F	Jeremiah 22:10-30	Sirach 42:15-25; 43:27-35
Sa	Jeremiah19:1-5, 10-15; 20:1-6	Sirach 51:1-12

30th Week

Su	Jeremiah 23:9-17, 21-29	Wisdom 1:1-15
M	Jeremiah 25:15-17, 27-38	Wisdom 1:16; 2:1-24
Tu	Jeremiah 36:1-10, 21-32	Wisdom 3:1-19
W	Jeremiah 24:1-10	Wisdom 4:1-20
Th	Jeremiah 27:1-15	Wisdom 5:1-23
F	Jeremiah 28:1-17	Wisdom 6:1-25
Sa	Jeremiah 29:1-14	Wisdom 7:13-30

	YEAR I	YEAR II

31st Week

Su	2 Kings 24:20; 25:13, 18-21	Wisdom 8:1-21
M	Jeremiah 37:21; 38:14-28	Wisdom 9:1-18
Tu	Jeremiah 32:6-10, 26-40	Wisdom 10:1-21; 11:1-5
W	Jeremiah 30:18-24; 31:1-9	Wisdom 11:17-26; 12:2, 11-19
Th	Jeremiah 31:15-22, 27-34	Wisdom 13:1-10; 14:15-21; 15:1-6
F	Jeremiah 42:1-16; 43:4-7	Wisdom 16:2-13, 20-26
Sa	Ezekiel 1:3-14, 22-28	Wisdom 18:1-15; 19:4-9

32nd Week

Su	Ezekiel 2:1-19; 3:11, 16-21	1 Maccabees 1:1-25
M	Ezekiel 5:1-15	1 Maccabees 1:41-63
Tu	Ezekiel 8:3-6, 16-18; 9:1-11	2 Maccabees 6:12-31
W	Ezekiel 10:18-22; 11:14-21	2 Maccabees 7:1-19
Th	Ezekiel 12:1-16	2 Maccabees 7:20-42
F	Ezekiel 13:1-16	1 Maccabees 2:1, 15-28, 42, 50, 65-70
Sa	Ezekiel 14:12-23	1 Maccabees 3:1-26

33rd Week

Su	Ezekiel 16:3-19, 35-43, 59-63	1 Maccabees 4:36-59
M	Ezekiel 17:3-15, 19-24	2 Maccabees 12:36-46
Tu	Ezekiel 18:1-13, 20-32	1 Maccabees 6:1-17
W	Ezekiel 20:27-44	1 Maccabees 9:1-22
Th	Ezekiel 24:15-26	Daniel 1:1-21
F	Ezekiel 28:1-19	Daniel 2:1, 25-47
Sa	Ezekiel 34:1-6, 11-16, 23-31	Daniel 3:8-23, 91-97

	YEAR I	YEAR II

34th Week

Sunday of Christ the King

	YEAR I	YEAR II
	Daniel 7:1-17	Daniel 7:1-17
M	Ezekiel 36:16-36	Daniel 5:1-17, 23-31; 6:1
Tu	Ezekiel 37:1-14	Daniel 6:2-29
W	Ezekiel 37:15-28	Daniel 8:1-27
Th	Ezekiel 38:14-16; 39:1-10	Daniel 9:1-4, 18, 27
F	Ezekiel 40:1-4; 43:1-12; 44:4-9	Daniel 10:1-21; 11:1
Sa	Ezekiel 47:1-12	Daniel 12:1-13

Suggested
Books
for Further
Reading

SUGGESTED BOOKS FOR FURTHER READING

THE BIBLE

The Catholic Study Bible — New American Bible
   (NAB)
Oxford University Press
New York
1990

   The best Catholic study edition of the Bible.
In addition to the notes of the NAB, it has a 576-
page study guide with cross references in the text.
Significant contributions by women biblical scholars. Some inclusive language in Revised New Testament. It was published too early to incorporate
revised inclusive-language Psalms. Maps.

The New Jerusalem Bible
Doubleday
New York
1985

   Excellent notes. Accurate and literary translation. Some inclusive language. Uses "Yahweh"
instead of "Lord." This is a departure from Christian tradition and offensive to many Jews.

The New Oxford Annotated Bible — New Revised
   Standard Version (NRSV)
Oxford University Press
New York
1991

The best annotated edition of the NRSV. Good introductions and extensive notes. Inclusive language throughout in regard to men and women. A true ecumenical study Bible. Contains all books regarded as canonical by Catholics as well as those books in Eastern Orthodox Bible that are not found in Protestant or Catholic Bibles. Maps.

The Oxford Study Bible
Revised English Bible with the Apocrypha (REB)
Oxford University Press
Cambridge University Press
New York
1992

A revision of the New English Bible planned and directed by representatives of Anglican, Catholic and Protestant churches of England, Scotland, Wales and Ireland. Excellent literary translation. Some inclusive language. Study edition includes 22 articles on the biblical world, an introduction to each book of the Bible and extensive footnotes.

Good News Bible with Deuterocanonicals/
        Apocrypha
American Bible Society
New York
1979

A sign of the new ecumenism in biblical studies. The American Bible Society, once regarded with skepticism by Catholics, publishes this Catholic edition, which contains books not previously found in most Protestant Bibles. Imprimatur by Archbishop John Whealon. Brief introduction to each book. Some inclusive language. Clarifies language of the Gospel of John regarding "the Jews." Attractive illustrations. Easy to read. Maps. Inexpensive.

BIBLE COMMENTARIES

The New Jerome Bible Commentary
Prentice Hall
Englewood Cliffs, New Jersey
1990

A thorough revision of the best Catholic Bible commentary in the English language. No one-volume commentary in any language is better.

The Collegeville Bible Commentary
The Liturgical Press
Collegeville, Minnesota

Aimed at intelligent lay readers. Solid scholarship. Published by the Liturgical Press, which for many years was the only press in America dedicated to introducing the Catholic laity to the Bible and liturgy as basic sources of spirituality. Liturgical Press also publishes the Little Rock Bible Study, which is the most widely used Catholic program for studying the Bible.

PRAYING THE PSALMS

Answering God (The Psalms as Tools for Prayer)
Eugene G. Peterson
Harper & Row
San Francisco
1989

Written by a Presbyterian minister whose learning is wide and deep. Ecumenical scholarship at its best. Interesting "Reports from the Field": reactions from people who are using the Psalms as the source of their own personal prayer.

Praying the Psalms
Walter Brueggemo
Saint Mary's Press
Christian Brothers Publications
Winona, Minnesota
1986

Brueggemo is professor of Old Testament at Columbia Theological Seminary, Decatur, Georgia. Deals honestly with problems a modern Christian has in reading these ancient Jewish prayers.

Missals

Saint Andrew Bible Missal
William J. Hirten
Brooklyn, New York
1982

The best missal for introductions, notes and commentary. Includes Ash Wednesday, and Easter Triduum — Chrism Mass, Holy Thursday (Maundy Thursday), Good Friday and Easter Vigil — all Sundays and major feasts. Does not have weekdays and minor feasts.

The Vatican II Sunday Missal
St. Paul Editions
Boston
1974

For Sundays, holy days and major feasts. Biblical introductions and pastoral instructions by Archbishop John Whealon.

The Vatican II Weekday Missal
St. Paul Editions
Boston
1976

St. Joseph Sunday Missal
Catholic Book Publishing Co.
New York
1974

Mass themes and biblical commentaries by John C. Kersten, SVD.

St. Joseph Daily Missal (two volumes)
Catholic Book Publishing Co.
New York
1975

      Brief introductions to biblical books read in weekday readings.

The Ministry of the Celebrating Community
Eugene Walsh, S.S.
Oregon Catholic Press
Portland, Oregon

      Excellent aid to praying the Mass.

Liturgy of the Hours

Liturgy of the Hours (four volumes)
Catholic Book Publishing Co.
New York

Christian Prayer (one volume)
The Liturgy of the Hours
Catholic Book Publishing Co.
New York
1976

Christian Prayer (one volume)
The Liturgy of the Hours
St. Paul Editions
Boston
1976

The Office of Readings (one volume)
1983

Shorter Christian Prayer
(Morning and Evening Prayer)
Catholic Book Publishing Co.
New York
1988

Shorter Christian Prayer
(Morning and Evening Prayer)
Collins
Liturgical Press
Collegeville, Minnesota
1987

EASTERN CHRISTIAN WORSHIP

Byzantine Daily Worship
Archbishop Joseph Raya and
Baron Jose de Vinck
Alleluia Press
Allendale, New Jersey
1969

The Byzantine Liturgy and Divine Office according to the use of the Catholic Melkites. Approved by Maximos V. Hakim, Melkite Patriarch of Antioch and All the East, of Alexandria and of Jerusalem. Letter of commendation from Athenagoras I, Archbishop of Constantinople, New Rome, and Ecumenical Patriarch of the Greek Orthodox Church.

BIBLE AND LITURGY IN THE HOME

Catholic Household Blessings and Prayers
Bishops' Committee on the Liturgy
National Conference of Catholic Bishops
Washington, D.C.
1988

Daily blessings. Days and seasons. Times in life. Blessings for various times and places. Common prayers. An excellent source of family prayer, solidly based on the Bible and liturgy.

Sourcebook for Sundays and Seasons
Liturgy Training Publications
1800 North Hermitage Avenue
Chicago, Illinois 60622
Annual

Unique. A gold mine of material for planning liturgies. Intended primarily for parishes and religious houses, but useful for families who want to enrich their spiritual life with the Church's liturgical year. Draws from Jewish tradition and Eastern liturgies. LTP is an invaluable source of outstanding liturgical publications for parish and personal use.

MARRIAGE

Together for Life
Joseph M. Champlin
Ave Maria Press
Notre Dame, Indiana
1988

A collection of prayers and Scripture for planning a Catholic wedding service. Texts for wedding within Mass or outside Mass. Father Champlin combines learning with pastoral experience.

How to Survive Being Married to a Catholic
Liguori Publications
One Liguori Drive
Liguori, Missouri
1986

Intended for the non-Catholic partner in a mixed marriage. Easy to read, but not superficial. Written with honesty and humor. Well received by non-Catholics.

MEDITATION — CONTEMPLATIVE PRAYER

Seeking the Face of God
William Shannon
Crossroad
New York
1990

One of the best introductions to contemplative prayer based on Scripture, with emphasis on Lectio Divina. Useful discussion of "Some Biblical Words and Theological Themes." By a priest of the Diocese of Rochester, who is president of the international Thomas Merton Society and general editor of the Merton letters.

Prayer of the Heart
George A. Maloney, SJ
Ave Maria Press
Notre Dame, Indiana
1981

Valuable guide to the Jesus Prayer and Eastern Christian spirituality. Jesuit Father George Maloney is director of the John XXIII Center for Eastern Christian Studies at Fordham University.

The Jesus Prayer
A Monk of the Eastern Church
St. Vladimir's Seminary Press
Crestwood, New York
1987

The author gives a history of the Jesus prayer and explains why this form of prayer has been so important in the history of Eastern Christianity and is now more and more appreciated by Christians of the West.

Sadhana, A Way to God
Anthony de Mello, SJ
We and God Spirituality Center
St. Louis University
St. Louis, Missouri
1978

A Catholic best-seller. Has been translated into more than 21 languages.

A Western Way of Meditation: The Rosary Revisited
David Burton Bryan
Loyola University Press
Chicago
1991

Dominican Father Wilfrid J. Harrington, noted Scripture scholar, writes, "David Burton Bryan has not written 'another' book on the rosary. He has written what is, quite simply, the best book available. I, for one, find myself, after a lifetime of rosary prayer — perhaps, sadly, not always rosary-meditation — introduced to a deeper and richer appreciation of it. This is a book that will make its mark."

Behold the Beauty of the Lord: Praying with Icons
Henry J.M. Nouwen
Ave Maria Press
Notre Dame, Indiana
1987

Spirituality for Lay People

A Man and His God

Martin W. Pable, OFM Cap.

Ave Maria Press

Notre Dame, Indiana

1988

Capuchin Father Martin Pable is convinced that many men have a deep spiritual hunger. Few spiritual books have been addressed specifically to modern men. This one is, and it is excellent.

Miryam of Nazareth

Ann Johnson

Ave Maria Press

Notre Dame, Indiana

1984

Breaks through stereotypes that have limited Mary as a role model for women of today. Links Mary with other great women of the Bible.

The Reed of God

Caryll Houselander

Christian Classics

Westminster, Maryland

1990

A book about Mary. Solidly based on Scripture. Written from a woman's perspective, but suitable for men also.

A Rocking-Horse Catholic
A Caryll Houselander Reader
Edited by Marie Ann Mayeski
Sheed & Ward
Kansas City, Missouri
1992

A 20th-century pioneer of lay spirituality,
Houselander's writings are as timely today as
they were 50 years ago.

SACRAMENTS

The Rite of Penance
Liturgical Press
Collegeville, Minnesota
1975

The Rite of Penance
Catholic Book Publishing Company
New York
1975

ACKNOWLEDGMENTS

The editor and publisher are grateful to the following for permission to use copyrighted material:

The Hierarchies of England and Wales, holders of the copyright of the *Knox Bible,* copyright 1949; the Oxford University Press and Cambridge University Press for the *Revised English Bible with the Apocrypha,* copyright 1989; the Division of Christian Education of the National Council of Churches of Christ in the United States of America, for the *New Revised Standard Version of the Bible,* copyright 1989; the Confraternity of Christian Doctrine for the *Revised Psalms of the New American Bible,* copyright 1991, and Psalm 8 from the NAB, copyright 1970; Old Testament Canticles, except the Canticle of Lady Wisdom, from the *Book of Common Prayer,* coypright 1979; *The Book of Canticles,* copyright 1979, the Church Pension Fund, used by permission; Prayers from the Byzantine rite from *Byzantine Daily Worship,* by permission of Alleluia Press, Allendale, NJ 07401; prayers from the Maronite Liturgy from *Fenquitho, A Treasury of Feasts According to the Syriac Maronite Church of Antioch,* copyright Diocese of St. Maron, U.S.A.; poems and hymns from the Gaelic, Henry Bradshaw Society, London, England; contemporary versions of the Lord's Prayer, Apostles' Creed, Kyrie, Gloria in Excelsis, Sanctus and Agnus Dei copyright by International Consultation on English Texts (ICET) 1975; English translations of Benedictus, Magnificat, Nunc Dimittus, Gloria

INDEX

The *Book of Catholic Prayer* was composed in 10/12 Pallatino, using FrameMaker sofware on a Macintosh IIci; printed by Oregon Catholic Press, Portland, Oregon.

Calligraphy by Robert Palladino.

ISBN 0-915531-02-X